Managing

Construction

Worldwide

CIB W-65   The organisation and management of construction

5th International Symposium, London, 7–10 September, 1987

PAPERS COMMITTEE

Chairman

Peter R. Lansley, BSc MSc FSS	Reader in Management Studies, Department of Construction Management, University of Reading

Members

N. Martin L. Barnes, BSc(Hons) PhD CEng FICE MBCS FCIOB	Martin Barnes Project Management
Barry G. Fryer, MSc ARICS MCIOB	Brunswick School of the Environment, Leeds Polytechnic
Professor Roger Flanagan, MSc PhD FRICS MCIOB	Department of Construction Management, University of Reading
Ian L. Freeman, BSc FCIOB	Building Research Establishment
Professor Ronald McCaffer, BSc PhD CEng FCIOB	Department of Civil Engineering, University of Technology, Loughborough

Secretary

Peter A. Harlow, CEng MIM MIInfSci	The Chartered Institute of Building

CORRESPONDING MEMBERS

P. Chemillier	CSTB, France
W. J. Diepeveen	Stichting Bouwresearch, Netherlands
G. Dressel	Institüt für Arbeitswissenschaft, Federal Republic of Germany
Professor A. Gaarslev	Technical University of Denmark, Denmark
Professor Y. Hammarlund	Chalmers University of Technology, Sweden
Professor M. Haruna	Kyoto University, Japan
L. F. Heineck	Servico Publico Federal, Brazil
A-H. Hosny	Ain-Shams University, Egypt
Professor I. D. C. Imbert	The University of the West Indies, Trinidad
Professor N. I. Ngoka	Anambra State University of Technology, Nigeria
Professor B. C. Paulson	Stanford University, USA
M. T. Pavlidou	Thessaloniki, Greece
Professor S. Peer	Building Research Station, Israel
P. T. Piggott	An Foras Forbatha, Ireland
V. G. M. Rao	Structural Engineering Research Institute, India
Professor A. D. Russell	University of British Columbia, Canada
Professor Y. Sey	Technical University of Istanbul, Turkey
Professor S. Singh	National University of Singapore

Managing Construction Worldwide

VOLUME THREE

Construction Management and Organisation in Perspective

Edited by
Peter R. Lansley and Peter A. Harlow

London   New York
E. & F. N. Spon

First published in 1988 by
E. & F. N. Spon Ltd
11 New Fetter Lane, London EC4P 4EE
Published in the USA by
E. & F. N. Spon
29 West 35th Street, New York NY 10001

© 1988 CIOB, Englemere, Kings Ride, Ascot, Berkshire
and CIB, Postbox 20704, 3001 JA Rotterdam

Printed in Great Britain at the University Press, Cambridge

ISBN 0 419 14020 4
ISBN 0 419 14030 1 (set)

British Library Cataloguing in Publication Data

Managing construction worldwide.
1. Construction industry—Management
I. Lansley, Peter R.   II. Harlow, P. A.
624'.068   HD9715.A2

ISBN 0-419-14030-1
ISBN 0-419-14000-X V.1
ISBN 0-419-14010-7 V.2
ISBN 0-419-14020-4 V.3

Library of Congress Cataloging in Publication Data

Construction management and organisation in perspective.
(Managing construction worldwide: V. 3)
Bibliography: p.
Includes index.
1. Construction industry — management — congresses.
2. Construction industry — management — case studies —
congresses.
I. Lansley, Peter R.   II. Harlow, P. A. (Peter Alan)
III. Series.
HD9715.A2M296   Vol. 3
624'.068 S   87-20548
ISBN 0-419-14020-4   (624'.068)

Contents

Preface

Introduction

There has been increasing interest over the last decade by both construction practitioners and researchers in how, and how well, construction organisations, institutions and industries function. Contracting, professional, educational, governmental and political organisations have all come under close scrutiny, not just by researchers but by those who manage them, those who work in them and by those who are served by them.

The questions which they have asked are important. For example, how can construction organisations cope with unpredictable markets and rapidly changing client requirements? What balance should be maintained between comprehensive pre-planning of projects and on-site short term planning by foremen and craftspeople? To what extent can traditional decision support systems be enhanced, even replaced, by modern computer methods and techniques of artificial intelligence? Is there a trade-off between the achievement of high levels of site productivity and maintaining organisational flexibility? What are the development needs of construction managers and professionals?

The list of key questions goes on, and it is long.

Knowledge

There are no simple answers. The questions are complex and a systematic knowledge base which can be used to deal with such questions does not exist. Contributions to a permanent base of knowledge are infrequent. Whilst typically they come from researchers, the richest knowledge, gained through the experience of those working in construction and related organisations, is largely unrecorded. Usually, at best, it is disseminated within a small circle of colleagues and acquaintances. Progress towards the widespread acceptance of good practice is slow.

Those who study organisations take different starting points, adopt varied perspectives, and draw on many disciplines and skills. Whilst none of these perspectives, or combinations of them, appears to be on the verge of generating the kind of knowledge that will be required to answer many of the key questions, the systematic study of construction organisations and management over the last decade has laid a foundation for the development of that knowledge base.

Strategic viewpoints

This third and final volume of the proceedings of the CIB W-65 Fifth International Symposium on the Organisation and Management of Construction, held in London in September 1987, is a further indication of progress towards an understanding of construction organisations and management processes. It provides, also, an indication of the considerable amount of work still to be carried out.

Unlike Volumes 1 and 2, which contain detailed reports of research programmes, this volume is principally devoted to strategic commentaries and reviews of the development and state of the art of construction organisation and management research and of priorities for the future.

A background for current research in construction organisation and management, and for the symposium as a whole, is provided by the comments and reflections of the chairman of the symposium – Professor Donald Bishop.

Both national and international contexts for research are provided by the papers from those who opened the symposium. These are by individuals who, because of their wide and varied experience, occupy strategic positions within industry, government institutions and research. Whilst, in the spirit of research and enquiry, these papers challenge practitioners and researchers to undertake better research and to use the outcomes more effectively; and industry, government and research institutions to mount comprehensive and more fully co-ordinated programmes, with which they do make clear that over the last decade, progress has been achieved.

Papers by keynote speakers provide a different series of perspectives. But they too highlight the excitement and exacting challenges of construction and construction research; the awe-inspiring engineering, environmental and political risks of the mega-project; the technical and commercial rewards of refurbishment; the construction needs of the developing countries; and, the education and training of construction industry personnel.

Whilst each of the opening and keynote papers brings forward the favourite issues and viewpoints of their authors, the product of their perspectives is to provide more than a mere sum of the parts. Through a process of triangulation they provide a consistent and telling statement of the opportunities, constraints and risks in construction; an understanding to which construction organisation and management research must contribute if it is to be of more than symbolic usefulness.

The papers by the rapporteurs of the workshop sessions held during the symposium provide an important step towards contributing to that understanding. By putting together the pieces of what are several very incomplete jigsaw puzzles, they provide a structure for appreciating the relationships between the individual papers.

Not only do these papers provide an important review of work presented at the symposium and a route map for understanding the work, but they also provide signposts for further necessary and fruitful areas of research. It is with the aid of these papers that the key questions posed earlier can be addressed.

Motives

A motive of the many people who have contributed to the three volumes which comprise the proceedings of the symposium is that readers will find some ideas which can be used to benefit the quality of the organisation and management in their own organisations and those they assist. Coupled with this aspiration is the hope that those who manage construction organisations, those who work in them, and those who serve them, will continue to ask more questions about how their organisations are managed and will articulate those questions more strongly. Only through such a process of questionning, and the consequent exchange between practitioner and researcher, will the knowledge base, which can answer those questions, be built and strengthened.

Peter Lansley
Chairman, Papers Committee CIB W-65 1987
Autumn 1987

Introduction to Volume Three

This volume, Volume 3 of the proceedings, *Construction Management and Organisation in Perspective*, is divided into five parts.

Part VI is dedicated to the chairman's report and reflections on the symposium.

The papers of the opening speakers are contained in Part VII and the keynote addresses in Part VIII. Part IX contains the reports of the rapporteurs.

A number of papers which were received too late for inclusion in the first two volumes are included in the final part, Part X.

Part VI
Chairman's report

ORGANISATION AND MANAGEMENT OF CONSTRUCTION :
CHAIRMAN'S REPORT - AND REFLECTIONS

Donald Bishop
Emeritus Professor of Building, London University, England

INTRODUCTION

Many readers and browsers of this collection of papers may not
be familiar either with CIB - the International Council for Building Research Studies and Documentation - or with the objectives of
the (mostly) triennial symposia on subjects currently in the mainstream of building research. In order to help them, this report :

- sets the scene by outlining the origins and purposes of CIB;
- examines the role and objectives of CIB's symposia;
- explains the two principal strands of this symposium : the
  plenary lectures and the workshops where papers presented ran
  the gauntlet of their peers. From these emerged the theme
  'industry and research', the hallmark of this symposium; and
- concludes with an assessment and some personal reflections.

CIB - NEVER HEARD OF IT!

In the early 1950s nearly all building research - structural
engineering being a notable exception - was carried out by
government-based research stations, many modelled on the then
Building Research Station.   The then dominance of BRE was
illustrated by Dr (later Sir) Frederick Lea's title : Director of
Building Research; and the same held true elsewhere, in Commonwealth countries especially.   In practice research subjects were
(and still are) tackled by individuals or by small teams.
Directors therefore saw advantage in establishing a forum to overcome this virtual isolation by providing opportunities for
reviewing programmes, for examining projects and for collaboration.   The need was met by CIB, the International Council for
Building Research Studies and Documentation, with a Rotterdam-
based secretariat supported by members' subscriptions.
At first meeting were informal, merely small gatherings of
specialists.   Some had tightly defined objectives, eg to produce
master lists for performance specifications; some were subject-
based, eg flat roofs or industrialised building; and more recenty
social science subjects were introduced, building economics and
the organisation and management of construction being examples.
Some, but not all, led to pooled programmes, an example from
personal experience the Trondheim Laboratory and BRE collaborated
when investigating the design of labyrinth joints in the '60s.
Now, and for some time past, arrangements are more formal.

CIB's larger membersip with 64 full, 202 associate, and 95 members which include national research establishments, research organisations and universities and polytechnics world-wide has led to formal procedures for the Council establishing working commissions. W-65 (Management and Organisation of Construction) is one; W-87 Post-construction Liability and Insurance is another. Each normally has a core of active specialists who meet relatively frequently, eg to mount studies or to arrange triennial symposia designed to generate interest and forge links between teams or research workers. These mesh with CIB's triennial congresses, the most recent of which was in Washington in 1986. They provide an opportunity to review priorities for building research as a whole and the progress and relevance of the twenty or so active working commissions.

Working commissions tackling broad subject areas - such as W-65 - normally attract attendance of more than 100. These now include both specialists and those with a general interest in a subject area as well as those from major research institutions (that of Richard Shaffer, the co-ordinator of W-65, has a mouth-watering research budget of $40m) to small university departments, to individual consultants. The circumstances are now very different from the early days when virtually every attendee would have been a specialist from a national research establishment.

Therefore the objectives of these broadly-based symposia now include :

- providing a forum for specialists to learn from one another and to forge working links with others tackling related subjects;
- encouraging newcomers to embark on relevant research - an increasingly important aspect now that CIB membership is so widely drawn;
- creating a collection of the papers reporting progress, in effect a state-of-the-art report;
- exposing the work reported to constructive criticism; and
- identifying priorities and growing points for future research.

HOW DID THE W-65 SYMPOSIUM SET OUT TO ACHIEVE THESE OBJECTIVES?

This, the fifth symposium mounted by W-65, was hosted by CIOB as part of its role to improve professional competence and to advance the discipline of building. The ways in which the CIB/CIOB Organising Committee (Annexe A) sought to meet the above objectives both followed and departed from precedent.

All would-be authors were required to submit substantial outlines of their papers for critical review. These were scrutinised by the Papers Committee (Chairman Peter Lansley) who pointed to ways in which content and presentation could be improved, and papers submitted were then read by at least two of the Committee,

4

this often leading to further revisions before acceptance. In the event 146 outlines were received, 125 of the 134 selected for development were offered as full papers and 102 were published by Spon in the two volumes issued to attendees as they registered. A further 15 late papers are printed in this volume which also includes plenary speakers' papers and the rapporteurs' reports.

The Symposia had three strands : workshops, plenary lectures and social events. At the heart were 25 workshops at which papers were presented and discussed.   Papers were assigned to the following topics - which corresponded to the original call for papers - and sub-topics :

Management and contracting systems	* serving the client * results from research * the developing countries * competition and co-operation
Planning and control	* planning for industrial development * planning and scheduling * planning and controlling resources, especially finance * the search for quality
Management information systems	* data management systems * use of computers * expert systems and artificial intelligence * the future; computers and expert systems
Productivity	* factors influencing productivity * new tools for productivity improvement * state of the art * productivity on site
Human factors	* organisation and environment: the company * organisation and environment: the project * the individual and the group * education and technology transfer

5

Each workshop topic was monitored by two experienced researchers, the rapporteurs responsible for reporting progress since the
last symposium and pointing to future developments. The last of
the five sessions in each sequence was devoted to a review of the
previous discussions in order to prepare the substance of the
rapporteurs' reports. These were presented in the closing plenary
session and are part of this volume of the proceedings.

Sharply focussed and detailed discussion in the workshops are
essential if ideas, research methods and progress are to be
objectively examined. Applied research must, however, be set
against current and future needs of society and the demands these
will make on industry. This element was met by the plenary
sessions which fell into two groups : those related to the
Symposium's topic areas and research policy. The titles of the
first group were :-

- 'Management of the Scheldt barrier' (the then largest
  infrastructure project in Europe) by Theo Van der Shaaf;

- 'The client, role, responsibilities and needs'
  by Christopher Benson, Chairman MEPC;

- 'Refurbishment, rehabilitation and renovation'
  by Norman Douglas, Managing Director Costain Refurbishment;

- 'Developing countries and international contracting'
  by Professor I D C Imbert, University of the West Indies,
  Trinidad; and

- 'Education, training and continuing professional development'
  by Dr Richard Shaffer, Deputy Director US Army Construction
  Engineerng Research Laboratory.

Together the plenary lectures made an impressive contribution
senior practitioners apart from Professor Imbert, the last two
generating very vigorous debates rather than questions eliciting
detail.

The crucial issues of the relationship between industry and
research was a recurrant theme of the research policy papers.
Pierre Chemillier, Director CSTB (the French equivalent to BRE)
and President of CIB, outlined the role of CIB before sketching an
academic framework for management research - and emphasised that
this subject has no standard solution because there is no standard
problem. Dick Shaffer, W-65's co-ordinator, indetified the
development of the subject as the co-ordinating committees'
principal long-term objective and the greater involvement of
industry as the immediate priority. This theme dominated the
other three overview speeches by David Trippier MP, Parliamentary
Under Secretary of State with responsibility inter alia for construction, Brian Hill, President CIOB and by Rex Watson, Director,

BRE. All contrasted the importance of the construction industry in any economy with industry's niggardly investment in research. Mr Trippier underlined current initiatives to improve performance and quality, eg QA and procurement policy and the opportunities now being generated by current inner city policies and by reviving the long-suppressed demand for private sector rented housing, both of which should give the industry confidence to invest in research.

THE SYMPOSIUM - WERE THE OBJECTIVES MET, WAS IT A SUCCESS?

The immediate objectives, stated above, were creating a research community, advancing the subject, and pointing to the future.

There is no doubt the first objective was fully met. The event attracted 230 attendees from 32 countries. Throughout the four days there was a high level of attendance at both plenary and workshop sessions. This held true even for the final plenary session - the lure of shopping, sightseeing, and homeward flights normally severely reduces attendance at final sessions. All coffee etc. intervals and social events were filled with animated discussion. Clearly links were forged.

It is more difficult to assess the second objective - the development of the subject area. Clearly the collection of papers was not intended to be read as a whole but rather to be used as a rich source by researchers, educators and industrialists. Experienced members of W-65's Co-ordinating Committee were unanimous in their opinion that the level of the published papers had been much improved on average by the more vigorous refereeing of the Papers Committee. Nevertheless any collection of papers contributed by individuals with very different experience and working in very different circumstances is bound to be of variable quality. Workshop sessions were arranged so that each contained one or more of the more challenging papers to give a lead to the discussion. As Chairman, I sampled each of the workshop sessions which were, without exception, stimulating and constructively critical. Their value can be assessed from the rapporteurs' reports because it is these that indicate fruitful avenues for further research.

The Symposium broke new ground in arranging a specific occasion for industry to present ongoing research. This was done by an exhibition 'Industry meets Research' in a large ante-room to the venue for one of the two social evenings. The stands of the 24 exhibitors thronged for an hour and a half or so - the only criticism being that too little time was given to this event.

The theme 'industry meets research' was the recurrent theme of the Symposium, dominating the hour's spontaneous discussion following Dick Shaffer's plenary papers. There was no hand-wringing, regretting the lack of interest of an apparantly unheeding industry, rather there was recognition that :

- much of the research reported had involved the active co-operation of industry, albeit only a few firms of any industry;
- greater involvement was a two-way afair demanding willingness by both research and industry;
- one direct route to make W-65's work more obviously relevant to industry would be for each attendee to recruit at least one industry firm to CIB membership. They would be welcomed to the Working Commission and hence able positively to influence international contruction management research. This would continue the evolution of CIB from a forum for governmental research organisation to one for a research-based community.

Whether or not the 1987 Symposium achieved its objectives can be judged only with hindsight. The acid tests will be more vigorous and co-operative research triggered by the Symposium and the greater involvement of industry as research customers, contractors and consumers. If these materialise the 1987 Symposium will have been a great success: if not the Symposium will have been an adequate milestone marking the progress of the subject - and an important event for those working in this area.

PERSONAL REFLECTIONS

Having the last word is one of the few prerogatives of a Chairman. I will exercise this in two ways.

First modestly to comment of the scope of W-65 as illustrated by the hundred or so published papers. Few mentioned profit, few addressed the continuity of organisations, few considered either the environment or society in which the management and organisation of all industries are embedded. Not for one moment do I accept profit maximisation as the only motivator: yet profit is a motivator and an absolute necessity in the medium and long terms. Profit given proper consideration, would have led both to studies of the management of continued existence and evolution of organisations to respond or (better) to anticipate changes in society's demands for building, a path blazed by Peter Lansley and Lady Lea. As it is, pride of place appears given to projects and programmes; perhaps giving a too restricted impression of the scope of this Working Commission.

Second, and this is a most pleasant task, to acknowledge all who worked unstintingly to ensure CIOB could fulfil its undertaking as host to this Symposium. Support of the Institute's senior officers was vital and always there, especially during the Symposium when the time given was noted and appreciated. The Organising Committee (at Annexe A) gave much time and thought to the pattern of the event moulding it on the basis of experience and breaking new ground. The Institute's permanent staff were both highly professionally competent and dogged in overcoming unexpected 'little local difficulties'. It is always difficult to single out individuals. This time it is easy. In a very real sense the Symposum was Joyce Ramsey's symposium. The Institute, the Organising Committee, W-65 and attendees are all indebted to her.

ANNEX A

ORGANISING COMMITTEE

Chairman

Professor Donald Bishop CEng   Emeritus Professor of Building,
MICE ARICS FCIOB   University of London, England

Members

A J Barry PPCIOB

Professor Roger A Burgess   Emeritus Professor, University
BArch FIBA PPCIOB   of Salford, England

David W Cheetham BScTech AMCST   Muspratt Laboratory, University
MCIOB MBIM   of Liverpool, England

B J Coates MCIOB   Ashby & Horner Ltd, England

Ian L Freeman FCIOB   Building Research Station,
                                       England

Professor Vir K Handa   Acting Co-ordinator, W-65,
                                       Department of Civil Engineering,
                                       University of Waterloo, Canada

B J Hill MA FRICS FBIM FCIOB   Higgs & Hill plc, England

Peter R Lansley BSc MSc FSS   Department of Construction
                                       Management, University of
                                       Reading, England
                                       (also Chairman of Papers
                                       Committee - see Volume I)

D Llewellyn CBE FCIOB   Walter Llewellyn & Sons Ltd,
                                       England

P T Pigott   Construction Division, An Foras
                                       Fobartha, Ireland

Professor Dr G Sebestyen	Secretary General, CIB, Rotterdam
Dr L R Shaffer	Co-ordinator, W-65, US Army Construction Engineering Research Laboratory, USA
Professor Victor B Torrance BSc PhD FCIOB FBIM FRSA	Department of Building, Heriot-Watt University, Scotland
Professor E Geoffrey Trimble BSc CEng FICE MIMechE MIstructE	Professor of Construction Management, Loughborough University of Technology, England
R Wharton BSc FCIOB	Chartered Builder
N E Wakefield PPCIOB	Y J Lovell (Holdings) plc, England

CORRESPONDING MEMBERS

Dr Janos Denes	Institute of Building Economy and Organisation, Hungary
Professor Raul Humar	
Dr Vernon Ireland	School of Building Studies, the New South Wales Institute of Technology, Australia
Mr Juraj L Marusic	University of Zagreb, Yugoslavia
Professor N M Nzioki	University of Nairobi, Faculty of Architecure, Design and Development, Nairobi, Kenya
Mr Dan Ove Pederson	Economic Division, The Danish Building Reserch Institute, Denmark
Dr Wang Pu	Shanghai Research Institute of Building Services, China
Mr N J Raufaste	International Technology Council, New York, USA

Dr Peter Rutland	The College of Architecture and Planning, King Saud University, Saudi Arabia
Mr Mufid Abdulwahab Samarai	National Centre for Construction Laboratories, Bagdad, Iraq
Mrs Karla Szoka	Co-ordintor, W-55, Institute of Building Economy and Organisation, Hungary
Mr S K Thakurta	Cannon Dunkerley & Co Ltd, Bombay, India
Professor Helen Tippett	Victoria University of Wellington, New Zealand

Part VII
Introductory addresses

OPENING ADDRESS by Mr Brian J Hill, President of CIOB

Mr President, Ladies and Gentlemen -
May I start this opening address by warmly welcoming you all to
the fifth International Symposium of CIB W-65.
I offer a special welcome to the international delegates,
some of whom I know have travelled many thousands of miles to be
in London for the next few days.
As president of the Chartered Institute of Building, I am both
pleased and proud to represent my Institute as hosts to this
Symposium - an event we have been looking forward to with keen
anticipation!
All of you who have studied the programme will be aware that the
theme 'Organisation and Management of Construction' has generated
of high quality of papers to support and develop this theme and
the discussions which will take place over the next few days.
At this point, may I express, on your behalf, our thanks to the
many who have worked so hard to make this Symposium possible.
There are many names that deserve mention but I can, in the time,
only personally thank Professor Donald Bishop who has chaired the
Organisation Committee and, secondly, Peter Lansley of the
University of Reading who has, with his Committee, been responsible for bringing together the many papers on such varied
subjects.
May I finally add my personal thanks to the staff of my
Institute who have worked so hard over many months on the detailed
arrangements for the programme and for the delegates.
Construction has always been the essential part of a nation's
economic growth and a reflection of the social aspirations and
demands of its people. It is an industry which knows no international frontiers. This simple fact is reflected today by the
presence of delegates from 31 difference countries - international
participation is, of course, vital to the on-going growth and
success of CIB.
Today, more than ever in recent years, we are aware of the need
for change and are able to challenge traditional practices and
customs of a industry which has historically been slow to adapt.
However, are we aware of the speed of such change -
necessitated by the economic and social change of a world that
bears little resemblance to that which existed at the beginning of
this century?
Some 80 years ago, economic wealth rested with a few countries,
of which this country was one, having prospered from the industrial revolution of the Victorian age.
The industrial growth of Japan and the USA were yet to come.
The independence and emergence of many new nations were not to
happen for a further 50 years. This century will be remembered
for the dramatic increases in world population and for the strong
demands for better education and health care. Dramatic changes in

communications have occurred. Nor will the historian overlook the influence and impact of two world wars. These are but a few of the changes that have influenced demands for construction in its many different forms.

Why do I make these broad generalisations of a century that has seen so many upheavals and still has 12 years, no doubt momentous, to run? It is because I believe that while we have seen changes in the development and management of our construction industry, we have yet to adapt and modify many traditional practices and techniques if we are to meet the challenge of the next century. Some of the doubts, questions and changes currently occurring are well-represented in the subject of the papers that are before this Symposium - and this we must all welcome.

What, therefore, are the demands that will determine the future role, structure and size of construction services for the next decade and beyond? I suggest the most obvious are :

- changes in the level of population and the size of the family unit in different parts of the world;
- changes in the purchasing power of people which is, or course, reflected in demand for industrial capacity, offices, education, health, leasure and better homes;
- local and international political decisions;
and finally,
- changes in technology.

Of these factors, given a continuing increase in world demands in real terms of three per cent per annum, the growth in population will be the most significant. By the end of the century, the world population will be about 6.1 billion, an increase of almost one-third since 1980. While the population in the States, Europe and Japan will show little growth, by the end of this century approximately one-third of the world's population will be in China and India.

While increasing population, linked with increasing national and personal wealth, will always generate demands for construction, of equal importance must be our realisation that both in the private an public sectors, the client is now far more sophisticated in his requirements and the services he asks for from our industry.

I have concentrated on these obvious causes of future demand but I wish to give proper emphasis to the many changes that we must make to meet and satisfy demand in the future. These are but a few examples :

- Today, we are challenging the traditional role of the client, his design team and that of the builder. We are seeing frequently the economic need to relate the management and procurement skill of the larger contractor to the proper and early development of the client's brief and the architect's

design.
- We are, therefore, seeing management contracting and project management developing to meet this demand.
- From these changes, it has been necessary to introduce new forms of contract responding to these changes in traditional roles.
- Clearly, there has been a need to build faster - we have to look for increasing productivity and improving the quality of buildings.
- 'Quality Assurance' is a reflection of the consumer or user of the building looking for better guarantees and protection.
- We have to be more responsive and responsible to the problems of design failure and faults on site - 'latent defects' is an issue that is with us and we must reduce its impact.
- More attention in future will go to reducing the 'design life' of new buildings and to creating industrial and office buildings which are highly flexible for a subsequent change in use.
- Space in your discussions has rightly been given to the need to develop further the use of the computer, both in the design and management of building projects.
- A further change is the inreasing conservation of buildings of public and historic interest. This necessitates the refurbish-ment of buildings to adapt them to a different use while retaining their architectural qualities.
   For example, on Wednesday night, you wil be attending a dinner in a building which, for several centuries, was a large brewery in the City of London
- In many cities, the regeneration of large areas of derelict land, no longer appropriate for its past use, is an increasing problem demanding a solution for many paties. Those of you who will visit London Docklands will see a remarkable transforma-tion underway bringing new life and economic use to large areas of derelict land - once the prime source of wealth to the City of London.

The list of changes is by no means exhausted by the few examples I have quoted. I have left to last the most serious change that we must encourge and that is the need for construction to spend more on research.
   Internationally, we are all aware that research into new techniques and materials is lagging behind.
   Only in Japan is investment into research and development at a high level against a background of construction being about 17 per cent of that countruy's gross domestic product.
   But, in Europe, research investment is very low and yet the average level of construction is about 10 to 11 percent of GDP.
   These are but some of the changes and problems that the construction industry must grasp if it is to efficiently meet demand.   Unless we do change more quickly than we have

historically, we have a high risk of failure in meeting economically the international demands to which I have referred. Some of the answers can emerge from the discussions you will have over the next four days.

Mr President, 'The Organisation and Management of Construction' was, I believe, a very appropriate and timely theme for this Symposium.

I wish you all well in your discussions and a memorable and enjoyable stay in London.

ADDRESS BY MONSIEUR PIERRE CHEMILLIER
Président du CIB

Monsieur le Président, Mesdames, Messieurs,
   Je voudrais tout d'abord remercier le Chartered Institute of Building (CIOB) et son président Brian HILL qui sont les organisateurs de ce Symposium. Mes remerciements vont aussi à l'Imperial Collège of Science and Technology qui nous offre ses locaux dans le centre de Londres. Mes remerciements vont enfin à ceux qui ont eu la lourde charge de préparer cette manifestation : M.LANSLEY et Mrs Joyce RAMSEY et, bien entendu, le professeur BISHOP, président du Comité d'organisation.
   Puisque je prends la parole en qualité de président du CIB permettez-moi de vous dire ou de vous rappeler ce qu'est le CIB. C'est une organisation internationale non gouvernementale créée en 1953 qui réunit des organismes publics, semi publics, privés ou des personnes qui tous ont en commun de prendre part à la recherche, à l'information ou à la pratique de la construction.
   Les principaux instituts de recherche dans le monde en font partie et j'ai plaisir à cette occasion à saluer ici à la tribune la présence de Rex WATSON, directeur du Bristish Research Establishement qui joue un rôle très important au sein du CIB. Le CIB comprend des membres titulaires, au nombre de 65, des membres associés et des membres individuels. Il a un Bureau qui conduit la politique de l'organisation, un Comité administratif et financier et un Comité de programmation des activités. Il a un secrétariat général qui est à Rotterdam et qui est dirigé avec une très grande efficacité par le Secrétaire Général M.SEBESTYEN et le Secrétaire Général Adjoint M.POLLINGTON.
   L'organisation est basée sur des Commissions de travail, au nombre d'une trentaine, qui réunissent périodiquement ceux qui sont intéressés à débattre d'un sujet scientifique, technique, économique ou sociologique ; ce travail en commun aboutit à des sortes d'états de l'art, à des méthodes de calcul, à des éléments de normalisation internationale, à l'organisation de symposiums ou plus simplement à l'échange d'information.
   La Commission W65 dont le coordonateur est M.SCHAFFER des USA est au coeur de ce symposium puisqu'elle contribue à son existence. Elle a pour domaine de travail l'organisation et la conduite du processus de production et de gestion des bâtiments et vise à introduire en la matière des méthodes scientifiques permettant notamment d'améliorer

la productivité.

D'autres Commissions traitent de sujets voisins et peuvent donc intéresser certains d'entre vous ; j'en cite quelques unes : la W 55 qui s'intéresse à l'économie, la W 70 qui traite de la maintenance et de la modernisation,la W86 qui travaille sur la pathologie,la W88 dont le domaine est l'assurance de qualité.

N'hésitez pas à vous adresser à M. SEBESTYEN qui est ici si vous souhaitez en savoir plus à ce sujet.

Le CIB à un journal qui s'appelle Building Research and Practice.

Il tient un important congrès tous les 3 ans ; le prochain aura lieu à Paris en Juin 1989.

Si le CIB a décidé de soutenir ce symposium de Londres c'est parce que le sujet qu'on va y traiter est à la fois important et d'actualité.

Le bâtiment traverse en effet aujourd'hui, une période difficile de mutation, où l'on découvre ce que l'on n'aurait jamais dû perdre de vue, à savoir que les techniques, aussi avancées soient-elles,sont insuffisantes pour résoudre les problèmes qui se posent.

Tous les pays sont confrontés à des défis nombreux et difficiles à relever.

S'agissant des pays industrialisés, tout d'abord, ces défis sont les suivants :

- la multiplicité des matériaux et des produits dont beaucoup sont par conséquent mal connus,ce qui engendre une pathologie inquiétante et oblige à un double effort de recherche et d'information technique

- l'évolution de la main d'oeuvre qui n'accepte plus d'exécuter certaines tâches et qui n'a pas l'habileté nécessaire pour exécuter les tâches nouvelles ; un encadrement difficile de cette main d'oeuvre, d'autant plus difficile que les chantiers sont plus petits et plus dispersés. la revalorisation des métiers du bâtiment pour y attirer des jeunes de qualité est un impératif absolu

- l'internationalisation des marchés qui provoque une concurrence très dure mais suscite aussi d'intéressantes coopérations et des échanges d'expérience et de savoir à travers ces coopérations

- la diversification de la demande des usagers qui n'acceptent plus des solutions types et recherchent des réponses appropriées à leur cas particulier, des usagers qui n'ont plus la docilité de ceux qui attendaient un logement en période de grande pénurie mais qui sont exigeants et qu'il faut donc convaincre par une offre alléchante

. l'informatique et l'électronique qui envahissent le champ de la construction et y constituent tout à la fois un outil très puissant et un incontestable risque si l'homme ne les maîtrise pas.

S'agissant maintenant des pays en développement, ils sont confrontés à deux problèmes majeurs :

. la nécessité de mettre en place une organisation sociale efficace, c'est-à-dire des structures qui définissent et répartissent clairement les rôles et les responsabilités ; cette nécessité est la conséquence inévitable du passage d'économies agricoles géographiquement dispersées à des économies urbaines concentrées ; sans un minimum d'organisation sociale il n'est pas possible de mettre en place une politique efficace et durable de la construction et de sortir de méthodes qui ne sont que des expédients

. la valorisation des ressources nationales en vue d'économiser les devises, ce qui implique des formes appropriées d'industrialisation, capables en même temps de faire passer la main d'oeuvre de techniques ancestrales encore valables en zones rurales à des techniques modernes appropriées aux grandes zones urbaines.

Tous ces défis ne seront relevés que par des organisations appropriées du processus de construction. Il faut les inventer car dans bien des cas elles n'existent pas encore.

D'où l'intérêt d'écouter les chercheurs, d'écouter les praticiens, d'échanger les expériences entre pays.

Cette double écoute et ces échanges sont l'essence même du CIB.

Je souhaite plein succès à ce symposium qui marquera, j'en suis certain, une étape importante dans l'histoire déjà longue du CIB.

ADDRESS BY MR DAVID TRIPPIER, MP, UNDER SECRETARY OF STATE

Mr President, the CIB is indisputably the world's premier international association for building research, and I am delighted that this year the United Kingdom has been able to host this, its fifth, international symposium. The theme, "The Organisation and Management of Construction", is one which I, as Minister responsible for the UK constructon industry, find a central and therefore recurring theme in the current pre-occupations of the UK construction industry.

It is right and proper that The Chartered Institute of Building should have organised this event for CIB, and I would like to congratulate Professor Donald Bishop, and his Committee, as well as those who have worked so hard behind the scenes, on such and impressive programme.

Looking at your programme for the next few days, I was struck both by the wide range of topics to be covered, and the numerous countries represented by the keynote speakers. Both of these features bode well for a stimulating and useful symposium. I look forward to its proceedings with great interest.

In addition to my responsibilities for construction, I also have responsibilities for inner cities. So, Mr President, I was very pleased to hear that many of you have already arranged to visit London Docklands later this week, and I hope that at some stage all of you manage to visit what is now the largest construction site in Europe. I shall certainly be interested to hear of your impressions and observations through your UK colleagues.

Mr President, I would like to say a few words about the three topics, first the Government's view of research and development, second, the question of quality in the construction industry, and last, the role of the construction industry in the regeneration of our inner cities.

The Government White Paper proposals welcomed increased international collaboration in research and development. The Government is also strengthening its own arrangements for improving the contribution of Government-funded research and development to this country's creativeness and capacity for innovation.

Over the last decade, there has been a consistent effort within the European Community to obtain harmonization in the Codes used by structural engineers in the design of buildings. This effort has involved 'callibration'; that is, a series of 'national' tasks designed to ensure that each country has safety factors which are appropriate to its own local conditions, materials, and industry techniques. The effort has also involved a joint programme to ensure that the Euro codes represents the latest and the best in the thinking both of practitioners and of researchers. The Building Research Establishment in the UK, together with industry associations such as the Timber Research and Development Association, have contributed greatly to this task. In many cases, this contribution has been through relevant commissions of the CIB, and through CEN, the European standard making body.

This work on the Euro codes is only beginning. There is now on the table, the Construction Products Directive which takes much further the process of harmonisation. This process will call up a substantial and continual joint effort to ensure that construction 'Euro products', if I may call them that, represent the best, and not some out-of-date compromise.

But CIB goes far wider than simply the European Community, and here again we have had useful experience of international co-operation. The cost of research - particularly the capital cost - increases exponentially. One way of keeping the costs within bounds is to share programmes. One example of this is the work of the International Energy Agency, which acts as a convener for research studies on energy conservation in buildings. This has made possible programmes which it is unlikely any single organisation or country would have been willing to do.

The belief of the UK Government is that public investment in science and technology will not achieve its full economic benefit unless, and until, industry undertakes the applied research and development which is required to capitalise on this investment.

The UK construction industry is noticeably lagging behind the mainstream of UK industry and its research and development efforts. I understand that the picture is broadly similar throughout the world, and there can be few countries where this can be regarded as satisfactory. We know you have problems; you know we have problems. For example, a few years ago, Germany and the UK shared knowledge on the problems of High Alumina cement concrete. Many of these problems arise not from the laboratory, but from the way people draw and calculate things in the design office, from the way in which people organise themselves and put things together on site.

The satisfactory organisation of what is a remarkably complication people-based operation is central to getting things right. The work of CIB Commission W-65 is all about that central problem, and it is good to see that the Chartered Institute of Building is responsible for the organisation of the symposium itself. To that extent, the UK contruction industry is itself backing the work of this Commission.

But the output of the UK construction industry is nearly 10 per cent of our Gross Domestic Product. In some countries, it is rather greater. Perhaps half of this very substantial figure is directly affected by questions of organisation and management. The contribution of the Chartered Institute of Building in running this symposium is a substantial one for the Institute itself. But it hardly seems to reflect the potential importance of the subject to that great part of the construction industry that is, alas, not represented here today.

The main problem seems to me to be the low level of the industry's own investment in research and development. This cannot be good, and I look to the symposium to generate practical ideas on how to change this situation.

My second theme concerns quality. The reduction of construction faults and defects is one aspect of quality which is high on our agenda in the UK. Here, we are developing Quality Assurance Schemes throughout the construction process. Quality Assurance techniques originated in the UK in the manufacturing industries, and its first application in the construction industry was in the manufacture of building materials and components. The availability of quality assured materials and components in the UK is growing very fast. My Department's Property Services Agency is the largest public sector client in the UK. Last year it placed over £1 billion worth of orders with the Uk construction industry - over a quarter of all non-housing public sector new orders. The PSA has set the lead in the UK in applying quality assurance to the construction process. Schemes are in place at the procurement and contracting end of the process, and PSA is now hard at work looking at ways of extending quality assurance to the design process. The benefits of the disciplines instilled by QA are substantial and wide in application.

Following an initiative by the Department of Trade and Industry called the National Quality Campaign, no less than 9,000 UK companies have been registered with the Department of Trade and Industry as having quality management system assessed to BS 5750 or to an equivalent standard.

BS 5750 has not only been recognised by the UK Government as the standard for quality systems, but it has now been taken up, I am pleased to say, as the basis for the International Standards Organisation's quality standard : the ISO 9000 series. I undertand that there is every possibility that the standard will also form the basis of a Eurpean Standard to be developed by CEN.

The Department of Trade and Industry has set up the National Accreditation Council for certificaton bodies, in order to help certification bodies demonstrate a consistent quality in their performance. We in the Government believe that the Accreditation system is a fundamental development which will build customers' confidence in independent certification systems. The National Measurement Accreditation service in responsible in the UK for the Accreditation of more than 500 laboratories carrying out tests, both in relation to certifcation and callebration. I understand that the UK systems of Accreditation for both the certifcation bodies and test laboratories has attracted a good deal of overseas interest.

Quality Assurance does not do away with the need for quality manpower. My own Department has taken a keen interest in the need to attract adequate numbers of good quality people into the construction industry, the importance of getting good graduates to go into small firms, and just as important, small firms to appreciate the value of graduates. The role of the builder in site management is central to improved industrial performance.

Last, Mr President, I would like to touch on the Government's views on the role of the construction industry in the regeneration of this country's inner cities. I believe that the revival of private sector activity is the key to restoring confidence, not just in potential investors, but in the people living and working in inner city areas. We cannot simply appeal to the social consciences of our major companies - although we have done so in the past and not without some success! The main aim must be to restore competitiveness to those areas by introducing well-targeted initiatives and by lifting burdens on businesses.

Most of our initiatives involve building projects and clearly we rely to a great extent on the ability and enthusiasm of the construction industry. Such projects, by virtue of their location - congested sites, strong local interest, a complex political environment and complex financial arrangements - make additional demands of the construction industry. If these are to be met, the industry may well need to nurture an even higher calibre of managers and develop project organisation to an even higher degree than is normally required.

This Government has set up a number of new Urban Development Corporations which have powers to assemble land and put in roads and infrastructure. The UDCs in England will also be given powers to grant planning permision for development. They will use these powers to tackle massive derelection in a single-minded way and create the conditions in which the task of development can be carried forward by the private sector.

Earlier this year, we launched Urban Regeneration Grant. This will be targeted on large sites of at least 20 acres - that's just over 9 hectares - and large buildings of at least 250,000 sq ft of floor space - that's about 24,000 sq metres. URG will tackle the comprehensive re-development of these very large derelict sites and buildings which have evaded treatment under other Government initiatives. I expect this to become a major feature in my Department's Inner City Programme.

I will be pleased if URG can repeat the success of the long running Urban Development Grant Schemes. One of UDG's principal aims is to lever private investment in inner cities by encouraging the private sector to tackle difficult sites. To date, a total of £125 million UDG has been taken up in 257 approved projects, which between them have attracted private investment of over £520 million. Our customers have included a wide range of companies from the construction and development world and this I believe demonstrates that the message is getting across.

We have also recognised the importance of increasing competitiveness by relaxing controls on business and by de-regulation. Enterprise zones give businesses rates and tax benefits, and the added advantage of a less bureaucratic planning regime. Local authorities can now follow this approach themselves by creating

Simplified Planning Zones to enable them to speed up and simplify the planning process.

Lastly, Mr President, one word about housing. The Government has radical proposals for combating the massive problem of the decaying and ageing housing stock in this country. But at the same time, we are looking at different ways of increasing choice of tenure on council estates, and giving people a far greater say in the way their estates are managed. Again, I believe there are great opportunities here for the private sector to become involved.

I am therefore greatly encouraged by recent initiatives which have come from industry itself. They are a clear and gratifying indication of the ability and willingness to take a long-term view, and to exploit the available opportunities. I believe that they can play an extremely valuable role in stimulating private sector interest in inner city areas, and furthering the concept of partnership between the public and private sectors. The role of Government is to enable - it is up to the private sector to do the business.

Mr President thank you for inviting me here today. The symposium programme is clearly ambitious, but looking at the calibre of the keynote speakers and the participants, a successful outcome should well be within their design limits. I very much look forward to seeing the results of your labours.

STRATEGIC OVERVIEW OF W-65 "ORGANIZATION AND MANAGEMENT OF CONSTRUCTION"

Dr. L. R. Shaffer, Technical Director
US Army Construction Engineering Research Lab, USA

W-65 strategic overview has five thrusts: (1) maintain interest of the top talent in the world in Organization and Management of Construction (OMC); (b) expand membership to fill voids not addressed by the current membership; (c) continue to take full advantage of CIB as a resource; (d) expedite the transfer of R&D into practice; and (e) facilitate younger members to assume leadership roles in W-65.

The W-65 program continues to attract top talent; 34 experts from 19 countries participate. However, less than the critical mass representation exists from South America, Africa, Japan and the Socialist countries. Less than critical mass representation exists from the contractors and the architect/engineer communities. W-65 is addressing the filling of these voids.

The CIB as a resource has been a magnificent aid to W-65. We have had an OMC-oriented session in every tri-annual Congress since 1974--W-65's birth year. The International Symposia series sponsored by CIB has been particularly helpful. The recent one in London was our fifth. The first was in the US in 1976, the second in Israel in 1978, the third in Ireland in 1981, and the fourth in Canada in 1983. The sixth is scheduled in Australia in 1990 and the seventh in the West Indies in 1993. A minisymposium was held in Turkey in 1982. These Symposia establish, expand and maintain the interacting of the top talent thereby enhancing friendships and profes-sional ties for a lifetime. The Symposia Proceedings present the state-of-the-art and are heavily used references. Indeed, the Proceedings for the London Symposium are being published by a commercial house.

The CIB program to foster the exchange of information facilitated the W-65 Task Group organization. Twelve Task Groups focus on specific subjects in OMC. One developed the Terminology in OMC published by CIB. Another became a

WC Technological Forecasting. A third developed the format of the OMC symposia. Another established a new research thrust in OMC, i.e. Theory of the Firm; it will be a main topic in the 1990 Symposium. It has been W-65 experience that if research is active in the subject the Task Group flourishes; if the Task Group merely defines an important subject the results are not nearly as satisfactory. W-65 has also fostered the between research organizations and joint programs.

The strategy to expedite OMC R&D results into practice is evolving. Information gained by academics and public agency conferees at Symposia and Congress is translated into practice in the conferee countries via their educational programs. Although complementing this program by encouraging practicing professionals to become W-65 members. Their participation in the Task Groups, Symposia and Congress will impact the nature of our programs. The 5th Symposium being sponsored by a professional association--Chartered Institute of Builders--is a good step. Another initiative is for facilitating research in continuing professional development involving OMC. This will involve a practical thrust.

The last strategy is to encourage the younger experts in OMC to assume leadership in the international activities of OMC. Those in the OMC leadership have been involved since the early days of W-65. Our professional careers are coming to a close; we must be succeeded by younger experts who are confident to address the problems of the industry through their visions--not ours. We in the twilight generation must accommodate to these younger experts. The Task Group program provides this opportunity.

Voila!--the strategy of W-65. Comments are welcomed. Strategies of other Working Commissions would be appreciated.

ORGANISATION AND MANAGEMENT OF CONSTRUCTION - A NATIONAL OVERVIEW

R G H Watson, CB PhD CChem FRSC

Building Research Establishment, UK

Summary
The present nature of the British building and construction
industry is reviewed, both its resources and its organisation.
The management of construction is then discussed in terms of the
relationships between six different management perspectives and
five essential resource types. Recent developments in the UK for
a number of intersections on this matrix are reviewed and needs
identified. Suggestions are offered for the emphasis of future
research - primarily related to relevance and application.

Resume
La nature actuelle des ressources et de l'organisation de
l'industrie britannique du bâtiment et de la construction est
sujette à examen. Les relations entre six optiques différentes de
gestion et cinq types essentiels de ressources font ensuite
l'objet de discussions. De récents développements au Royaume-Uni
concernant un certain nombre de recoupements de cette matrice sont
examinés et les besoins sont identifiés. Des suggestions (portant
essentiellement sur la pertinance et l'application) sont avancées
quant à la mise en valeur des recherches futures.

INTRODUCTION
It is with some trepidation that I address this audience both as a
keynote speaker yet as a Chartered Chemist, only relatively
recently introduced to the problems of the Construction Industry.
However, I take comfort from the fact that the Building Research
Establishment has played a leading role for many years in the
issues you are to debate this week. I am perhaps simply mirroring
the experience of my Establishment in what I shall say. This will
first of all deal with the present nature of the British building
and construction industry; then the developing role of
construction management practices and finally the role of research
in seeking improvements in these practices.

The Industry
In the UK we spend nearly 24 billion pounds a year (or giga-pounds
to scientists) on building divided roughly equally between new
build and maintenance and repair (the refurbishment of existing
property being an area of growth). The breakdown is:-

	G£/y	
Private Commercial	3.8	
Private Housing	3.3	
Private Industrial	2.4	
Public non-Housing	3.3	
Public Housing	0.7	
Maintenance and Repair	10.1	(of which half on housing)
	23.6	

This money is spent through the labours of:-

    225,000 supervisors (managers, designers, surveyors etc.)
    600,000 directly employed manual workers
    600,000 self-employed workers (labour-only subcontractors)
            (the ones we know about)

and this represents a major drift in recent times towards
"trade-contractors" who act as subcontractors to the main
contractors. This move towards a different labour structure is
also reflected in the growth in the number of firms involved - now
about 160,000, having doubled in the last ten years, during which
time the number of firms employing more than 300 workers has
halved.

Roughly half the total spent on building is on materials.
Although this has not changed in volume much in recent years an
increasing proportion is being imported. Some recent commercial
buildings have as much as 70% of their material costs borne by
imported material such as air conditioning systems, curtain
walling and so on - the "high tech" bits!

The contractual basis for spending this money has also been
changing, especially in the private sector. A move in the early
1980's towards various management forms of contracting with a
professional management organisation acting for the client has
slowed and been replaced by a move back towards more traditional
relationships. These have changed, however, with better informed
clients led by the British Property Federation taking a more
positive role, and a more demanding one, in their relations with
the designers and constructors. The growing fragmentation of the
industry and increasing complexity of its products has increased
the number of separate participants involved. Coordination of
their individual contributions demands high standards of
management of design and construction. So how is the area of
"construction management", dealt with by CIB Working Commission 65
itself, developing?

Construction Management
Perhaps we should remind ourselves that the context of this
subject for W-65 are the objectives and scope quoted in the CIB
Compendium:

"To develop effective calculations and techniques for evaluating various organisational forms utilised in the planning, architecture, engineering, construction and ownership stages for both conventional construction and for industrialised construction and:

To provide tools for comparing alternative organisation structures and management doctrines in the enterprises."

I shall treat "organisational forms" in the pragmatic British way as elements of management - its structure in fact - and would like to comment on construction management as itself a coherent professional sub-discipline of professional management. Professor Geoffrey Trimble, in his paper to an ARCOM seminar at BRE last year, **(and I shall return to ARCOM itself later)** pointed out that since he accepted a Chair in Construction Management twenty years ago he has been trying to make it a respectable academic subject. This conference illustrates the number of organisations that have rallied to that banner.

In 1981 the UK Science and Engineering Research Council was sufficiently persuaded of its respectability to support a specially promoted programme of research on construction management. Alongside the SERC stands our Building EDC whose then Chairman, Sir Monty Finniston, addressed the ARCOM conference I referred to. The report produced last year by its Research Strategy Committee also recommended extra research effort in the area of construction management. Last year also saw the launch of a new International Journal of Construction Management and Technology, sponsored by the British Chartered Institute of Building, with a distinguished editorial board. So clearly construction management is now well established as a respectable subject; but what does it appear to involve? Although Professor John Bennet's recent book on the subject defines no less than a hundred concepts at the heart of construction management I have chosen to take a very simple view in a matrix of resources:-

Knowledge
Money
Manpower
Materials
Time

on the one hand - and the managers of these resources:-

Client
Designer
Constructor
Supplier
User

and being cynical let us add a sixth:- **Lawyer!**

I would suggest that the particular factor that distinguishes construction management from other forms of production management is the complexity of the interaction of these management centres with one another and with the circumstances of the building process itself. Before I turn to the issue of the research needed in the UK again, I must develop some of the more obvious intersections in this matrix.

Knowledge

I have used "knowledge" rather than "information" because we must manage people's use of what they already know, as well as what we tell them. The effective management of knowledge as a resource seems to me to be the most important single issue in construction management. All that I have heard since joining BRE three-and-a-half years ago suggests that the great majority of failures and defects in buildings and the building process arise from failures to apply what we already know to the solution of the, admittedly complex, problems of construction. The industry concludes, it seems, that it needs better informed clients, and a large number of Client Guides have been published.(1) Our research was the basis of the guide "Thinking About Building" that the Building EDC published two years ago, in which they emphasise that:-

"using the construction industry is like buying custom-built production equipment..... The act of creating the building you need is therefore not simply the making of a product it is the giving of a service", and this underlines the point I made earlier about the speciality of construction management, perhaps now seen as a combination of production management and service management skills. The reader of this EDC guide is led up the seven steps to success in their relationship with the industry:-

Select your in-house project executive
Appoint a principal adviser
Take care in deciding requirements - in Brief
Be realistic about timing
Select suitable procurement path
Choose organisations to work with you with care
Take advice on choice of site/building.

But such advice is probably only helpful to a powerful client, and perhaps we now need more Guides for the professionals in Design and Construction?

Thus, studies by the IAAS at York,(2)(3), of how architects manage knowledge, which were published last year, show how difficult it is to communicate new knowledge to them, yet they are the spear-head of innovation. An important source of their information is the trade literature produced by materials and systems suppliers. However, we have not yet achieved the level of "catalogue building" possible in the United States so that it is often easier - but more costly and more risky - to design "specials". This "customised" tradition in the UK is perhaps one reason why imports of well-tried components from Europe and North America are increasing. More important is the management and organisation of the design process, and we have seen in the UK how progressive evolution of building system designs can ultimately ensure very good products – as in the school buildings programmes.

The opportunity for advance in such management of knowledge arises in the way in which the Industry embraces information technology. Computer aided design is well established, and the understanding of how it should interact with "paper and pencil" methods is growing but it is only used to the full in relatively few projects. Indeed I understand that BRE is aware of only one major contractor who makes full use of CAD in transferring information between designers themselves and between them and the site, in the UK. Expert systems may then offer the additional opportunity to introduce state-of-art technology into the design process without requiring separate information searches by the architects. The pragmatic British have, for some time, been developing standards for the presentation of contractual information in drawings, specifications and bills of quantities. The recommendations we shall see published this Autumn by the Coordinating Committee for Project Information will fortunately be compatible with the needs of computerised information management – without which some of our major projects could not be handled efficiently.

We have also seen rapid advance in the part played by the Industry's professional institutions in the management of knowledge by their members – most recently by the Continuing Professional Development programme of the RIBA who are catching up with the RICS, CIBSE, ICE, ISE and CIOB in this general area. The role played by the CIOB itself in organising this Symposium illustrates the Institutional support for information exchange in the building industry.

The "Constructor's" role is well illustrated in a series of papers in "Building" this summer by Ian Macpherson,(4) the project director at Broadgate, one of our major commercial developments. He emphasises the way in which knowledge was shared amongst all those involved, and indeed the clients, Rosehaugh Stanhope Developments, and the construction managers Bovis found opportunities for studies by Reading and Brunel Universities of the training of both skilled workers and managers. Provision of construction managers with the knowledge and skills now needed is not keeping pace with demand in the UK despite the success of the relatively few Departments of Building science and/or technology in our Universities. To some extent this reflects the status of the industry perceived by young people looking for challenging careers. This was one of the important messages of the BEC/CIOB Joint Committee on Higher Education chaired by Sir James Lighthill, which reported last year.(5) Those of you in this major industry can have no doubt of the challenge and rewards it offers – but this is not the perception of the ubiquitous man-in-the-street in this country. In my brief acquaintance

with building - looking at the buildings around us, and visiting
building sites, I am sure that we have a lot to be proud of.
Perhaps our management of knowledge should start by broadcasting
this pride more effectively.

I said earlier that perhaps my list of "managers" should
include lawyers. The increasingly litigious culture that we
suffer, and rising personal indemnity premiums for professionals,
helps to sustain the view that industry creates more than its fair
share of problems. But it also reflects the peculiarity of a
building - if it doesn't work you cannot send it back under
guarantee! The knowledge of many outstanding building
professionals is then harnessed to lawyers' search for redress.
Much better, by far, to organise that knowledge and experience to
avoid the cause of failure in the first place.

The management of knowledge by suppliers is, in part, the
business of their individual industrial management, but it
interfaces with construction in the guidance they are able to give
designers and users about how their materials behave and should be
handled. It is clearly essential that this process is effective
and that the quality of materials and the technical support
available in their use is clearly established.

The last person I have considered - and sometimes the last
person to be considered by the Industry - is the user. Yet in his
hands lies the responsibility for getting the best out of a
building, and knowledge is the key. I was much encouraged last
year to be associated with the publication of a guide to owners of
Timber and Brick Homes prepared by the Timber & Brick Homes
Consortium.(6) Later that year BRE produced guidance on how to
avoid condensation and mould growth in homes, much of it about
sensible user behaviour. A long way from construction management?
Perhaps, but the ability to describe accurately the building he
occupies and how he should use it to a user is itself a test of
the control management has exercised in its construction.

Ultimately we also have to consider as "users" those who enjoy
the built environment that the Industry achieves. In the UK this
is governed by planning regulations that themselves are a
management issue in construction.

Money
Despite the availability of clear analyses of life-cycle-costing
techniques for construction, such as that by Dr Flanagan and Dr
Norman from Reading, published by the QS Division of the RICS four
years ago,(7) total building costs are not yet established as a
primary design consideration as opposed to the first-cost of a
building. Those who attended the seminar held by the Institution
of Civil Engineers last year will perhaps recognise the different
perspective held by developers and researchers. My further
difficulty in understanding the way in which builders are paid for
their work through surveyors' measurement leads me to conclude, as
you will already have done, that this part of my matrix is best

left to someone better informed. However, I cannot leave this
topic without some reference to the problem of relating cost to
value as an issue for all those involved. Often the total cost of
a project is determined initially on broad judgements, but as
these estimates are refined when detail is known additional
finance may not be possible. Cost-cutting excercises then ensue
that may have serious consequences for the value of the final
product, either in its durability or in its usefulness. As Ian
Macpherson reminds us(4) such damaging cost-cutting exercises can
be avoided by early introduction of well established value
engineering techniques into the project. Experience shows that
the same quality and purpose can often be achieved more cheaply
than was at first thought possible. No doubt some of you will
continue to discuss this issue next week at the CIB W55 SYMPOSIUM
and we look forward to the results of a study that the RICS has
sponsored of practice in the USA.

Manpower

I have already spoken about the problems in the UK of providing
enough adequately educated and trained people to satisfy the needs
of the industry, and the importance of the clients' and designers'
use of the skills of their staff. In construction management the
constructors bear the major burden of man-management, often in
small groups of independent subcontracted workers. In a paper
published in the first issue of IJCM&T (to which I referred
earlier), Fryer and Fryer(8) quote a study of 50 construction
managers which showed that they perceived the ability to deal with
people as one of their most important skills. These skills
include an understanding of human relations which should be
included in the training for managers in construction. The need
for "a consultative approach which allowed all members of the
building team to develop a motivation towards quality work" was
one of the conclusions of the work BRE did for the Building EDC on
"Quality on Building Sites"(9). Managers also need to know what
people should do, what they are doing and what they have done. We
also showed that many problems (over a quarter of those observed)
arose because operatives did not know what they were supposed to
be doing. Other studies have shown the difficulty of being sure
about what is happening, or has happened, on a building site.

Materials

As a one-time materials scientist this is an area in which I would
like to spend most time, but I believe the principal issue is
management of the information available about how materials behave
in buildings and how they should be handled in fabrication and
subsequent use. Quality assurance is most advanced in this
section of the Industry.

There are however interesting issues raised in the handling of
materials. The choice of sea-dredged aggregate for concrete at
the Sizewell nuclear power station was influenced by the need to
avoid traffic on local roads; when I first arrived at BRE a
colleague, Ted Skoyles, taking me round building sites, pointed
out the number of bricks ground into the mud at more than 10p a

time! Between these extremes there are a wide range of
opportunities for good management. And there is much such
management when we consider that building a major project in inner
London, for example, is equivalent in material-handling terms to
erecting a super-tanker in Leicester Square.

Time

The last of my 'resource' headings, but this is the all important
determinant of the rate at which all the other resources are
consumed. It is also the resource over which management of
construction has had the most decisive influence in recent years,
and seems likely to continue to do so.

Last year the Building Employers Confederation published(10)
work by the University of Reading showing cases where the speed of
construction in the UK has matched that of the USA. This work
reinforces BRE findings contained in the Building EDC booklet
"Faster Building for Industry" published four years ago(11). Two
quotations:-

"The research has shown that the British construction industry
can deliver quickly and efficiently in the right circumstances",

and:-

"We believe this research clearly demonstrates substantial
scope for improving the general pace of construction of industrial
buildings without sacrificing quality or increasing cost",

with the underlying message that where a client demanded fast
build, the need for high quality construction management was a
necessary consequence, and such management delivered fast build
with no penalties. You can see this in a number of recent
developments in the UK.

Research

That researchers have pointed out such success is the final theme
of this paper because too often research is associated with
post-mortems.

The SERC specially promoted programme in construction
management that I referred to earlier led directly to the
inaugural meeting of ARCOM at the South Bank Polytechnic in May
1983, and I am delighted that BRE has been able to host two of
their conferences. I see this Association as a powerful body for
identifying with the Industry what problems need to be addressed,
identifying with Academia and the Professions which areas of
knowledge need refreshing, and seeking effective application of
the results. Internationally, CIB 65 can play something of the
same role, as long as it pursues the CIB aim, declared in its Long
Range Plan last year, to achieve relevance. I was concerned,
therefore, to see the report of the W65 Task Group (a) meeting
last year in Italy, when the lack of interest in their research by
the building industry was deplored - at length. I suspect that

this is due not only to an apathetic industry, but more to a
misdirected research community - however unpopular that view may
be to this audience. What I think we must realise is that it is
difficult to show that research on management of construction has
made any contribution to recent advances in industrial
performance. The contribution that the researchers are seen to
make, as BRE has done for years now, is to provide objective
monitoring of what is happening at the management intersections I
have described. This may then quicken the tempo of learning from
experience. Our research therefore needs to concentrate on the
observation and reporting of success.

This also means that we need to discover how to improve
management of knowledge in the Industry - and to learn ourselves
how to manage the knowledge we generate about succes so that it
will be received and understood by a welcoming audience. In the
area of thermal performance of buildings the UK Energy Efficiency
Office has shown how demonstrations in the form of building
projects can put the research message across. But the message has
to be a positive one - positive feedback amplifies the signal,
negative feedback attenuates it! The challenge we face as
researchers is to show how effective management in construction
(when all concerned are confident that they understand the
problems they face, when all are up-to-date in the technological
state-of-art, and apply good practice in design, construction and
management) can keep a business out ahead of the competition!

REFERENCES

1. . for example:
   "A Client's Guide to Management Contracts in Building",
   CIRIA, SP 33, 1984.

   "Thinking About Building", NEDO, 1985.

   "Better Briefing Means Better Buildings", J J N O'Reilly,
   BRE Report, 1987.

   "Building for Industry and Commerce", CIOB, 1980.

2. "Using Experience and Publications in building design",
   Heather Marvin, BRE Information Paper 13/85.

3. "Information and Experience in Architectural Design",
   Heather Marvin, IAAS, University of York, Research Paper 23,
   June 1985.

4. "Broadgate" Series, Ian Macpherson, "Building" May 15 to
   June 19, 1987.

5. "Degrees in Building Management: Demand, Provision and
   Promotion",   Report of the BEC/CIOB Joint Committee on Higher
   Education in Building, August 1986.

6. "Timber and Brick Homes Handbook", The Timber and Brick Homes Information Council, January 1986.

7. "Life Cycle Costing for Construction", Roger Flanagan and George Norman, QS Division, RICS, July 1983.

8. International Journal of Construction Management and Technology,Vol 1, No.1, 1986.

9. "Achieving Quality on Building Sites", NEDO, January 1987.

10."A Fresh Look at the UK and US Building Industries", R Flanagan, G Norman, V Ireland and R Ormerod, Building Employers Confederation, September 1986.

11."Faster Building for Industry", NEDO, June 1983.

Part VIII
Keynote addresses

THE SCHELDT BARRIER

T Van der Schaaf

1. Introduction

This paper deals with the management of design and construction from 5 control instruments:
quality and performance, time, money, organisation and information.
Experience in this subject will be discussed in relation to the Storm-surgebarrier mega project in the Eastern Scheldt.

2. The project

The main project characteristics are listed below:

. technical
- closure of the barrier under any condition
- 25 percent reduction in tide
- maximum load incidence of $2,5 \times 0,0001/yr$
- guaranteed lifetime of 200 years

. delivery
- in 1986

. costing
- original estimate (1976 prices) - Dfl. 3,0 bn
- outturn cost (1987 prices) - Dfl. 5.7 bn
- cost overrun without inflation 30 o/o

. organisation
- matrix
- participation of civil engineering contractor consortia in design matrix

. client
- Government of The Netherlands represented by Rijkswaterstaat, a division of the Ministry of Transport and Public Works.

. <u>contractor consortia</u>
  - civil and marine engineering
    by Dosbouw vof comprising:
    . Ballast Nedam Groep N.V.
    . Baggermaatschappij Breejenbout N.V.
    . Hollandse Beton Groep N.V.
    . Van Oord Utrecht N.V./ACZ Marine Contractors B.V.
    . Dirk Verstoep N.V.
    . Royal Volker Stevin N.V.

  - gates and electromechanical operating systems by
    OSTEM vof, comprising:
    . Grootint B.V.
    . Hollandia-Kloos B.V.

The barrier is a mega-project because of the fact that
the project displays the following characteristics:
- long execution time (more than 3-5 years), which can
  lead to changes in the design. It is impossible to
  work out every design detail in advance. The extent
  of certain technical problems only becomes clear
  during construction;
- major impacts outside the project - such as water
  management, natural environment, national or
  regional economy, labour market, etc. - mobilizing
  political interest and causing the project to become
  a periodic topic of discussion in the political
  arena;
- the application of advanced technologies which have
  not, or not fully, been tested in prototype. Hence
  there are no historical cost data which would
  normally provide a basis for the estimate;
- the once-only nature of the project in which one is
  unable to fall back on past experience gained in
  similar projects: accurate estimates are therefore
  not possible;
- great complexity, which involves a large number of
  interrelated processes;
- application of a (extensive) project organisation
  with complicated communication and information
  channels, procedures, etc. and explicit task
  qualifications in relation to the existing line
  organisation;
- large budget;
- high risk on the part of the principal for
  calamities, negative cost developments etc.;
- limited possibilities for insurance coverage.

3. Quality and performance control

3.1 Design

3.1.1 Working Methodology

During each stage of the design, the designer adopts a methodology which involves the following steps in the design cycle diagram below, and by repeating the cycle, generates the correct solution in a systematic manner.

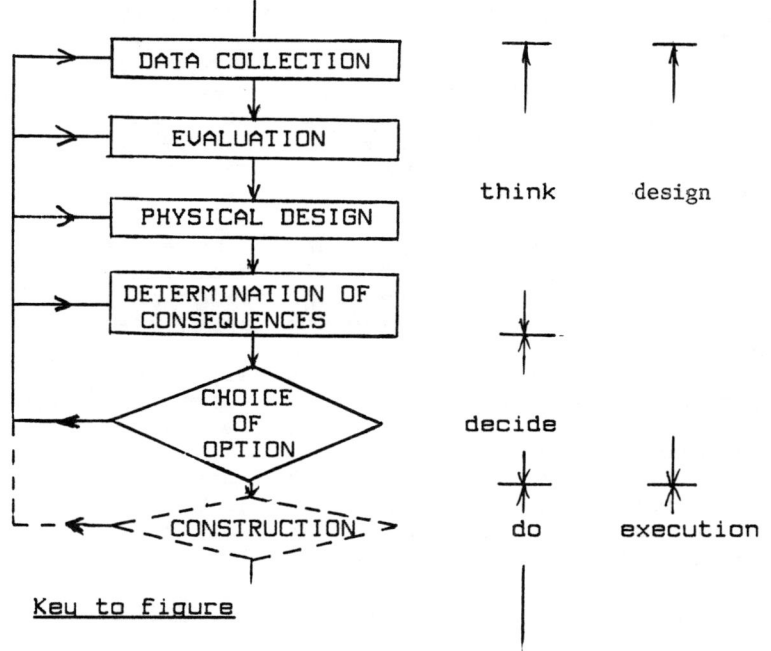

Key to figure

- the collection and analysis of data, boundary-conditions, criteria and goals;
- the evaluation (determining the concreteness, and/or the relative weighting) of boundary-conditions and criteria; determining of design philosophy;
- the physical design of the project, taking previous stages into account;
- determining the consequences of the design for diverse aspects;
- the choice of option and comparison of consequences (examined in the light of the pre-conditions).

43

It should be noted that : with respect to preparation
of a project:
- during each design stage, insufficient account is
  often takes of the requirements and wishes to which
  the design will be subjected in subsequent stages.
  This leads to loss of quality when the design is being
  worked out in detail since limitations on design
  freedom often mean that an optimal solution can no
  longer be realized, and that extra construction and
  maintenance costs are incurred because construction
  and maintenance personnel are often confronted with
  design flaws;

- in some cases a certain (familiar) solution is seized
  upon without thorough analysis of the problem having
  been conducted; too little effort is made to
  incorporate the various pre-conditions into the design
  in an integral manner.

In general one does not spend enough money on quality
assurance in the design phase of the building process.
The client appreciates a thorough design review in an
unadequate way; it costs time and money. Insight
knowledge of the connection between the material
choices and the care for a good detailing of the
design and the maintenance costs in long term for e.g.
the infrastructure such as sluices, scope protection,
dikes etc., is not well known.
A lot of attention is payed to the duration on a long
run to keep the maintenance cost low. This leads to
high investments on infrastructural works which are
able to survive their economical life time anyhow.

3.1.2 Analytic-policy oriented and methodical
approach

In order to arrive at better balanced and more
insightful project preparation, it is proposed that an
approach to design be stimulated which is (a)
analytic-policy oriented and (b) methodical.

a. Analytical-policy approach to design

An analytic-policy oriented approach implies, among
other things, that: during each stage of design the
design activities are carried out in the phases: -
analysis of the problem, development of alternatives,
determination of consequences, and choice of option.
One must not hastily adopt solutions at a project's
outset, but rather after first conducting a sound

analysis of the problem, generate a solution based on
the pre-conditions. One should not submit solutions to
the designer as if they were pre-conditions, but
rather involve the designer in the project at an early
stage;
- suitable methods and techniques are employed in the
  various phases. (see also b. below)
- design activities are not only informed by
  retrospective considerations involving previous
  design stages, but also by anticipation of subsequent
  stages in the design process;
- a number of mutually comparable alternatives are
  worked out in detail and presented as such;
- the role of uncertainty factors in the evaluation and
  weighting of consequences for the design is made
  explicit;
- the criteria adopted and the reasons for selecting a
  certain alternative are made clear;

One can stimulate an analytic-policy approach by:
- establishing a plan at the outset of the project
  which clearly states how the above-mentioned
  guidelines are to be put into operation;
- spreading awareness of state-of-the-art know-how and
  experience;
- drawing up a manual for the analytic-policy approach
  to the general plan.

b. Methodical approach

One should develop and promote the use of methods and
techniques which are useful in:
- analysis of the problem, e.g. methods according to
  which inventories could be made of the consequences
  of proposed alternatives (among others, methods of
  system analysis), and methods for the development of
  quantitative yardsticks (among others, target-setting
  analysis);
- the generation of alternatives and variants;
- the determination of consequences, by means of, for
  example, theoretical model-building and forecasting
  methodologies. It is of importance that current
  consequence-determining methodologies be optimalized
  (by means of, among other things, systematic
  evaluation of the design products.).
- the comparison of alternatives. In particular, tools
  for establishing a hierarchy of the alternatives for
  each of the individual criteria, e.g. multi-criteria
  analysis.

3.2.   Execution

The management in the executive phase has to follow the rules of 4 important systems:
. the system of cost management
. the system of schedule management
. the system of quality assurance
. the system of human resource management

These systems have many conflicting rules and where this situation occurs very often a compromise is reached.
Many times the quality is a victim of such compromises. During the actual execution it will become apparent that many activities are interwoven and influence each other. Stagnation of the progress of a single activity can delay the progress of many others, and resulting indirect losses could prove to be far greater than the losses which a single activity might cause.
The construction practice is very famous of the talent of improvisation; the influence of such talent leads to higher costs and less quality; in addition to that there is not very much attention payed to the design of preventive measures.

3.3   Experience at the Storm Surge Barrier

3.3.1 Feasibility study

As a result of the political discussion, in November 1974, a decision was made to investigate the feasibility of the alternative solution of the closure of the Eastern Scheldt. This study should be carried out in 1 1/2 year and the criteria were:
- a structure, normally open and only to be closed during severe storms had tot be technically feasible;
- the cost of the structure should not exceed the cost of full closure by more than 1.2 billion guilders (with a contingency of 20 o/o);
- the structure had to be completed in 1985.

The final decision was planned to be made in 1976.

3.3.2 Policy analysis

Apart from this study, another study was started. At that time, a general feeling was apparent, that whatever the result of the feasibility study, the decision itself had to be better founded. The most important decision to be made was the choice between

3 alternatives:
- fully closed Eastern Scheldt according to the original plan;
- half open dam (flood barrier);
- open Eastern Scheldt with heightening of the dikes.

To prepare for this decision a policy analysis was started with help of the Rand Corporation, Santa Monica, USA.

In this analysis, the 3 alternatives were compared, based on a great number of aspects such as safety, environmentol impact, fishery, watermanagement, shipping, recreation, cost, economy and planning. The result of this study was a major contribution to the final decision made in June 1976.

3.3.3 Organisation

It was clear to the management of the project that it was impossible to carry out this study without the help of all resources available. This meant that beside of Rijkswaterstaat, the researchinstitutes and a number of large contractors were involved in this study. In a very short time a lot of alternatives were investigated. Futuristic looking design alternatives and other concepts just looking simple but often inconsistent with physics passed in review. This 1 1/2 was a crazy time. There was no question of any systematic research or approach. After some time it became clear that the available knowledge was insufficient to make a fully new design concept of the closure of the largest estuary of the Deltaproject. But just like in other disciplines, the bold step forward is made in such a situation. The whole organisation was convinced that it was possible to make a structure which could normally let pass the tide and that would only be closed during severe circumstances. And this conviction is essential to be succesfull. The design delivered to the Government after this 1 1/2 year was not a worked out pre-design; it was more or less a design idea, feasible in the mind of the designers and founded on belief and self-confidence. It must be said that this self-confidence was also apparent in the policy analysis and after all it will be clear that this self-confidence was justified.

3.3.4 Implementation

After the decision in June 1976 which was in favour of the half-open dam, the struggle for success begun vehemently. A projectorganisation was set up. Rijkswaterstaat and the contractor, a combination of 6 large Dutch contractors in civil engineering, worked together in a matrix organisation. In a short time, the design ideas had to be transformed into detailed designs which were to be built in the deep water with the strong currents of the Eastern Scheldt. So many problems had to be solved, that no carefully planned systematic research was possible in the first 2 years. Basic and applied research were carried out simultaneously. Research on boundary conditions was not finished at the time that these boundary conditions were used in the applied research. The period of the middle of 1976 to the end of 1977 can be characterized as the second phase of the original feasibility study, but the organisation was much more clear and consistent than in the period before. From the beginnen of 1978, the systematic approach was apparent in the whole organisation. Designgroups had clear tasks, the coordination of the research activities was well organised and the managament controlled progress.

3.3.5 Risk analysis - a way of thinking

Risk analysis is the systematic investigation of uncertainties inherent in a process. To specify the type of uncertainty under investigation, the discipline may be referred to as reliability analysis, sensitivity analysis, failure analysis, etc. The subject of analysis may be a thing, such as a pump, or a nuclear power station, but also a process, such as driving a car, or building a flood barrier. A process like motoring is not a likely subject for risk analysis, not because it is free of risks, but because the inherent risks (personal injury through accidents; getting stranded with engine trouble; incurring parking tickets, etc.) are sufficiently known. Our experience of the contingencies of motoring is so complete that there seems to be no point in conducting desk studies on the subject. The evidence from real life suffices. In the case of motoring a certain, largely unconscious, balance has developed between the need for prevention of undesirable consequences and acceptance of the risk of their occurence. Constructing a flood barrier with closable gates across a tidal esturay is very different in this respect. Apart from convential techniques, the construction involves a great many new ones; here lack of experience causes much uncertainty, as the risks involved are largely unknown. However, many of those working on the project have been developing ideas on the subject, and it is the task of the risk analyzer to bring out this latent knowledge by systematic inquiry. The next question to be answered is whether the risk situation is acceptable and, if it is not, what should be done to improve it. Risk analysis enable us to recognize, to discuss, and to influence risks..

In a well-planned project the aspects quality, money and time should be able to influence one another. If that is indeed the case, setbacks in one sector can be compensated from the other two. As a result of the legal framework which was the basis of the project mutual influencing of the three factors became nearly impossible. This was a severe constraint for the freedom of design. As a result of the systematic risk analysis these limitations could be overcome to a large extent. A comprehensive risk analysis of a project includes the same three aspects. The quality part comprises a risk analysis of the technology, in design as well as execution, in which undesirable events result in either a loss of quality, or time, and/or money.

3.3.6 Risk analysis in the design phase

The design philosophy was that the barrier was one part of a total sea defence system, to which dykes and other construction work such as the locks in the Eastern Scheldt basin also belong.
The strength of the various barrier components and the barrier itself is well balanced. This was accomplished by means of a risk analysis of the barrier and its components. Probabilistic methods greatly influenced the design of the barrier.
It proved possible to establish the joint probability density function of the storm surge level, the basin level and the wave energy, to be in the region of very low probability, by a combination of physical and mathematical modelling techniques.
The probabilistic load determination provided more realistic loading combinations; these were 40 per cent lower than the deterministic values previously used.
The introduction of probabilistic design methods and a more industrial approach to construction required a high level of attention to quality control.

Previously, quality control had been based on experience and expertise, in effect on intuition. The industrial approach to construction led to more determined scientifically-based specifications. Quality control for the barrier construction was centred on so-called quality control groups, which consisted of personnel involved in design, research and execution.
As a result, new quality control specifications were defined for new working methods as well as for materisals such as sand, gravel, slag and quarry stone.

A crucial factor in all this is the assumption that during the execution phase no major deviations in product quality from the strength specified in the design will occur. However, there are all sorts of influences which may alter the structure in unforseen ways. A risk analysis of the design phase therefore logically and necessarily entails a risk analysis of the execution phase. The aim of risk analysis in the execution phase, apart from safeguarding quality, is to reduce the need for improvisation during construction. Unexpected occurances during construction often call for quick action and improvisation. However personally rewarding such challenges may be, they usually cost time and money. The project managers therefore saw it as their duty to restrict the improvisational element as far as possible, by having it included in the risk analysis.

3.3.7 Analysis in the execution phase

As stated earlier, an important objective in the executive phase is the prevention of execution errors impairing the quality of the product. The errors in question are chiefly of the kind that remain unobserved, so that the loss of quality caused by them goes unobserved and unrepaired. The analysis aims at identifying those executional operations in which unobserved errors may occur, and at designing measures to reduce or even eliminate the probability of their occurance. The second objective, reducing the need for improvisation, involves the detection of any remaining "blind spots" in planning, and of probable sources of malfunction in people and technology. Usually such problems will show up during the execution phase and be solved in due course, but their adverse effects in terms of extra time and money may be substantially limited if the problem can be detected and dealt with an earlier stage. It is especially at points where one section of a project has to link up with another, and where there is a discontinuity in organisation, that such blind spots do occur. By incorporating a risk analysis group in a staff group which has access to all sections of the project it is well placed to detect this kind of linkage problem. Where malfunctioning of people and technology is concerned the analysis is based on the assumption that correct functioning is the norm and that the effects of incidental failures have to be investigated. If, in addition, some insight into the probability of failure is desired, the group may advise on the use of reserve equipment, or help to establish "emergency" procedure. Such procedures are of particular importance in failure situations, which often call for quick decision-making on the spot. The risk analysis procedure sets out as a stock-taking operation, by reviewing a process in general, but eventually it works towards results on three different levels:

- day-to-day operation: creating an awareness of problems; working out small-scale technical alternatives; making reserve materials available.
- sectional project management: preparing for quick decisionmaking in emergency situations; earmarking funds for preventive measures; incorporating risk factors in executional strategy.
- overall management: including risk assessment as a factor in the choice between alternatives; working out alternative courses of action in the event of a high risk assessment for the main course; holding means of production available with a view to the assessed risk of impaired quality of the product.

Recommendations for top-level decisions can be realistic only if they are borne out by experience at lower levels. An analysis which does not "get down" to details, if necessary to the very "nuts and bolts", cannot be anything but vague and non-committal. Risk analyzers are faced with long chains of causes and effects. The question is where to begin: from the loose bolt and upwards to the probable catastrophe, or from the catastrophe down to its probable causes? Practice has shown that it is best to start in the middle. Define clear, recognizable failures. Assess the consequences (tree of events) and at once link them to possible remedies.

Only in this manner it is possible to keep a firm grasp on the problem in hand. The risk analysis about design, time and money is part of the task of the owner. The analysis of the execution is carried out by the owner and the contractor together. In the projectorganisation of the Flood Barrier, risk analysis, both qualitative and quantitative plays an important role in most of the decisions. The management has gained experience in how to handle risks since the introduction of the probabilistic design method in 1978. Since then, risk analysis has become an important element in the decision making. We are convinced that this way of consistent thinking has contributed considerable to the relatively small exceedance of timeschedule and budget.

4.   Management of planning

4.1 Planning techniques

The most common and widely used techniques available for planning are: bar charts, network analysis and line of balance for repetitive construction work.

Bar charts are the easiest to understand and the most wisely used form of planning tool. It shows a list of activities with the start, direction and finish of each activity shown as a "bar" plotted to a time scale. The level of detail of the activities depends on the intended use of the plan. It is used for progress control, for calculating the resources required for the project and for estimating the work content interms of manhours or machine hours.

Network analysis is more applicable to complex operations. The smaller, self-contoured steps of a network of such analysis compared with a bar chart, opens the possibility of using computers for the calculations.

Line of balance is a planning technique for repetive work. The basis of technique is to find the required resources for each stage at operation so that the following stages are not interfered with and the target output can be achieved.

4.2   Planning the Storm Surge Barrier

4.2.1 Piers

For the construction of 66 piers the line of balance
technique was used.
Each of the 66 piers was devided into 7 construction
stages and one stage for final finishing activities.
The studies for the construction of the piers in
connection to the construction works in the gulleys
indicated that for each pier a total of 290 working
days was available with an interval of 8 days between
them
It was decided to work according to a so called
conveyor (assembling line) belt system which means:
one shift and its staff will always remain at the same
construction stage. To cope with downtimes in the
conveyor system, slack-time between construction stages
is required to deal with delays in one stage in view of
the next stage.
The gain in time obtained by the repetition effects
could be used to get the abovementioned required
slack-time. The totsal working time for a pier could be
reduced to 242 working days; equipment and staff
employed are based on this last figure for economical
reasons.

4.2.2 Planning the assembly

Due to circumstances it was decided to design and build
a prefabricated barrier.The elements of which the
barrier is composed are very large. The machines that
have been build to build the prefabricated elements are
large in comparision with the width of the three
channels in which they worked.
It became clear at a very early stage that the
limitations imposed by the space the machines occupy
would govern the assembly pace. Due to the
undesirability to cross anchor wires the working
vessels could not work closer to each other than 1000
m. Another determing factor for assembly planning was
the velocity of the tidal currents that could be
accepted with regard to scouring occurring in the
narrowing channels. It became evident that the best way
to represent the assembly plan was to put it down in
the way of a road-time diagram, very much like railways
and airlines do.

53

The plan was based on progress estimates of each
assembly unit. The progress estimates were forecast
after a study of each handling sequence and based on
annual w eather worse than average.

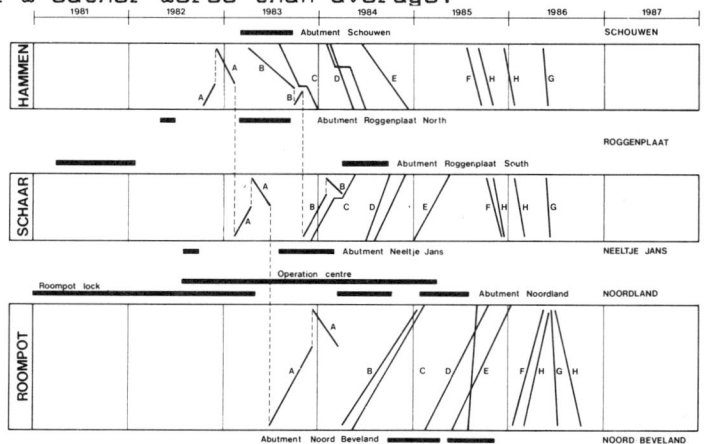

*The road time diagram was computerised to allow quick assessment of deviations from the
target progress: (A) "Cardium"; (B) "Ostrea"; (C) rock sill; (D) box girder bridge and capping
unit; (E) drop gates; (F) sill beams; (G) upper beams; and (H) cap rock placing.*

The consequences of deviations from the target progress
were very complex and, as these were certain to happen,
an effort had been made to computerize the road-time
diagram in order to enable a quick assessment to be
made of the effects on the other operations. THe
existence of a computerized road-time diagram enabled
the project management to implement in advance various
progress rates in the plan. In this way the sensitivity
of the plan could be tested and an eventual completion
date could be forecast with a certain probability. Thus
the probabilistic approach that was applied to the
design of the barrier, was also applied to the time
schedule.
To maintain schedule control it was needed:
- to update daily the job progress
- to bring potential problem areas to the attention of
  project management immediatly
- to take corrective actions to recoup or assure schedule
  maintenance
- to hold regular schedule revieuw meetings with the
  management
- to reforecast the schedule to highlight delay in
  projectcompletion dates or change to or addition of a
  critical path.

5.   Instruments for cost control

In every project cost control strongly depends on the
ability to cope with uncertainty.This applies especially
to mega-projects because of their long duration, the
large number of people involved, their diverse impacts
and their once-only nature.
The following subjects which enfluence cost control will
be discussed: technology, organisation, environment and
contracting.

5.1   Technology

The employment of new technology generally leads to cost
overruns. The lessen to be learned here is to employ new
technology as little as possible. The second lesson is to
establish the main features of the design as clearly as
possible and subsequently to change as little as possible
in these main features. In this way chain reactions can
be prevented and disturbances are localized.
The third lessen is to control continuously the
interaction between design and construction.
Aspects of the practical employment of extrapolated
techniques deserve special attention. Those working with
them must have fail in then. Close cooperation between
design and execution staff is essential.
This means evaluation of the construction aspects during
the design phase. However, this also means a constant and
structured feed-back during construction to starting
points in the design.
What is said in the above does not mean that the
application of new technology does not have its positive
aspcts, i.e. the generation of new knowledge and of
marketable expertise and products.
Large-scale projects should be grasped as a means of
stimulating technical development, with a view to export
opportonities.
However, little empirical research into the spin-off has
been carried out and it is difficult to indicate its
signaficance beforehand. It is clear, though, that the
spin-off is systematically underrated.

5.2   Organisation

Assessment of time, cost and quality

Important is to create a cost conscious atmosphere in the
organisation.
For good cost control it is necessary to:
- know what has to be done
- know what has been done
- know which remains to be done
- know what's wrong early and why
- to take corrective action

In every large project the totsal work must be split up
into a number of manageable parts. At the same time
however the separate elements should be constantly
synthesized, as the responsible sectors tend to
overstress the risks and to treat costs as secondary.
There is a need for people with a sharp eye on how
problems are solved in the design phase, as there is a
natural tendency to devote too much attention to matters
already familiair. It is important to discover the "white
spots" in the whole, as these can often be the cause of
unpleasant surprises. During the construction phase costs
are strongly emphasized. This should not, however,
detract from the quality of the work. In this case it is
expedient to carry out sensitivity analyses in which
certain alternative construction processes are considered
in terms of their consequences for time, cost and risks
with the aid of computer programs.

Restrictions in time, money and quality contribute to
efficient cost control in mega-projects. There should,
however, be a balanced assessment of these three aspects
at all phases of the project. During construction of a
mega-project the cost aspect should not be
over-emphasized by making irresponsible concessions to
the quality of the construction.

Financial management

The normal procedures used by the public services proved
unsuitable for this mega-project. Changing that system to
fit better with the project requirements, costed much
effort.
Nevertheless a solution has been formed in a special fast
procedure for the approval of expenditive proposals.

- External auditing

Intuition always plays a role in decision-making, especially when working with a tight time schedule. Technical audits, made in consultation with experts at home and abroad, increase confidence in certain solutions. In addition a periodic management audit should be held. Procedural agreements on the working methods are important for the smooth functioning of audits. This does not mean that (fundamental) differences of opinion do not emerge, but proper discussion of these will lead in itself to an improvement in the management system, contracting procedures, etc.

5.3   Environment

By this we mean influence exerted from outside the project organisation. Three categories may be distinguished: nature, politics and inflation.

- Nature

Nature manifests itself in air, water and soil; the behaviour of these elements is dynamic and the scale of the movements different. The uncertainty this causes for the project is reduced as far as possible by choosing construction methods which are independent of the stochastic charactereistics of nature.

Central problems often spring from natural circumstances such as type of foundations, hydraulic and meteorological conditions. Such problems are seldom caused by restraint in construction processes or by aspects of materials.

In general the removal of uncertainty by reducing vulnerability involves an increase in cost. Furthermore the extensive network of obseervation posts which has been built up in the Eastern Scheldt and the North Sea should be mentioned. This meant an increased predictability of disturbances due to improved prediction techniques in the field of meteorology and hydrology.

- Politics

In general mega-projects influence the social system to
such an extent that they generate conflicts, which often
leads to political boundary conditions inexpedient to
cost control. Moreover some parts of a mega-project run
the risk of becoming less acceptable due to the long
duration of the project. This leads to a shift in
functional demans. One way of handling the uncertainty of
political boundary conditions is to have a built-in
flexibility. However this always leads to extra costs,
which can be prohibitive in mega-projects.
There is always tension between the project leadership,
which looks primarily at the relative cost overrun and
the line organisation c.q. the political arena, whick
looks primarily at the absolute cost overrun.

Go/no-go decisions are particurly difficult in
mega-projects. Initially because of great uncertainties
and later on because the changeover to another
alternative is time-consuming and results in political
struggle. Strict time limits set for political reasons
lead to the danger that peoople think too quickly in
terms of solutions without penetrating the problem
beforehand.
One has to realize that mega-projects are politically so
sensitive that conditions set beforehand turn out to be
more restrictive than is desirable. Furthermore a no-go
decision based on cost increases would mean exceeding the
time limit for the project, as there would not even be a
pre-design for the alternatives. As the project
progresses, cost estimate uncertainties do decrease, but
at the same time the point-of-no-return may be reached.
The management has to establish with the client the
objectives with regard to the importance of achievement
of performance, cost or time targets.
The management decisions, large and small, should be
taken with the most important objective as starting
point; everyone in the organisation should be aware of
that objective.
The project's basic objectives must be carefully watched
over. Any shifts in emphasis which may occur, from the
performance (preliminary design phase) to the cost or
time norm (execution phase), for example, must be
formally approved.

The client, seeking to limit uncertainties, will benefit from a phased decision-making process as follows:

* pilot study   duration approx. 2.0 % of completion
                                            time
                 costs   approx. 0,5 % of total costs

* preliminary
      design   duration approx. 20.0 % of completion
                                            time
                 costs   approx. 5.0 % of total costs

* final design and execution

In the pilot study and preliminary design phases, alternative solutions should be developed alongside each other. Their elements must be developed evenly. The working approach is a process of refinement by which the desired aim is to be reached in a systematic manner. This can be achieved by division into phases whereby the end of each phase is followed by an assessment which leads to guidelines for the subsequent phase. The development of the project is brought about in stages.

Too short a period of preparation allows insufficient latitude for an approach to the problem on the level of basic principles, necessarily resulting in reliance on existing techniques and materials, and consequently limiting the opportunities of finding an optimal solution.

It would seem desirable that an external, independent body assesses the report which forms the basis for investment decisions. Special attention should be given to how uncertainties have been handled. This would also provide substantial help to the client in his supervisory task.
For reasons of proper management of public works the salaries of used servants involved in design and supervision should be added to the constrction contract's budget.

- Inflation
Inflation forms an important element in the cost development of mega-projects. The longer a project takes, the greater the chance of cost overrun; moreover, any extra work involved is also hit by inflation. It is advisable to agree at the start of the project on price compensation procedures so that suitable provision can be made in the budget.

5.4   Contracting

Contractors

In the case of normal projects a contractor carries out
the work according to a detailed decription of the works
after he has obtained an order for the work via a tender.
In the case of mega-projects the relationship is
generally different and this can best be illustrated with
the Eastern Scheldt example. A frame-contract was drawn
up in the period 1976-1977 between the government and a
combination of contractors. A large part of the storm
surge barrier falls under this agreement. The arguments
for this approach were:
- It was considered desirable to commit the Dutch
  contractors with their know-how from start to finish,
  considering the complexity of important parts of the
  project and the long construction period.
- There was a dynamic market in 1975-1977, characterized
  by a rapid growth and pull of activities outside the
  country. The committments made then were in the
  interest of the continuity of the work and an assured
  price level.

The following applies with regard to cost control of the
work under the frame-contract:
- The construction agreement with the contractor should
  be formulated so that cost factors are unambiguous to
  both parties. The size of the contractor's cash flow
  (liquid revenue - cash expenditure) must be in
  proportion to the actual results of his efforts. A
  compartmentalized contract is the most appropriate in
  this respect, provided that it includes an incentive
  factor.
- a gradual downward cost trend is achieved with
  recurring activities (the advantage of the learing
  curve) by dividing the total work in a number of
  successive packets and entered into a contract;
- the work, involved in each part of an agreement is
  contracted out to the combination for a fixed price.
  Where this is not possible (for activities where the
  risks cannot be properly assessed) an attempt is made,
  via built-in premiums, to influence the speed of
  production, while taking into consideration the quality
  criteria set by the principal.
- the contractor, as co-signatory of the frame-contract
  has a joint responsibility to strive for as low a price
  as possible and for overall cost control.

It can be concluded that the early involvement of contractors in the development of advanced projects in which aspects of execution play an important role serves to increase the client's confidence in the aspects of technology, scheduling and cost proving satisfactory at the project's completion.
Pre-requisites to such involvement are:

* mutual good faith;

* mutuality of discussion partners on a similar level, especially where costing aspects are concerned;

* establishment in advance of the terms and conditions under which the project is to be carried out.

6.   Organisation

For good project management is required: good people, effective systems and management support.
Advanced projects require a balanced personnel mix.
The working team must be assembled on a broad basis from:

* researchers;

* practically-oriented, typically older, designers and engineers;

* theoretical-scientific oriented, typically younger, designers and staff.

The team on the decision-making and steering level must:

* be small in number;

* consist of experienced members covering all aspects;

* be available on a full-time basis;

* be closely acqainted with the problem at hand.

Personnel with a total overview must be developed at strategic points.
The large number of interested parties, the extensive serial repecussions and the exceptionel risks demands a specially-equiped team for the project. This team must be tailor-made with change in mind. Such changes must occur concurrently with the design - execution - delivery stages of the project.

A challenge to the project management team is to be at
work on a project with very many different people, very
many different discipline, contractors, research
institutes and authorities and to care that always the
cross-connections get right; these are the connections
through which people of different disciplines yet make a
product which is linked up with one another.

Above and beyond its tasks in the areas of technology,
delivery-time and costs, the project organisation has
tasks involving the issue of reports on target-setting
and on the securing of support from interested parties.

Project organisation Eastern Scheldt Storm Surge Barrier: pulling together the various strands

An organisation chart of contractor in relation to
client, design staff and supervising staff is given
below.

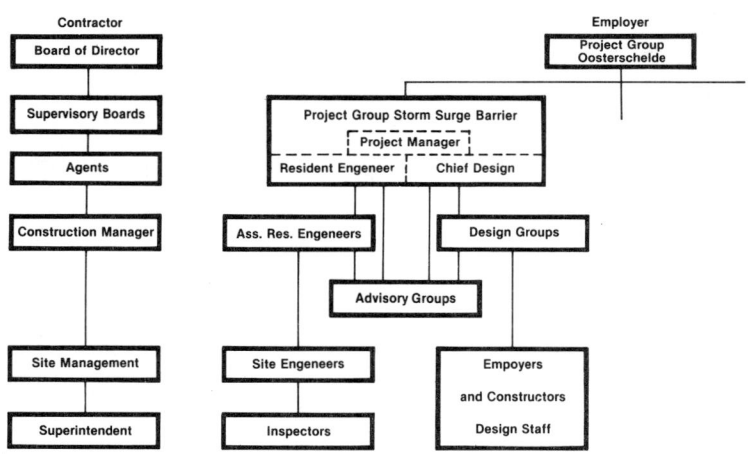

The design process took place in mixed groups
representing the civil engineering contractor and the
employer. These groups report to a design board that sets
out the main principles and checks the design of the
various groups for consistency with the main principles
and for cost.
Decisions are made at all levels of the design
organisations by consensus of the different disciplines
of engineering. This process of decisionmaking is
time-consuming, but it has the enormous advantage that
the design is accepted by all participants. General
acceptance of the design adds greatly to the motivation
of the design managers that consecutively are in charge
of constructing what they have designed.

During construction however the roles of employer and
contractor become more distinct. The contractor is given
a fixed price contract for a portion of the job and his
personnel is in charge of operations with the aim of
profitable progress.

The designers become inspectors and as such must not
interfere with the construction line of command. They
must be so informed at each decision level so as to
render them able to judge the soundness of the
contractors'decision with regard to quality, time and
cost.
This requires a change in the employer's organisation at
the time when the construction progress is so fast that
quick decisions must be made. Authority of a single man
taking decisions must replace the group decision-making
progress of the design period.

The above process of changing the organisation is a
continuous activity, as some elements of the construction
pass from the design to the construction stage earlier
than others.
Therefore during the construction time the organisations
of both the employer and the contractor have gradually
been changing from being design-oriented to
construction-oriented.

The assembly contracts are divided into five groups. The
manager of each group is also in charge of supervising
the prefabrication of the appurtenant elements.
The five groups are of similar relevance.

Each group has three decision levels. Decisions can be
made autonomously by each group manager as long as the
effects of his decisions do not affect the other groups.

This is not often the case therefore many cross-references have to be made, controlled by the project management. The decisions are governed by quality specifications and tolerance rules derived from an overall tolerance guideline. The five construction groups consist each of about 30 government employees. They are supported by just as many civil servants providing information, or furnishing support facilities to the constructions groups.

The information and support functions are listed below.

			REGULAR ORGANISATION	
	ADVISORY GROUPS		RIJKSWATERSTAAT	CONTRACTORS
			REGULAR MANAGEMENT	
PROJECT ORGANIZATION	PROJECT MANAGEMENT	1	STUDY AND RESEARCH	
		2	DESIGN AND WORK PREPERATION	
		3	SUPERVISION	EXECUTION
		4	MAINTENANCE AND SERVICES	
		5	PLANNING	
		6	COST ESTIMATION	PRICING
		7	ROUTINE ADMINISTRATION AND ACCOUNTING	
		8	ORGANISATION / PERSONNEL	
		9	SURVEY / UNDERWATERINSPECTION	
		10	SECRETARIAT / REPORTING	
		11	INFORMATION / PUBLIC RELATIONS	
		12	AUDITING	
		13	RISK ANALYSIS / TOLERANCES	
	PROJECT MANAGEMENT VERSUS REGULAR MANAGEMENT			

7.   Management of information and communication

The output of processes are largely depending on the circumstances existing during the course of the process. Factors influencing this circumstances are:
- the organisatonal rules (tasks, procedures, responsibilities)
- the material and immaterial means supporting the process
- the people with their individual personalities, their experiences, their motivation and their behaviour and culture as members of a group
- the provision of information as institutionalized with insures the delivery, processing and storing of information and knowledge.

The lifeblood of a project is information as it is the interface between everyone concerned with the project. It is necessary to relegate the means used to handle all information to the project to people with great appreciation of its importance.
Good information and communication is vital to project success, to ensure common understandig, to inform of job deviation or job progress, to record action, outcome or feedback.
Important are the periodical reports which cover in detail the overall status and progress of each phase of work.

Decisions should be properly communicated and as soos as they are taken all persons involved should be informed as to why certain arguments have been rejected; otherwise there will be a loss of motivation.

Each mega-project enjoys abundant attention from the media which is at times admiring ("this is a great enterprise") and at times critical ("everybode kew all long that it would go wrong").

The development of a public work project, as the Eastern Scheldt Storm Surge Barrier is, is governed by political decision and guided by established procedures.
As government agencies make no active use of the media, negative publicity can create tensions within the project organisation.

The political importance of the Eastern Scheldt Works is emphasized by the fact that the Minister of Transport and Public Works to parliament every half year on the communication between the project organisation and the Minister and on the other hand in the external communication between the Minister and parliament. This tension crops up in every mega-project. The project organisation looks primarily at the relative cost overrun, while the line management and the political environment looks primarily at the absolute cost overrun. A small relative cost increase (1% of the original Eastern Scheldt works budget comes to 50 million guilders!) means a successful project, but in a mega-project this leads at the same time to severe financial problems.

REFERENCES:

- Design Report Storm Surge Barrier Eastern Scheldt
  (in Dutch, published by the project organisation 1987)

- Proceedings of the Delta Barrier Symposium
  Rotterdam 1982

- Proceedings of the 8th Internet World Congress
  May 1985, Rotterdam

- Wearne, S.H. Control of engineering projects
  (Edward Arnold Publishers Ltd 1974 Londen)

- Harris, F. and McCaffer,R. - Modern Construction
  Management - (Granada Publishing Limited, Londen 1977)

REFURBISHMENT, REHABILITATION AND RENOVATION

Norman Douglas FCIOB

Director Costain Construction Limited (Refurbishment Division)

Managing Director Costain Renovations Limited

The subject allotted to me falls into the hands of a speaker, who you will find is not academic, but is a total Builder and Contractor.

Accordingly, my observations will be biased from the Contractors side of the Industry, for which I offer no apology at this stage. My comments will also be concentrated on the United Kingdom, as my experience Internationally is very brief, as compared with a career in this country, mainly specialising in the Refurbishment, Rehabilitation and Renovation spheres of the UK Building Industry.

I hope, however, that factors, problems and demand will have some relevance to industries of all those countries which the participants of this Symposium represent.

DEFINITION
Refurbishment, Rehabilitation and Renovation may be regarded as the process of changing a building, or indeed an area previously unusable or unsuitable, to a condition where it becomes usable at a standard acceptable to the community.   It may involve substantial change of use. This heading also includes Improvement which is less dramatic and does not usually involve change of use.

I would also suggest that Repair and Maintenance enters into this section of the Building Industry, which implies the continuing up-keep of building stock to existing standards.

HISTORY AND BUILD UP
The Refurbishment, Rehabilitation, Renovation - Improvement - Repair and Maintenance, (for which there can be no physical hard and fast lines between categories), must have existed in the Building Industry, almost as long as the Industry itself.

Any study of ancient buildings and monuments in this country today, will almost without exception indicate major changes, improvements, extensions, refurbishment and renovation of the present building.   In many cases, there may have been several buildings on the site during its history.

It is in comparatively recent times, with the advent of technological advance in building systems, materials and Management skills, that recognition seems to have been given separately to the area of Refurbishment within the contracting side of the Industry.

Sociological changes throughout the centuries have demanded alteration, improvement to existing building stock.   In modern times change has been much more radical and rapid.

In recent history (say the last 40/50 years), we have seen a number of changes within the Sector.

There was a severe shortage of buildings and works as a result of the Second World War.   Little maintenance of buildings had been carried out, and repairs had been curtailed to emergency war-damage repairs.

Immediately post Second World War, the Industry concentrated on War Damage Repairs and the reinstatment of dilapidations caused by non-maintenance during the war period.   New building was restricted and controlled.   Countries suffered from political and financial crises.   Gradually national economies were re-inflated, and by the mid 1970's, the severe shortage of buildings and the urgent demands for additional stock had been met.

Since the mid 1970's the demand for new buildings has been lower, leaving repair, maintenance, refurbishment and improvement with a higher proportion of the Industry's work load.

In a mature economy, once there are sufficient buildings and works, there must be more emphasis on repair, maintenance and improvement rather than on new construction.   At the same time the long life of construction products, implies to some degree a long interval between new construction and replacement.

On the other hand, the age and condition of some stock of buildings, and the fact that some is no longer suitable or required for the purpose for which it was originally intended, means there is a demand for rehabilitation and improvement. In addition there has been a reaction against new building and in favour of refurbishing and rehabilitation for aesthetic reasons.

There has also been a reaction against new building caused by the defects and failures of buildings designed and constructed in the period of the "demolish and redevelop" syndrome of the late 50's, and 60's. There have been signs that clientele now go out of their way to adapt buildings for new uses and changing requirements, rather than consider new.

Legislation and movement towards "Conservation" which has
been intensified by English Heritage, formerly known as the
Historic Buildings and Monuments Commission, has contributed
to the increase of specialist refurbishment and rehabilitation
activities over several years.

Local Authorities have strengthened their requirements with
regard to the retention of traditional building for purely
aesthetical reasons. The imposition of differing grades of
preservation, affects not only residential but all aspects
of community building.

In the 1980's, a number of new initiatives have been taken by
Central Government, amongst which "The Urban Programme" was
launched in July 1981 under which local authorities were asked
to develop schemes for securing economic regeneration, improving
the physical environment and ensuring that local services and
amenities are geared to the particular social needs of the local
communities in urban areas. Private sector involvement is
encouraged in these schemes, and for which substantial grants
have been given.

The current government is embarking on a whole new programme
of Inner City regeneration.

Thus whole areas are now the subject of rehabilitation, a
sector which is becoming ever more available to the Building
Industry, as may be witnessed by activities in the London Docks.

The need for improvement and repair and maintenance in housing
was documented in the "English House Condition Survey 1981".
The report indicated that there were 1.1 million dwellings
unfit to be lived in; 0.9 million dwellings lacking one of
five amenities; and 1.0 million dwellings requiring repairs
in excess of a value £7,000 (per dwelling).   With Government
encouraged improvement grants, both in the local authority and
private sector, the last few years have seen an increasing
market with rehabilitation of dwellings.

A further demand has been created by statutory requirements,
demanding the upgrading of building due to building regulations,
fire precautions, safety, offices and premises acts, asbestos
regulations and energy saving.

One last point is that there is usually a cost advantage –
albeit often small – in rehabilitation as opposed to new building.

All these separate factors have, and are continuing to, expand
the requirements of Refurbishment, Rehabilitation and
Renovation, in that now this sector carries out half the
Industry's Work Load.

THE CURRENT SCENE

Thus what for many years was considered to be within the general activities of building construction, initially confined to hastily assembled gangs of tradesman, more lately to small and medium sized Contractors, has now emerged as a recognised specialist sector of the Industry. Refurbishment, Rehabilitation and Renovation **are** not treated separately in the National Statistics of the Construction Industry, but are included within the figures for New Construction.

Repairs and Maintenance, however, are considered separately.

Out of a total estimated output for new construction and repair and maintenance combined of over £24,000 million per annum, repair and maintenance account for above 50% of the total. It is also noted that currently 20% to 25% of design work being carried out in Architects Offices, is in the refurbishment, rehabilitation sector.

Specialisation of the Sector, has probably resulted by major contractors, realising the potentiality of refurbishment, coupled with the reduction in new work, which also coincide with a general recession in the Industry, turned to the sector in numbers. Most major contractors have recognised the potentiality by forming new divisions, and selecting differing recognition of the specialist activity by names such as Refurbishment Divison, Special Works, Specialised Works Division, Special Contracts Division, etc. In the case of my own Company, works in this sector of the Industry were commenced 54 years ago, by the formation of a separate company which did not use the name of the main company until only 12 years ago, when it was changed to Costain Renovations Limited, and only just recently we have succumbed to the current mode by recognising it as the Refurbishment Division of Costain Construction Limited – which in its turn is the recognised Building Division for UK and Europe within the Costain Group. Many of the "specialist sectors" of major companies are now active in repair and maintenance in Term Maintenance Contracts.

Recognition by Major Contractors, I believe, has crystallised the "specialisation" of the sector, and the need for specialist skills of Management, both at site level and administratively is essential. The need for specialist skills to be retained and renurtured from the traditional skills of the Industry (i.e. stone-masonry, woodwork, plumbing, fibrous plastering, decoration, etc.) is equally important. It has also emphasized the importance of previous experience in the sector, and of the added problems to be encountered when estimating and carrying out refurbishment projects.

All types of clientele (Industrial, Commercial, Administrative, Public, Educational, Institutional and Residential) are covered by this Sector of the Industry.

Refurbishment, Rehabilitation and Renovation projects are variable in their scope. They vary from a simple refit of a retail store or superstore, involving no structural alterations, through to schemes which require all but the external walls to be demolished and a new internal structure built in its place.
Refurbishment and improvement of old listed buildings often entails the strengthening of old foundations. Once having stripped original finishings, a need for the replacement of structural components and treatment to eradicate rot and decay can be discovered : floors need restrengthening, load bearing walls bonded and strapped.

Again by way of variation, the Refurbishment Contractor may find himself re-fitting a Shopping Centre only completed 15 years ago, or even carrying out the fitting out of a store or office complex, the shell and structure of which have only just been completed.

Refurbishment contracts often have an element of new build encompassed in extensions or infill to the newly refurbished building. This usually has the qualities required of a new build operation, but with the added complications of more difficult access, co-ordination of modern detail and materials with existing and the need for programme co-ordination with the remaining past of the building.

Indicative of an organisation specialising in refurbishment and re-fitout work is the current cross section of work at present within my own organization.

Total 33 Contracts ranging from £300,000 to £13,000,000 in value.

3 Commercial	Properties – complete refurbishment with an extension built.
4 Commercial	Properties – retaining the external walls, complete re-newing internal structure and finishing.
3 Commercial	Properties – complete refurbishing, little or no structural work.
3 Commercial	Bank Buildings – complete refurbish including ancilliary offices.
1 Commercial	Conversion of old Convent School to small business units.
1 Commercial	Refurbish and refit existing warehouses for workshops and offices.

1 Commercial	Demolish building - rebuild to previous traditional style all finished with moulded cornices, window surrounds in "stucco" finish.
1 Hotel	Refurbishment of bedrooms and corridors.
3 Residential	Properties - complete refurbishing internally and externally to luxury finish, one with new swimming pool in basement.
1 Ambassador's Residence	Complete refurbishment to high quality finish, including renew roof.
1 Foreign Embassy	Refurbish existing, erect new large extension, all to high quality finish.
1 Government Building	Prestige refurbishment to a very high standard with major works infilling to light areas. Major Mechanical and Electric Services installation.
3 Retail	Food Supermarkets - refitting of existing shop with construction of new extensions.
1 Retail	Fitting out of new Shopping Centre-Concourse.
1 Telephone Exchange	Convert to commercial use.
2 Underground Stations	Complete refurbished - each contract consisting of 5/6 Stations.
1 School	Refurbishment of Science Laboratories in 5 different Schools in different locations.
1 Local Authority Flats	General refurbishment to multi-storey block of flats.
1 Local Authority	Term maintenance contract on houses, schools, public buildings.

Of the 33 Contracts, 16 are in full occupation by the Client throughout the contract period, the remainder vacant. The majority are of a "fast track" programme requirement.

CONSTRUCTIONAL MANAGEMENT PROBLEMS IN RELATIONSHIP TO REFURBISHMENT, REHABILITATION AND RENOVATION.
Every building project is different, possessing its own problems and difficulties. I maintain that variation is greatly increased on refurbishment work when compared to new work. Problems are further increased when carrying out refurbishment work in, or very adjacent to occupied buildings.

I summarise some of the "additional problems" which occur when compared with "new work".

Labour
1.   Work often difficult, and executed in uneconomical "small lots".
2.   Often access is restricted, as are working hours when alterations and extensions are being carried out to a building, or adjacent to a building, in which persons

are in occupation, and who cannot be disturbed by noisy
building operations.   Overtime working may be
required when a building is empty at the weekend.
3.   On the other hand it may not be possible, or you are
prevented by legal injunction, from working later than
certain hours each day or at weekend, for the fear of
disturbing nearby residents.
4.   Removal of rubbish and debris may be difficult,
particularly when working on upper floors with no direct
access to the outside.
This is particularly relevant to demolition activities.
5.   The nature of the work will preclude the extensive use of
many items of mechanical plant and power tools, resulting
in labour intensive operations and its effect on a
predicted level of productivity.
6.   The work can be more dangerous, dirtier and difficult,
requiring the payment of enhanced rates to operatives.
7.   When "matching up" to existing work in brickwork,
carpentry, plastering and all trades, a greater basic
craft skill is required than for new work.   This aspect
is becoming a greater problem "day by day", particularly
when the industry is tending to "overheat", (as witnessed
in London particularly at present).

Materials
1.   Unloading, distributing and getting materials into position
may present difficulties, with a considerable amount of
double handling and hoisting involved.
2.   Problems may arise in trying to match up new materials
with existing, e.g. existing bricks being imperial size
and new bricks being metric size, skirtings, architrave,
flooring, etc.
3.   Materials are often purchased in small quanitities.

Mechanical Plant
1.   Items of mechanical plant and equipment such as hoists
and scaffolding etc., may be subject to excessive periods
of standing time.

General Facilities and Services

1. Protection items may be costly, with following trades working in close proximity to newly finished work. Original work required to be maintained may likewise be a costly item for protection (i.e. polished wood surfaces, balustrading, doors, wall panelling, marble fireplaces, decorative ceilings, etc.).

2. Storage may be restricted, resulting in goods and materials being stored off site or in adjacent buildings.

3. If in occupation additional costs are often incurred in providing temporary services and the maintenance of existing services such as electricity for staff. Temporary dust screens, walkways and other protective measures must also be allowed.

4. Security is an increased problem, particularly when the building is in occupation, ensuring that it is properly locked up and secured at the end of each working day. (The pilferage of marble fireplaces, York Stone paving, traditional panelled and cased doors, historical chimney pots, and even vintage sanitary fittings, has become widespread, not only on sites but also from unoccupied vintage houses. The stolen material becoming the basis of a flourishing black market).

5. Supervision and co-ordination of the work force, sub-contractors, becomes difficult as operatives are often working in isolated areas and rooms throughout the building and not in immediate contact with foreman or chargehands.

6. With the nature of much of Refurbishment Work, the problems with regard to maintaining acceptable standards of Safety and Welfare are increased. Demolition, Temporary Support Work always add to hazards and maintaining the required standards of safety.

7. In connection with contractural obligations, the content and extent of the work may not be (and possibly cannot be) clearly defined, which can lead to dispute at a later date, or delay in payment for the works which can have an adverse effect on cash flow. In this context the responsiblity for defects and condition of the building may also be a matter for dispute if not clearly defined at time of tender bid.

8. The remeasurement of large areas of work due to provisional items being taken in the description, specification and quantities for a project, where the nature and extent of the requirements are uncertain at the time of tender.

9. When programming work load, planning resources and management requirements, an essential difference in refurbishment, is in the early build up of labour, materials procurement and sub-contractors. With new work there is a steady build up of trades commencing probably slowly with demolition, piling, steel frame, concreting, brickwork, etc., and not until the building is water-tight is there an appreciable multiplicity of trades, and this is

74

approximately halfway through the contract period.   Thus
there is a gradual build up and more time for procurement
and planning.   Refurbishment, generally apart from an
initial demolition or stripping out operation, requires
a multi-build up of trades in the first weeks of a contract,
putting extra pressure on the procurement and planning
activities.

These factors must be considered by the Refurbishment Contractor,
not only through the period of the contract, but of course at
the time of submitting his bid.

The essential differences may be summarised as:

Access, Materials supply and restriction, Storage, Noise,
Protection, Productivity, Safety, Security, Selection of
Labour, and last but not least, Management.

MANPOWER
The boundaries of skills in the Building Industry have changed
little over this century, and from time to time suggestions
have been made for a division of skills more in keeping with
modern requiremnts.   20 years ago, a study by the Building
Research Station pointed towards the need for a change in trades
and their training, including a requirement for broadly based
trades able to undertake a wide range of building work, possibly,
for example, wet trowel trades and dry trades.   The different
requirements of repair and maintenance and new work were also
shown.   I can see no evidence of widespread change to these
recommendations.   I understand there are some syllabi covering
trowel trades, except plastering, but any move to institute
courses where craft students may change from one craft to
another, simply does not operate. Flexibility is very limited.

Within trades there have been changes in requirements.   The
increasing proportion of refurbishment, rehabilitation, renovation,
repair and maintenance in the work load requires different types
of skills.   The existing training is geared towards skills for
new work and not for repair or rehabilitation.

Furthermore, the tendancy for skills to be split up on site,
and hence in trainees' experience into sub-skills (e.g.
shuttering carpenter, first and second fixing carpenter and
joiner) means that the generally skilled carpenter is getting
scarce, but he is just the type of person required for
rehabilitation work.

It is my opinion that action must be taken so that the necessary
skills should be available for the construction and renovation
of high class buildings and old buildings.   Dare I suggest the
consideration of a registration scheme for such a purpose or

putting the clock back and increasing the periods of
apprenticeship?   The first part dedicated to new construction,
the latter part to traditional trades.

Sub-Contractors
The practice of sub-contracting has grown throughout the Building
Industry.   This covers not only specialist labour and material
sub-contracting but also the employment of labour only
sub-contractors.   This tendency has effected the refurbishment
sector of the Industry, equally to new construction.

This helps the contractor in a number of ways: first it enables
him to choose specialist trade inputs when he wants them from a
range of specialist firms, who will have more "skill and know
how" than he can command;   second, he can obtain the advantages
of low prices by competitive bids;   third, it enables him to
keep his own work force small and minimise the costs of under
employed operatives on the payroll;   fourth, it allows him to
keep his working capital requirements down;   and lastly, it
gives him greater flexibility on the type of work to be undertaken
and in its execution.   The flexibility is particularly applicable
when employing labour only sub-contractors.

There are also disadvantages to the contractor.   Sub-contracting
requires supervision and management of a different type to that
on a site with directly employed operatives.   Although it may be
easy to negotiate a price for fairly straight forward work, it
is often difficult to do so for refurbishment, repair and
maintenance.

MANAGEMENT
Because of the multiplicity of inputs to a building site, the
fact that each project is a one-off operation open to many
vagaries and the difficulties of managing numbers of men working
together, often for the first time, the number of "ad hoc"
decisions that have to be taken by site managers is very great.
Moreover, the diversity of conditions from one site to another
and the particular characteristics of each site mean that these
decisions have to be taken by the man on site, often without
reference to seniors at head office, or to any information, apart
from his own personal knowledge, and often in response to some
particular problem necessitating quick action.   I suppose this
is why management generally on construction sites is often
described as crisis management.

By comparision, most factory and industrial processes are carried
on by clearly defined past practices and often are dictated by
fixed plant and machinery.   There are relatively fewer management
decisions, and those large ones that are taken are often helped
by a group decision with colleagues with a reasonable time period
in which to consider.

The cost of poor management on site is measured, not in the
direct costs of management, which are basically the managers'
remuneration and are small as percentage of the total costs,
but by increases in total costs of other inputs to the
construction process or failure to reduce costs. Poor management
increases the cost of materials, because of wastage due to bad
storage, pilferage or lack of care in use.   It increases the
cost of labour because of low productivity, poor workmanship
resulting in the need for rectification, and wastage of time
between jobs because of inadequate planning of the flow of
operations.   It can increase the cost of sub-contractors because
poor planning may mean they cannot start on site on time and
therefore can generate claims against the main contractor.   It
can increase the costs of plant, because of low utilisation and
improper maintenance.   All these things taken together, and
combined with the need for constant vigilance on such matters as
labour relations, safety, welfare requirements, and bad weather
precautions, may mean that the costs to the company of a poor
management team on site are very high indeed and can turn a
potentially profitable contract into one making a substantial
loss.

All these factors may well be said apply equally to new
construction and refurbishment.   I submit that the changes of
incidence of potential loss are greatly increased with
refurbishment operations.   Clients anticipated performance
programmes for refurbishment work, are invariably a great deal
more ambitious than for new construction work.   The refurbishment
contractor is therefore much more vulnerable to the performance
of management in the carrying out of "fast track" contracts.

My own experience indicates that craft skills provide the majority
of site management at the "work face" in refurbishment.
The proportion of craft based managers increases on the smaller
contracts, where there is a requirement for only one or a few
site based staff.   On major projects there is a larger proportion
of academic or technical type front site manager, but this manager
is backed by a level just below him of "craft trained" type
managers, again nearer the work face.   Thus there is a more
predominant requirement of craft based managers in refurbishment
and rehabilitation.

The qualities and qualification of Head Office and technical
staff are not quite so different to those required for new
construction.   It is important, however for them to gain
knowledge and skills of the major differences between the
different sectors of the Building Industry.   They should be
particularly mindful and capable of dealing with the added
problems and peculiarities of refurbishment and rehabilitation.
The demands and effects of fast programmes and early procurement
activities should be uppermost in their experience and knowledge.

There is concern within the Building Industry that for a sector
such as refurbishment, rehabilitation, repair or maintenance,
constituting a major proportion of the work load, all skills and
management training are directed to new construction skills. The
Sector itself must do more to project its image to compete with the
more "glamour" attractive large and new construction sector.

There is current concern as to the source of site technical and
administrative managers for the refurbishment sector. The
Construction Industry Research and Information Association
recommended in 1981 that apart from drawing attention to "The
development of methods of repair, maintenance, replacement and
refurbishment for various types of structures and installations,
but particularly buildings, bridges and sewers", also were of the
opinion that there should be an "Investigation of the type,
background and training of managers and supervisory staff in the
refurbishment and rehabilitation sector and of the future needs".

COSTS
Is refurbishment, renovation and rehabilitation, profitable to
the contractor?

Notwithstanding the trend of liquidation of companies within the
Industry, particularly amongst the smaller firms who carry out
such work as the whole or major portion of their business, trading
results generally tend to show this sector equally profitable as
new construction.

To differentiate between results for the differing sectors through
published accounts is difficult, if not impossible, but results
of my own organization (within a larger general building
construction unit) show net profit potential only in line with
results for new construction.

Cash flow, however, can be substantially under pressure, due to
slow payment for extra or more expensive work, which was not
covered in original bid documents or has been uncovered in
subsequent construction.

The proportioning of building costs is different. For instance,
labour costs are higher in the refurbishment sector as compared
with new construction when reflected as a percentage of the whole
cost, but there is a corresponding reduction in the percentage of
material costs. Percentage proportion of direct site on costs,
that is to say, site management, scaffolding, plant, establishment,
attendant labour, safety, welfare, etc., is higher (i.e.
increasing from say 10% to 13%/14% on average). General
Overhead Costs are higher by a fraction, but the net profit
result appear to be similar.

What are the costs to the Client?

The Cost of Mechanical Services, Electrical Services, Lifts and special finishing and furniture costs is significant.

Economic balance between redevelopment and refurbishment often requires an objective judgement.

CONCLUSION

Undoubtedly Refurbishment, Renovation, Rehabilitation is "in". Unthinking redevelopment is "out". There will always be a demand, fluctuating as economic factors and fashions dictate, but always an important, and maybe at times the predominant sector of any nation's Building Industry.

Developing Countries are now also realising the need to conserve and rehabilitate some of their older buildings, rather than demolish them and rebuild.

I have endeavoured to portray the picture of a typical UK Contracting Organization specialising in this sector of our large and varied Building Industry, the problems which are excerbated in this sector of the Industry, and probably one of two suggestions as to how performance and potential may be preserved and improved for the future.

I cannot but feel that in the sector of Industry I have described, which carries out 50% of the work load, it is incongruous that training of craft skills and management are based on " new construction". Such a comment may apply to methods of tendering, and form of contract, for they too seem to have been developed from new construction principles.

It is pleasing to note that Heriot-Watt University are at present conducting research into the Refurbishment section of the Industry. They are to be encouraged, and others too who consider, like myself, that the Refurbishment sector of the Building Industry should be reviewed as a separate entity; in many ways born of the same basic skills of new constnruction but so different in application.

To quote from Mr Owen Luder, a past president of the Royal Institute of British Architects:-

"All countries have building stock. The buildings will vary in age, condition and suitability in different parts of the world. Materials, climate, social habits and economics are different, but underlying problems have a remarkable degree of similarity. We can all learn from each other. The more we accept that the world is now a global village in which we all have a part to play, the quicker the problems will be resolved."

COST PER M2	OVERALL COSTS INCLUDING M & E SERVICES LIFTS, ETC.		NET BUILDING COSTS LESS M & E SERVICES LIFTS, ETC.	
	RANGE	AVERAGE	RANGE	AVERAGE
COMMERCIAL REBUILD Elevations retained but internals demolished and rebuilt	£862–£1282	£1045	£761–£893	£816
COMMERCIAL REFURBISHMENT Repair, some alteration, extension and refurbishment throughout.	£712–£1016	£865	£481–£769	£687
DOMESTIC REFURBISHMENT Ditto as last, but to a luxury standard throughout.	£746–£962	£793	£472–£768	£572
INDUSTRIAL REFURBISHMENT General refitting out, to a change of use to Industrial Purposes.	£138–£185	£158	£110–£127	£118
COMMERCIAL Refitting out of Office Accommodation to up-dated standard.	£318–£578	£388	£237–£504	£305
RETAIL Stripping out re-fitting of retail properties to up-dated standard.	£725–£866	£866	£385–£464	£464
COMMERCIAL NEW BUILD To vary high standard, to a traditional style of design.	£1260–£1361	£1339	£1019–£1097	£1037
COMMERCIAL NEW BUILD Basic unfitted office block - open areas only.	£760–£896	£818	£495–£696	£593

The above prices are for net building costs, in the one column, inclusive of M and E Services, Lifts, finishing costs, and the other column without these items. They include for site on costs overheads and profit, but do not include for professional fees, finance or development charges.

Care must be exercised in reviewing overall costs of projects when quoted as a cost per area of building. As previously outlined, there are so many variable factors from contract to contract.

I have endeavoured to list a series of cost per square metre, for 8 categories of work recently carried out by my organization.

The table gives a ranging of costs and an average cost per sample for each category.

As may be seen, there is a wider ranging of costs in some of the categories, due to differing standards of finishings or requirements.

It does, however, indicate that to enter into a rebuild situation where external walls are required to be retained, and the internals completely renewed, is generally more expensive than the general multi-storey open spaced new office block building.

General refurbishment, with limited structural alterations and additions does compete favourably. To build, however, in a traditional manner with enhanced finishings such as stone or stucco moulded features, decorative plasterwork and hardwood traditional joinery is more expensive than a general rebuild and infinitely more expensive than basic refurbishment contract.

INTERNATIONAL CONSTRUCTION AND DEVELOPING COUNTRIES

Ignatius D.C. Imbert, ME, PhD, MIEI, MASCE, FAPETT

The University of the West Indies, Trinidad

Summary
The characteristics and infrastructural needs of developing countries
are examined and the involvement of the developed world in satisfying
these needs through construction work discussed. The history of such
work, classified as international construction, is traced, the
adverse effects of technological importation given prominence, the
appropriateness of contract provisions examined and the importance
of feasibility studies emphasised. Management and supervisory
problems, with particular reference to cultural influences, are highlighted, solutions indicated and the use of international labour
productivity factors recommended.

Sommaire
Les propres et les nécessités de la sous-structure des pays en voie
de développement sont examinées et on discute le rôle du monde
développé en satisfaisant ces nécessités au moyen de la construction.
On suit l'histoire de tel travail, classifié comme construction
international, et on met en évidence les effets adverses de
l'importation technologique. La convenance des provisions des
contrat sont examinée et l'importance des études de la practicalité
des projets sont soulingés. Les problèmes d'administration et de
surveillance, relatifs en particulier aux influences culturelles,
sont accentués, les solutions sont indiquées et l'emploi du facteurs
de productivité international est recommendé.

Keywords
Construction, contracts, cultural, developing, international,
management

INTRODUCTION
The word *international* did not come into vogue until the late 18th
century when the English philosopher, Jeremy Bentham, came up with
the notion that a new word should be used to describe transactions
between citizens of separate nation-states (2). This derived from the
growing realisation that the trading of goods and services between
nations was an activity separate and distinct from trading between
persons or organisations in the same country. Such trading had indeed
been in existence for centuries, having had its origins in ancient

civilisations. The Phoenicians, for example, travelled on their ships
throughout the Mediterranean and beyond, marketing their products,
at least five thousand years ago. In the 20th century, international
trade has become a major concern of all countries and it is
increasingly evident today that the economic health of any country
depends on its ability to transact business successfully across its
borders.

International trade has become very complex and its ramifications
are not understood by many. Among those who do are the large
organisations in the developed world many of which operate
transnationally. They are often to be found in the construction
industry and, in some cases, act in concert with their governments,
even to the extent of receiving subsidies designed to secure export
earnings. Indeed, construction contracts in other countries are
frequently considered as foreign trade and government shareholdings
in organisations involved in such contracts are not uncommon.

The involvement of large (and not so large) organisations in
construction outside their national borders, including the establishment of subsidiaries in other countries, may be properly classified
as international construction. It is the purpose of this paper to
discuss some of the more important aspects of such construction as
it relates to developing countries. It is worth noting here that
organisations in the more advanced developing countries are learning
by example and are themselves becoming involved in construction in
the less advanced ones.

CHARACTERISTICS OF DEVELOPING COUNTRIES
The term *developing countries* is loosely used to describe the countries
which lie outside the relatively small group of highly developed,
industrialised nations (4). They range from countries which are large
in area, varying considerably in climate and topography, to ones which
are small islands. Some are located in the temperate zone whereas
others are in the dry and wet tropics. Many are densely populated
and becoming increasingly so while others are sparsely populated.
Some have well-educated and literate populations together with
partially good infrastructure and facilities but many have not. A
few are on the threshold of becoming modern industrial states while
several are economically backward and others are desperately poor.

The diversity indicated in the foregoing is itself made greater
by a variety of political, social, psychological, cultural, linguistic,
historical and religious factors. Thus, developing countries cannot
be 'lumped together' as a homogeneous group and should rather be
treated on an individual or regional basis. Nevertheless, they do
exhibit certain common characteristics, a notable one being their
technological dependence on the developed world. This dependence
has, in fact, been suggested as a basis for identification of
developing countries by one author (9). Indeed, it can be argued
that, once a developing country attains a substantial degree of
technological self-sufficiency, it is well on the way to becoming
a developed country and the term *developing* should no longer be applied
to it.

Technological dependence is itself directly related to another common characteristic of developing countries, namely, the under-development of human resources. Technological self-sufficiency can only properly develop and grow if there is a sufficiently large pool of people skilled enough to understand, assimilate and generate scientific and technical knowledge and use it for the processes of production. This was emphasised by the late President Kennedy who, in a speech soon after his inauguration in 1961, stated that the 'missing link' between development and underdevelopment was 'skilled manpower'. This missing link-situation has been identified as the most serious impediment to the advancement of developing countries and the implementation of projects therein (1,11).

The causes of the underdevelopment of human resources in developing countries are many and various but three important ones may be identified. Firstly, many of these countries underwent colonial rule by European powers during the period when the latter were themselves making the major technological advances which have given them their present dominance in the world. It was certainly not in their political and economic interests to encourage the development of scientific and technological know-how in the colonial territories. These territories were rather to be kept in technological and economic dependence by being producers of primary products and sources of cheap labour whereas finished products requiring technical skills and expertise would remain the preserve of the colonial rulers. This was also true of technical skills and expertise required for other areas of activity such as construction, most of the important work being undertaken and managed by technical experts from the colonising countries. Although the days of colonial rule have theoretically disappeared, the fact that less than 10 percent of technological research and development worldwide caters for the requirements and demands of developing countries indicates that things have not significantly changed. Secondly, the planners and executors of economic policy in developing countries, while understanding the importance of physical infrastructure in development, are seldom consciously aware of the relationship of skilled manpower to its provision or of the role of such manpower in reducing technological dependence. Even less do they understand that technological skill has political and economic significance, is a key factor in the exercise of power and affects a country's relationship with the rest of the world. Thus, technology policy is not explicitly utilised as a central instrument of planning for social and economic development but instead is usually institutionally divorced from direct developmental efforts. This approach is clearly a legacy of the colonial past. Thirdly, because of inadequate financial resources, most developing countries have been unable to set up, improve or expand the educational and training programmes and institutions which are essential for the creation of an appropriate reservoir of skills. For the same reason, there is also a dearth of institutions such as research-and-development institutes, consultancy companies and centres of information and industrial extension which are themselves part of the process of development of human resources.

NEEDS OF DEVELOPING COUNTRIES
The populations of developing countries constitute the majority of
the human race and, if the demographers are to be believed, will
become increasingly so with time. At the present rate of growth,
the world's population of about 5,000 million is expected to total
over 6,000 million by the end of the century and the bulk of that
population (somewhere close to 5,000 million) will be living in
the developing world. If these large numbers of people are to
achieve a minimally acceptable standard of living, it does not need
a seer to visualise that major efforts are required to provide basic
physical infrastructure and other amenities such as shelter, food,
water, sanitation, health care and education.

It has been estimated that an increase of at least 60 percent in
infrastructure and facilities is already necessary if present per
capita services in the developing world are even to be maintained
over the next decade (7). Since the level of these services is
already generally low, it does not need too much imagination to
realise that, with the projected population situation, the increase
required to achieve an acceptably higher level may easily exceed
100 percent. This is a daunting task and faces the construction
industry with a challenge of considerable magnitude. The nature of
the challenge can perhaps be perceived if one considers projections
which indicate that cities like Calcutta, Sao Paulo and Mexico City
will have populations of approximately 19, 26 and 30 million
respectively at the turn of the century, with millions of people
living in sub-standard housing and having limited access to clean
water and adequate waste disposal. What this situation may mean
in terms of threats to the health of entire urban areas is mind-
boggling, to say the least.

INVOLVEMENT OF DEVELOPED COUNTRIES
The scale of construction indicated in the foregoing as being
required in developing countries is of a magnitude beyond the
capacity of most of them, particularly in terms of financial, human
and technological resources. Even where the financial resources
exist, as in the case of the oil-producing countries of the Middle
East, deficiencies in the other resources constitute a major problem.
Thus, assistance is usually sought and obtained from the developed
countries, either directly or through international institutions such
as the World Bank. This assistance covers all areas of the
construction process and ranges from feasibility studies, economic
analyses, planning and design to actual building and commissioning
of facilities. It is usually arranged through contracts with
construction organisations and frequently involves the use of
advisers and consultants from international agencies or government
aid institutions. The latter also often assist in the provision
of specialist training programmes, either locally or in the developed
countries themselves.

Assistance from the developed world, while usually meeting
developmental needs, is nevertheless fraught with many difficulties
and dangers. Among these are the effects of the technological
importation which necessarily accompanies it. If such importation

does not encourage the development of local technological efforts, it effectively becomes disadvantageous in the end, despite any ostensibly practical benefits which may ensue from particular projects. One major disadvantage is that the capacity to innovate, by synthesising different methods and techniques so that they become appropriate to local construction needs, is actually displaced. Foreign knowledge is, consequently, applied without being absorbed by the local construction industry and, once its purveyors have quit the scene, is of little real value. Thus, we have a *pseudotransfer* of know-how which, wittingly or otherwise, is of advantage to the developed world in that it maintains the state of technological dependence and enhances the position of construction organisations from that world with regard to work in developing countries.

If one examines the matter of pseudotransfer closely, it transpires that, despite the number of organisations involved in external-aid construction over the last few decades, little progress has been achieved in the transfer of skills and knowledge to local populations, especially in the area of management. What gets transferred instead are alien cultural forms, social information and methods of operation which are subtly communicated to the receiving societies, affecting their productive and social patterns long before the full implications are understood. The more technologically dependent a society, the more this occurs, with possible consequent loss or disturbance of its cultural identity and use of inappropriate or unsuitable methods, techniques and materials.

The problem of inappropriateness or unsuitability of imported technology has begun to be recognised as a matter of major importance in developing countries and is creating much concern. Not only do methods and techniques often conflict with local culture and other conditions but also frequently do not take into account the level and variety of skills available. Moreover, the use of capital-intensive operations and high-grade, factory-made materials often runs counter to basic social and economic objectives regarding employment. In this context, it must never be forgotten that abundant supplies of labour constitute one of the major resources of the developing world and that the employment of people is both socially desirable and politically important.

One of the contributing factors to the situation described here is the insistence by many aid agencies and donor nations that designs take place where the funds originate. This usually causes the entire construction process to assume a developed-world orientation. It also inhibits, and often prevents altogether, the transfer of skills and knowledge. This state of affairs can be changed by a more enlightened approach whereby local participation becomes an integral part of design activity. Such change is already beginning to take place, albeit at a slower rate and on less wide a scale than required.

HISTORY OF INTERNATIONAL CONSTRUCTION
The involvement of developed countries in construction in the developing world is, as indicated in the introduction, part of the activity classified as international construction. Although, because of developmental needs, this involvement has shown remarkable growth in

the last few decades and is now fairly wide-spread, it is by no means a new phenomenon. It has its genesis in the many military and public-works projects undertaken by colonial governments well before the beginning of the 20th century. More recently, and particularly in the period between the World Wars, infrastructural projects were undertaken through the agency of expatriate engineers who staffed the senior ranks of public works departments or consulting engineers who sent their representatives to direct and supervise the work of local labour. Design work was almost always done in the *mother* country. The British colonial system of operation in Africa, Asia and the Caribbean is a particularly good example of how construction work was undertaken during the period. The Americans, although not strictly a colonial power, had control of much construction work in Latin America and the Pacific islands and operated similarly, mainly through Federal agencies and private companies.

In the period immediately following the end of the Second World War, international construction activity followed the pattern set between the Wars. In the case of Britain, for example, the government set up a Colonial Development and Welfare Programme through which work was sponsored and financed. The Crown Agents acted on behalf of the government, British consultants and/or contractors being engaged for all major work and expatriate engineers continuing to occupy senior public works posts. As colonies and protectorates, both British and others, began to become independent one after the other in the fifties and sixties, there now appeared a large number of new governments on the world scene. The dramatic increase in the United Nations membership during that period gives living evidence of this. All these governments soon realised the need for major infrastructural development; as did governments of other countries, such as those in Latin America, which had achieved independence much earlier but still remained relatively underdeveloped. Thus, demand for experienced designers and builders grew apace. As indicated earlier, the vast majority of these had to come perforce from the developed world. Because of the need for co-ordinated development and efficient use of funds, the period also saw the emergence of institutions such as the World Bank, African Development Bank, Asian Bank, Inter-American Development Bank and the United Nations Development Programme. These now finance a considerable amount of international work in developing countries, as do other institutions such as the European Development Fund and a variety of government aid organisations.

The advent of these institutions, coupled with the obvious need for development, led to a considerable increase in the scope and quantity of international construction in developing countries and, by the beginning of the seventies, several developed countries were involved in such construction. These included not only the former colonial powers but also others in Europe, North America and the Far East and this pattern has continued to date. With the coming in the seventies of the petro-dollar boom in the Middle East and elsewhere in the developing world, a marked expansion in international construction took place and, although its momentum has diminished because of lower oil prices, its extent is still considerable. This is due to the reality that infrastructural development and the provision of basic

facilities are not only an absolute necessity for economic survival
and social harmony but also, as indicated earlier, beyond the resources
of most developing countries.

Paradoxically, both the oil-importing and oil producing ones are
caught in the same cycle of dependency. Many of the first had their
economies severely battered by the dramatic increases in energy costs
in the period from the mid-seventies to the early eighties and have
had no choice but to depend on external aid. They are among the
poorest and most technologically backward countries in the world and
seemingly will have to depend on such aid for the foreseeable future,
both in financial and technological terms. Most of the second,
mesmerised by sudden wealth in the same period, engaged in profligate
expenditure and too large a number of projects and now find themselves
in severe financial straits without the technological capacity which
could have been created by that wealth. Thus, they too now have to
depend to a large extent on external aid. The ones in the Middle East
are perhaps the only exception to this, as far as financial resources
are concerned.

A recent historical development which is worthy of mention is the
entry of private companies from the developed world into the fields
of tourism and manufacturing in developing countries. In the case
of tourism, there has been considerable investment in the construction
of hotels, yachting marinas and recreational facilities in areas such
as the Caribbean, Central America and the Pacific islands. Such
construction is generally undertaken by companies located in the same
developed countries as the investors and is usually accompanied by
local governmental investment in the infrastructure required to cater
to tourism. The infrastructural work is usually funded by loans from
international agencies and is normally conducted by means of international construction. With respect to manufacturing, many companies,
lured by cheap labour and the existence of natural raw materials,
have set up subsidiaries or entered into joint-venture projects
throughout the developing world. This has naturally led to a
considerable amount of construction, most of it undertaken by companies
from the developed world.

NATURE OF CONTRACT PROVISIONS
As indicated earlier, construction operations undertaken in developing
countries by organisations from the developed world are usually
arranged through contracts. These may come about through the tendering
procedures of international agencies, bilateral agreements between
governments or the initiatives of private investors. The history
of these international contracts has clearly shown that due attention
has often not been paid to their appropriateness (10). This is quite
apart from the associated problem of inappropriateness of the imported
technology which is usually an inherent part of international
construction and which has already been discussed.

In general, contract agreements and provisions are based on standard
procedures which have a developed-world bias. This bias exists despite
the allegedly international nature of contract documents such as those
produced by the International Federation of Consulting Engineers and
widely used by the international and regional agencies which are the

principal sources of finance for major projects in developing
countries. In fact, because of the constraints imposed by the requirement to have so-called international standard forms of contract, little
or no provision is included in them to allow for amendments to cater
for local conditions. Thus, what appears on the surface to be a
laudable attempt to establish standards which can be used internationally actually allows developed-world standards to predominate,
the scope for contract provisions appropriate to particular developing
countries being thereby significantly reduced.

By their very nature, the contract documents used are often very
complex and lengthy, refer to standards, codes of practice and
specifications which are not easily available, understood or
applicable and which are usually inflexibly applied. Misinterpre-
tation and disagreements frequently result, situations not being
improved by language barriers and communication difficulties. In
many developing countries, local advisers do little to help,
preferring to rely on the provisions in the documents either as a
way of ducking the issue or in the mistaken belief that this is the
only way to achieve high standards. What is really alarming and
indeed tragic is the fact that, although bitter experience (some
of it very costly) has clearly indicated the necessity for contract
documents to be as simple as possible and tailored to suit local
conditions, developed-world practices are such an ingrained part
of the system that it is very difficult to create serious change.
There are several reasons for this situation not the least of which
are the prevalence of certain economic attitudes and the education
and training of professionals and other construction personnel.

If we look first at economic attitudes, we find that attention
is usually concentrated on profit-making and related financial matters
such as credit arrangements and cash-flow, with the resulting tendency
that designs, methods, techniques and practices are chosen for
economic convenience. Thus, unless prior information and experience
indicate otherwise, local needs and interests are usually disregarded.
Moreover, the profit-making motive often leads to exploitation in the
form of provisions which ensure that certain equipment and materials
can only be imported from particular donor countries. It should, of
course, be recognised that, without the profit-making motive, many
construction organisations in the developed world would probably not
concern themselves with work in developing countries. Since, as
already indicated, many of these countries do not possess the technological capacity to implement the variety of projects needed for
their development, this would be a serious loss. With respect to
education and training, especially in the case of architects and
engineers, basic theory is usually taught hand-in-hand with developed-
world practices so that the two are intertwined in the learning
process. This is true not only of the developed world but also of
many parts of the developing world where much of the education and
training at the higher levels tends to have a developed-world
orientation. The philosophy that built facilities, having the same
theoretical design basis, can be produced in a variety of practical
ways, each suited to a particular social setting (3), is only slowly
beginning to gain ground. Indeed, if this philosophy were to become

part of the educational system in the developed world, it would lead not only to the appropriateness of contract provisions in international construction in the developing world but also to a better social understanding of the developed world itself and thus to more suitable and innovative approaches to construction practice in that world.

It is important to note at this point that the use of the term *contract documents* tends to be rather restrictive in that it often refers to matters such as the conditions, drawings, quantities and specifications which form part of an agreement between an owner and a builder. These are in fact only the outcome of a series of other contracts which relate to agreements for the performance of work such as feasibility studies, topographical surveys and design. These are extremely important elements of the construction process and have an enormous influence on the actual building phase, especially where specifications, methods, techniques, practices, time and cost are concerned. Project management contracts relating to the entire gamut of operations which constitute the construction process or part thereof are also becoming increasingly popular and can now be considered as an integral part of the process. Thus, the term *contract documents* should be used in its widest sense so as to cover all aspects of construction.

With particular reference to feasibility studies, these constitute one of the best ways of ensuring that local conditions are properly evaluated and suitable contract provisions for implementation of projects made. They also help to avoid preconceived notions of methods of undertaking work in developing countries. In particular, studies of projects executed by local government departments and private designers and builders can reveal a considerable amount of information and data not otherwise available. For example, locally executed projects generally contain as much labour intensity as is permitted by their nature and it is more than worthwhile for in-depth studies to be made of the economic and technical feasbibility of methods which will substitute as much labour as possible for capital. Not only are such methods usually more appropriate, especially in dealing with the employment problem, but also they are often more successful. Other examples relate to the suitability and substitution of more appropriate local materials (13) and practices and the accuracy of cost estimates for projects in particular countries or regions.

One of the major problems with feasibility studies is, of course, their cost and the securing of finance for them often creates considerable difficulty. Increasing awareness of their desirability and, indeed, their almost essential nature has, however, alerted international and regional agencies to the need for providing funds in their budgets for the purpose and such funding is usually provided to developing countries in the form of long-term soft loans. Governments in a number of developed countries have also set up agencies to subsidise their national consulting companies for undertaking studies which appear to have promising outcomes for their own construction industries. Large private investors, such as the previously mentioned ones in tourism and manufacturing and those

engaged in extracting and marketing natural resources, have also
become fully aware that their projects may go awry if in-depth
preliminary studies are not undertaken. Thus, they now increasingly
make provision for such studies in their budgets.

INFLUENCE OF FEASIBILITY STUDIES ON DESIGN
One noteworthy consequence of feasibility studies which frequently
occurs is the revelation of areas of indigenous expertise whereby
advice on the most suitable ways of implementing projects can be
obtained and applied. This is particularly important in the field
of design and helps to avoid many of the pitfalls and errors
occasioned by inadequate knowledge and understanding of local
conditions. A few examples will serve to illustrate the point.
    The first example relates to water resource development, an area
in which the typical developed-world approach is to design dams,
reservoirs or large pipe-borne systems from the nearest rivers. In
many areas of the wet tropics, however, household water supply may
be better achieved by small rainwater catchment systems. Design of
such systems is based on a determination of catchment areas and
storage capacity appropriate to precipitation patterns and water
demand, the most efficient and economic design being that which causes
the fewest periods of deficit in supply for a given investment in
labour and materials or, alternatively, satisfies a given level of
demand for the least investment (3). The second example is that
of designers who specified deformed steel bars and a certain type
of cement for a major complex in Africa (12). It transpired,
however, that only smooth bars and another type of cement were
locally available. This led to considerable confusion and much time
and money were lost. Some simple detective work could have easily
determined the facts and an alternative design prepared. The third
concerns the design of pavement base courses using crushed rock
when only finely graded gravel or sand is available. Knowledge
of the facts can lead to designs based on material stabilisation
or the performance of existing pavements. The fourth example deals
with the design and installation of automatic devices for providing
constant flow of water to farmers from irrigation canals with
variable water level (6). Experience has shown that these devices
do not function efficiently when levels are low and, in many observed
cases, farmers have actually removed them because they are considered
to be obstructions. Local knowledge would obviate such problems
and lead to different designs. Fifthly and finally, there is the
example of a geotechnical design for a project in a particular
developing country which required sophisticated testing procedures
for its implementation. Preliminary investigations would have shown
that equipment for such testing was not available locally and a
decision could then have been made to import such equipment or
abandon the design altogether. Alternatively, correlation factors
between tests in the country of design and ones conducted locally
could have been established and an appropriate design prepared.
    One positive result of feasibility studies and the associated
interaction with local experts is the increasing number of joint-
venture arrangements between international construction organisations

and local ones. These arrangements, although still small in number, are not only proving to be of mutual benefit but also help to raise the level and increase the scope of indigenous skills and services. This is a development which should, in any case, be one of the objectives of external aid in an increasingly interdependent world.

MANAGEMENT AND SUPERVISORY PROBLEMS
The success of a construction project, just as that of any other form of endeavour, depends on its management, whether that project is undertaken in one's own national environment or beyond its borders. Projects undertaken beyond national borders do, however, pose special problems with regard to management and these problems and their solutions constitute a major part of what characterises international construction. Many of the problems posed for organisations from the developed world occur irrespective of the location of a particular project, be it in another developed country or a developing one. Examples of such problems are the difficulty of dealing with more than one currency and language, the necessity to operate within local laws, regulations and social customs, the obtaining of permits for remission of capital and profits and for movement back and forth of personnel and equipment, the requirements for importation of materials, the selection and recruitment of suitable personnel, the requirements for housing such personnel and satisfying their other needs and the limited existence of the diplomatic skills which are essential for dealing with local politics, power structures, bureaucracies and labour. These examples, and many others too numerous to mention, give some indication of the managerial skills required in international construction anywhere. These skills are required to a particularly great degree for projects in developing countries where the problems are often intensified by factors such as cultural differences, geographical size and distance, inadequacy of services and infrastructure and difficulties in communication.

There are no specific formulae or principles which can be itemised as being the basis for successful management of international construction in developing countries and this makes the selection of suitable managerial personnel a very difficult task. Nevertheless, there is abundant evidence that management which is strong, dynamic, flexible, knowledgeable and intuitive succeeds best. Such management is strict in the field, shows imagination in dealing with administration and organisation and relates meaningfully to the local population. Astuteness is perhaps the quality which best encompasses the attributes mentioned here. In those cases where there are mandatory or indicated requirements that local subsidiaries be set up, sometimes with majority local directorates but having major managerial inputs from the *mother* organisation, such astuteness is of paramount importance. Special reference should also be made to the need for management to avoid over-staffing projects during the building phase with foreign supervisory personnel. Such personnel usually fall into the category of site managers and engineers, office administrators, construction superintendents and top foremen. Their role in making or breaking projects is often not fully recognised and it is considered useful to highlight some of the problems associated with that role.

The relationship between foreign supervisory personnel and their subordinates is subject to cultural influences which determines the degree of success achieved by such personnel (8). The subordinate group is often multi-cultural and/or multi-ethnic. This situation may be peculiar to a particular country, as happens in many parts of Africa and Asia, or may be the result of subordinates coming from different countries to work in one location. In one particular case in the Middle East of which the author has heard, there were workers from six different countries who not only spoke different languages but also exhibited significant differences in education, ability, experience and psychological make-up. Such situations are difficult enough for highly skilled and psychologically adjustable supervisors. How much more difficult they must be for those whose education and work experience have taken place in a particular developed-world environment and who, therefore, have no framework within which to analyse their subordinates' behaviour. Thus, although most of them are technically competent, they are often ill-prepared to function effectively, even where the local environment or work force may be homogeneous. It seems, therefore, that success can best be achieved by keeping the numbers of such personnel to a minimum and making every effort to recruit suitable locals.

Because of the previously described diversity of developing countries, one should not generalise about supervisor-subordinate relationships and the suitability of leadership styles. Different relationships and styles work effectively in different cultural settings. This makes it all the more important that particular countries or regions receive careful study by top management before projects are started and supervisory personnel selected. A particular aspect of country study which should be emphasised is the effect of differing motivational forces on construction workers. In the developed world, economic motives tend to be dominant whereas, in many societies in the developing world, people often have different views of material gain. The bases for these views may be religion, social norms, status with groups, family or tribal structures or the importance of gaining the favours of traditionally paternalistic or authoritarian leaders. These bases differ from society to society.

Another aspect of cultural influences is the effect on the process of communication. People from highly developed countries generally like to settle issues face-to-face while the cultural or social norms of some developing countries emphasise harmonious relations between people, at least on the surface. There is also the fact that, in particular developing countries, status differences within the culture may inhibit subordinates from free expression in discussion or in reaction to supervisors. Thus, supervisors need to be aware of behaviour patterns in a particular setting if they are to function successfully. Even in what appears to be a homogeneous region such as the Caribbean, where the author lives and works, there are major behavioural differences from island to island. Not only are these occasioned by differences between linguistic culture but occur even within the same culture.

It is to be assumed that people placed in supervisory positions are intelligent and perceptive enough to absorb training and thus acquire the knowledge and understanding required to function effectively in other cultures. The problem is that few organisations in the developed world provide special training for supervisory personnel chosen for work in developing countries and problems, consequently, ensue. Experience is, of course, creating change and more and more organisations are being alerted to the need for such training. The author suggests that the United States Peace Corps orientation programmes are one good model to follow and that supervisory personnel be given total immersion courses to familiarise them with particular cultures and conditions. They should also be given training courses in human relations, cultural adaptability, political sensitivity and understanding of mission.

LABOUR PRODUCTIVITY FACTORS

This paper cannot end without a brief mention of labour productivity factors. Such factors are affected by variables such as national culture, owner characteristics, methods of financing, work practices, equipment type and availability, government regulations, climatic and topographical conditions, forms of contract and style of management. A recent paper on the subject (5) shows how widely the factors vary between countries and, therefore, how necessary it is to conduct preliminary studies to determine likely labour costs in particular countries or regions before the building phase of any project begins. Moreover, these factors can be of considerable benefit in the preparation of designs, the writing of contract provisions and specifications and the choice of methods and techniques of construction.

CONCLUSION

The paper has given an overview of international construction as it relates to developing countries. In doing so, it has discussed the characteristics and needs of those countries and the involvement of the developed world in satisfying these needs. It has looked briefly at the historical development of international construction in those countries, discussed the nature of contract provisions and emphasised the importance of feasibility studies. It has made special mention of management and supervisory problems, especially those caused by cultural influences, and pointed out the importance of becoming familiar with international labour productivity factors. It is hoped that the paper will contribute in some way to an understanding of the problems of international construction in the developing world and point towards probable solutions of those problems.

REFERENCES

1. Abdalla, M.H. and Cockfield, R.W., Implementation of capital projects in developing countries - problems and potential solutions, Proceedings CIB W-65 Fourth Symposium, Vol 3, Waterloo, 1984, pp 677-686.

2. Hamman, N.N., Multi-national working: the challenge of work overseas, Proceedings of Conference on Management in the Construction Industry, London, Macmillan, 1979, pp 125-130.

3. Heggen, R.J., Appropriate technology: a modest proposal, Journal of Professional Activities, ASCE, Vol 107, No EI1, Jan 1981, pp 7-10.

4. Imbert, I.D.C., Management and organisation of construction in developing countries, Proceedings CIB W-65 Third Symposium, Vol II, Dublin, 1981, pp C2 181-192.

5. Koehn, E. and Brown, G., International labour productivity factors, Journal of Construction Engineering and Management, ASCE, Vol 112, No 2, June 1986, pp 299-302.

6. Kirpich, P.Z., Developing countries: high tech or innovative management, Journal of Professional Issues in Engineering, ASCE, Vol 113, No 2, April 1987, pp 150-166.

7. Lewis, R., The human habitat: vision and reality, International Journal for Housing Science and Its Applications, Vol 10, No 2, 1984, pp 103-114.

8. Maloney, W.F., Supervisory problems in international construction, Journal of the Construction Division, ASCE, Vol 108, No CO3, Sep 1982, pp 406-418.

9. Mansell, D.S., Engineering constraints in the third world, Journal of Professional Activities, ASCE, Vol 104, No. EI4, Oct 1978, pp 281-292.

10. Morgan, P.R. and Kamil, M.H., Contract arrangements in the third world, Journal of Professional Activities, ASCE, Vol 108, EI4, Oct 1982, pp 243-250.

11. Powell, D., Problems of economic development in the Caribbean, British-North American Committee, London, 1973.

12. Reed, P.M., The american engineer overseas, Journal of Professional Activities, ASCE, Vol 108, No EI2, Apr 1982.

13. Spence, R.J.S. and Cook, D.J. Building Materials in Developing Countries, Wiley, 1983, p 138.

EDUCATION AND TRAINING IN CONTINUING PROFESSIONAL DEVELOPMENT

Dr L R Shaffer, Co-ordinator, W-65, USA

INTRODUCTION

It is most appropriate that this topic be featured on the final
day of the Symposium. During the first three days we have been
treated to some very impressive research in the organisaation and
management of construction. A treasurehouse of knowledge,
innovation and inventive-ness has been laid at our feet. We have
benefitted greatly; we have a renewed vigor to pursue our
vocations.

However, if this were to be the ultimate result the Symposium
must be termed a failure. For the Symposium to be a success its
results must be incorporated into the practice of organisation and
management of construction in our societies. The UN International
Year for Shelton (1987) has articulated that the current critical
problem facing the societies in the developed countries is the
rehabilitation of their decaying built environment and in the
societies in the developing countries it is the unprecedented
demand/load on the existing infra-structure and housing caused by
uncontrolled urban growth. These problems can be solved only be
affordable construction. The research presented in this Symposium
is fundamental to making construction more affordable. Thus for
this Symposium to be successful the research must be incorporated
into the fabric of the construction industries in our countries.
The craftsmen must be trained to apply them; the young
professionals in our schools must be educated in them so as to be
able to assimilate them efficiently in his/her practice.

With our research in the organisation and management of
construction not being complete until its practical application
attention to Training, Education and Continuing Professional
Development (TE/CPD) is appropriate. The W-65 Commission has
recognised this issue. One of the three subject areas it
established in its meeting in September 1986 was Technology
Transfer, ie the research in TE/CPD directed to expedite the
transfer of results of research in the organistion and management
of construction into practice. This keynote will present some of
the issues to be enjoined by the Commission. The CIB has also
recognised this issue with the newly established Commission W-89
BUILDING RESEARCH AND EDUCATION.

The issue is not a new one. Technology Transfer has been an
extremely popular topic of research. One colleague advised me that
he found that 745 papers have been published on the subject since
1973. The previous W-65 Symposiums and the CIB Congresses since
1977 have included 39 papers on the TE/CPD. Yet the capability of
the industry to incorporate and translate research results into
construction practice to provide the affordable construction to the

scale required in our society is an unsolved critical problem. And
the requirement for the solution today is more severe than ever
with the developed countries facing monumental infrastructure
rebuilding for the first time and the developing countries
desperate requirements in housing, sanitation and logistics,
becoming even more desperate - if that is possible. The
environment for the urgency for solution is upon us. It is
sincerely hoped that this body in its deliberations in the
workshops following this keynote will identify some solid
foundations in TE/CPD on which to translate the research in
organisation and management of construction into practice as
effectively and efficiently as required.

OUTLINE

This keynote begins with a comment on the state-of-the-art in
TE/CPD in the 38 countries in Table 1 whose TE/CPD programs were
reviewed to provide this comment. The keynote then presents and
evaluation of the state-of-the-art. Finally, some initial thoughts
are given as items for discussion for making TE/CPD as robust as
they must be.

STATE OF THE ART : DEVELOPING COUNTRIES

TE/CPD programs in the developing countries reflect their
economic and social characteristics, ie paucity of capital;
abundant labour supply, albeit not necessarily skilled; the lack of
construction industry infrastructure and the cultural and social
environments of the region. But they all maintain the same
keystone, ie the developing of an in-country capability to be self-
sufficient in the organisation and management of construction in
full cognizance of these characteristics. Local populations are
trained as craftsmen, as foremen and supervisors and as organisers
and managers of construction by local professionals and educators,
whenever possible. Labour intensive vice machine intensive
construction operations are the norm. A study by the World Bank
concluded that labour-intensive construction methods are both
technically and economically feasible - a substantiation of the
keystone of TE/CPD in developing countries.
The keystone is effected primarily through a combination of
short courses/worskhops and on-the-job training programs. The
ultimate goal is for the educators/trainers and the trainees to be
of the local population. The popular technique for training
craftsmen is on-the-job training wherein contractors employ a
prescribed number of apprentices. In many countries their
employment is encouraged by government programs. Typical is the
program in Swaziland where a registration system requires a
contractor to sponsor two to eight trainees. Another approach to
providing practical skills to young school leavers to find other
forms of non-agricultural employment exists in the Brigade Program

of Botswana. These Brigades are self-supported and where construction is their main focus the Brigade takes on contract work. They are proving to be good training ground to provide skilled tradesmen.

In educating local populations to be competent in the organisation and management of constructon a menu of workshops, seminars, co-operative arrangements, diploma and post-graduate programs are employed. These address the fundamentals in our profession which according to the survey of the national experts in organisation and management of construction in nearly all the Asian countries, inlcluding the Peoples Republic of China, are the organisation of the firm; contract conditions; preparation of proper bids; management of finances; management of human resources; labour and management; human relations; management of materials; management of equipment; project management and public relations. These are taught in some cases as a joint classroom/advisory service as in Botswana where an 11-week course includes four weeks of class work training in topics in construction management and seven weeks on-the-job applying these skills. This program is being developed by a governmental agency.

These are taught in some cases in short courses sponsored by contractor and trade associations as by the Malawian Building Contractors and Allied Trade Associations. These are taught in some cases in diploma courses in close co-operation with industry as in the Technical University of Istanbul which established a chair in Construction, Elements, Equipment and Administration 43 years ago and a chair in Construction Management in 1976. These are taught in some cases as a post-graduate and diploma level program as in the University of the West Indies which includes short intensive courses using video-satellite hook-up. And video-training is being established in Indonesia and Malaysia. These are taught in correspondence courses as in the National Institute of Construction Management and Research in Bombay. Clearly no mode of TE/CPD is being ignored.

These programs are dependent upon the availability of sufficient local talent to provide TE/CPD. Where such was not possible the International Labour Organisation furnished staff. Where such was not the case organisations of universities in Norway, Sweden, Denmark, Netherlands, UK have trained local populace as trainers.

STATE-OF-THE-ART : DEVELOPED COUNTRIES

The SOA in TE/CPD in the developed countries is a well-established regime which includes all of the modes used in the developing countries but in a more rigorous fashion. This is seen in the training of craftsmen which is accomplished totally in vocational schools or in formal apprenticeship programs. But the exciting TE/CPD program in France can be used to dramatize this difference in degree. France's program in TE/CPD has perhaps the richest heritage - dating to the French Revolution of 1789 when the

Marquis of Condorcet stressed the need to continue education in the whole course of life in the Legislative Assembly in 1791. In 1794 the Conservation National des Arts et Metiers was established for anyone who wanted to improve his qualifications by enrolling in evening and Sunday courses. In 1971 it was proclaimed that continuing education of engineers was a national obligation and a legal liability of the employers. The law states that all firms, both state and private, must spend 1.1 per cent of their wages and salaries on continuing education which can be either in-house or outside. Those who do not meet the 1.1 per cent are required to pay the difference to the Treasury. In 1984 the expenditure was $4.5 billion where 30 per cent of the courses dealt with management, and finance; 34 per cent in science and technoloy and 12 per cent in human relations and psychology. 20 per cent of the engineers are always in continuing education programs; the engineers range from 30 to 65 years in age.

The developed countries also include significant in-company TE/CPD. In Japan the construction firms have developed training schools for their employees in accordance with their culture of a lifelong association of employer/employee. Hitachi, for example, has four institutes which offer courses of 10-day lengths.

In the developed countries numerous universities provide both degree and diploma courses in engineering management. In the US there are in excess of 60 such schools and many of these offer flexible schedules to accommodate the practicing professional. Examples of such flexibility are epitomized by those in the UK. For example, the University of Reading has a Master's level program for two years requiring four visits of one week each per year - a self-professional development course. Another version is such as done at the University of Manchester Institute of Science and Technology, University Collge and Heriot-Watt where a Master's program entails ten week blocks of one day per week over a period of two years.

Professional societies are also very active in CPD and many grant Continuing Education Unit credit for their offerings. The teachers are practicing professionals - not usually academicians. These can lead to a Master's Degree. And finally, in the US the National Technology University has been established with numerous universities involved where the medium is totally electronic. Individual programs are developed using electronically transmitted courses from several universities. Programs in management are included albeit not construction management to this date. Clearly, TE/CPD in the developed countries is a robust industry.

An Evaluation of the State-of-the-Art :

Clearly our TE/CPD efforts are robust and effective. Our construction industries are vibrant resources in our societies. In times past they may have been totally responsive to our societal needs. But there is some question as to their ability to respond in the future and even today perhaps.

For example, in the US the cost of rehabilitating the infrastructure has been estimated to be $300 billion. This is a price too expensive for the US society - yet the problem is acknowledged. The US construction industry is not able to provide affordable construction. In a constrction field of the laboratory in which I serve as Technical Director there is a programmed backlog of validated new construction of approximately $700 billion a year because US Congress does not have sufficient funds to provide these new facilities were they to be built with the current state-of-the-art of construction technology. Again a failure in providing affordable construction.

In this inability to provide affordable construction the result of inappropriate research or because of less than adequate TE/CPD? The answer is "Probably Both" but the Business Round Table in its study on US Construction Industry Cost Effetiveness concluded that it was more the lack of adequate TE/CPD. The statistic that on the average it requires 17 years in the US after a successful demonstration for a technology to become commonly used in practice may have influenced its conclusion.

The evaluation is that the TE/CPD of today has served the industry and society well but appears to lack robustness to serve the industry and society well in the future.

Initial Thought for an Adequate TE/CPD for the Future

These thoughts are presented as bases for comment on TE/CPD in either developing or developed countries. They are presented as being valid goals in either environment. Of course they do not present mechanisms to meet these goals. Your comment on their validity and on suggestions for implementing mechanisms for those which are of value is sought.

Thought *1 : The challenge is so severe that any hope of developing adequate TE/CPD in the future requires a super-ordinate goal - a goal which supersedes for example the criteria in developing countries of establishing an in-country construction industry or in developed countries superscedes a major basis of competitiveness between organisations. The super-ordinate goal is that research in organisation and management of construction which makes construction more affordable be incorporated into practice as soon as possible.

Thought *2 : A visionary capability must be fostered in TE/CPD. Innovation in the construction context is standard practice and pervasive in the industry. However, innovation in the TE/CPD is an ad hoc fits-and-starts activity. Formalized procedures dominate TE/CPD; for the future these are not sufficient. A visionary capability pervasive in TE/CPD is required for stability in the industry.

Thought *3 : Career long learning must be mandated and facilitated. (The French model needs close examination.) Research and organisation in management and construction incorporated into practice will change professional practice continuously. Practicing proessionals must be strongly encouraged to stay abreast of these developments and apply them in their procedures as soon as possible. The researchers must be strongly encouraged to package their results into products which have been translated into formats which can be absorbed readily by the practitioner.

Thought *4 : Fragments of the industry working on a team basis in the research and in TE/CPD is essential. Research in organisation and management for construction must be a collective effort involving adademia, industry, labour, finance, et al. to assure that the right problems are being researched and that the opportunity provided by advanced technology is being researched. Only team-developed research will lead to practical application in the shortest time possible. The human relationship associated with team work is a fundamental element.

Thought *5 : To expedite the knowledge know-how to the practicing professional every advancement in technology must be exploited. Expert systems which translate knowledge into helping-hand guidance for applying research results is one possibility. Data banks which can be assessed to answer questions on a day-to-day basis is another. Expanded use of video-based TE/CPD is still another.

CLOSING STATEMENT

TE/CPD is the most vital problem facing the research community in the organisation and management of construction throught the world today. The critical problem in tommorow's industry is the inability of today's TE/CPD to transfer the know-how of research centers into industry effectively. This is the challenge of TE/CPD. It is our challenge. We must address it aggressively. There is no one else capable or available to do so. If we fail there is no question that quality of life on this planet will deteriorate substantially. It is a rare obligation and opportunity which may not be matched in any other profession - only us in the organisation and management of Construc-tion. Thank you.

ACKNOWLEDGEMENT

Dr V Handa, University of Waterloo, Canada and Chairman of W-65 Task Group in Education in Organisation and Management and Construction, provided valuable assistance in developing material for this address. His contribution is gratefully acknowledged.

BIBLIOGRAPHY

1.   Andrews, J A, "Research - New Knowledge and Trends", Vol. 4, PROCEEDINGS, CIB W-65 1984, Waterloo, Canada.
2.   Building, Civil Engineerng and Public Works Committee, General

Reports 1983, 1987, ILO, Geneva 22.
3. Construction Management and Technology News *6,7,8,9, International Labour Organisaton, Geneva 22.
4. Construction Today, April 1987, Institution of Civil Engineers, London.
5. "Education and Training in Construction", PROCEEDINGS of the CIB W-65 Second Symposium on Organisation and Management of Construc-tion, Vol III, Haifa, Israel, May 1979.
6. Gaarslev, A "Means of Construction Management", PROCEEDINGS of CIB W-65 Third Symposium on Organisaton and Management of Construc-tion, Section B, Dublin, Ireland, 1981.
7. Handa, V, "Rapporteur's Review - Education and Training in Construction" PROCEEDINGS, CIB W-65 Second Symposium, Haifa, Israel, Vol IV, 1979.
8. Jepson, W B, "Technology Transfer and Constrution", International Journal of Construction Management and Technology, Nov. 1986.
9. Papers, International Federation of Building and Wood Workers, Mandated 1981.
10. Reif, Colin Helping Towards Self Reliance ILO Genera 22, 1981.
11. Second World Conference on Continuing Engineering Education, Paris Proceedings, European Society of Engineering Ecucation, Brussels, Belgium, 1983.
12. The Construction Industry, The World Bank, Washington, DC 1984.
13. The Construction Industry in Asia : A Survey, Asian Productivity Organisation, Tokyo, 1983.
14. Wissema, J G "Improving the Diffusion of Knowledge in the Dutch Building Sector", PROCEEDINGS, 10th CIB Congress, Vol 8, Washington DC, 1986.
15. 1986 World Conference on Continuing Engineering Education, Orlando, Florida, Proceedings, The Institute of Electrical and Electronics Engineers Inc., New York, N.Y.

TRAINING/EDUCATION/CPD PROGRAMS REVIEWED

Botswana	Israel	Sri Lanka
Brazil	Japan	Swaziland
Canada	Kenya	Sweden
Cyprus	Malawi	S. Africa
Denmark	Malaysia	S. Korea
Egypt	Nairobi	Tanzania
Ethiopia	Nepal	Thailand
Gambia	Netherlands	Turkey
Hong Kong	Nigeria	United Kingdom
India	Pakistan	United States
Indonesia	Phillipines	West Indies
Iraq	Singapore	Zimbabwe

Part IX
Rapporteurs' reports

MANAGEMENT AND CONTRACTING SYSTEMS

Rapporteurs : W J Diepeveen and V Ireland

Stichting Bouwresearch, The Netherlands and The New South Wales
Institute of Technology, Australia

INTRODUCTION

The workshops on Management and Contracting Systems were well
served with stimulating papers. The authors and the editors
deserve to be congratulated on the significant improvement in
quality of papers by comparison with previous CIB W-65 Symposia.
Attendance at this workshop ranged from twenty-five to forty
people and a total of twenty-three papers were presented. Some
general observations will be made and then the papers will be
reviewed as a group.

NEED FOR GREATER RIGOUR

As a general rule greater rigour is required. This can be seen
in the following areas :

Need for use of common definitions

It became very obvious, particulary in the presentation of the
papers on the topic of choice of a contractual arrangement, that
there was a great deal of confusion caused by the lack of use of
common definitions. Much of the confusion was caused by different
uses, from one country to another, of terms such as project management, construction management, management contracing, design
and construction, turnkey, etc. It is the view of the rapporteurs
that the Glossary of Terminology should be extended to distinguish
between these terms and then published extensively with a plea for
common use.

Need for use of more rigorous statistical techniques

Many of the papers received lacked the use of rigorous statistical techniques. Many were simply a report of the observations
of authors. Some which used simple techniques such as correlations did not go to the more rigorous approach of partial correlations, which involved correlating Y and X1 while X2, X3, X4 ....
are held constant. Surveys were seldom random. There was a
suspicion that good researchers may then find what they are
looking for.

Need for development of common measuring scales

A further step in achieving greater rigour in the discipline is the development of common measuring scales, which is an unspectacular task; however it is essential to the laying of foundation stones of a discipline. Scales have been developed in other disciplines which have allowed replication of experiments and the establishment of some degree of certainty about relationships between variables. Examples are scales for measuring intelligence quotient in psychology, or a common approach to measuring stress in engineering. Obvious examples in management and contracting systems are buildability or constructability, degree of fast-tracking, extent of co-ordination, building complexity, time of construction, profit, overheads, etc.

TITLE OF WORKSHOP

Many of the papers extended well beyond the scope of organisation and management of construction. This is almost inevitable since what is done during feasibility and design has a large influence on the organisation and management of construction.

This questions whether management aspects during feasibility and design should be reflected in the title of the Workshop.

ASPECTS NOT ADEQUATELY REPRESENTED

The Workshop decided that some areas were not well represented by the scope of papers submitted. It was felt that the management of sub-contractors and the role of sub-contracting generally deserved more study. Furthermore it was felt that the electronic and communications aspects required more study.

A view was expressed that systems should be investigated to protect techniques developed, in a similar manner to that protecting patents for manufactured items. It was felt that research and development of management systems is inhibited by the likelihood that ideas developed will be learned and used by competitors.

Finally it was felt that research is required into methods that can be used to attract skilled craftsmen to the industry. It was considered that attraction and training of skilled craftsmen is a problem in many countries.

RELATIONSHIPS WITH INDUSTRY

The Workshop acknowledges that communication with practitioners can be difficult, which is illustrated by so few practioners attending the Symposium. However, it was concluded that the researchers must take the initiative in bridging the gap by producing results which are of practical value and which can be readily communicated to industry. Papers may need to be made understandable and easy to reference by a communicator who comes between the research community and the practitioners.

The development of an interfacing group between industry and research was also considered to be helpful in directing areas for research.

CONTENTS OF PAPERS

Categorization

Papers fall into the following areas :

Developing countries

```
China     - Walsh (project management)
          - Wilkins (joint ventures)
India     - Mohan and Sofat
Malaysia  - Yong (turnkey)
Nigeria   - Wahab
```

Specific project

Giritli, Sozen and Galin (bridge over the Bosphorus)

Choice of a contractural arrangement or organisational form

Bentil and Herbsman (construction management)
Davidson and Mohsini (minimisation of conflict)
Hauptfleisch (South Africa)
Ireland (CM in Australia and USA)
Naoum and Langford (management contracting)
Rowlinson (industrial buildings)
Suite (finance, design and construction)
Walker and Langford (public sector case study)

Estimating

Taylor and Bowen (parameter based measurement)

Number of tenderers

Wilson, Atkins, Sharpe and Kenley

Barriers to entry

Bishop

Management of the firm

Birrell (evaluation of other contractors)
Eastham (tender prices)

Peer (allocation of overheads)
Kangari and Farid (risk management)
Skitmore (decision evaluation system)

Developing countries

Walsh provides invaluable insights into the Chinese construction industry, pointing out that difficulties occur for foreign
contractors due to the lack of a commercial, financial and legal
framework which contractors are used to; great competition for
foreign reserves; the Chinese wish to do as much work as possible
themselves; the local design industry is unsophisticated; approval
periods are difficult to predict; resrictions on materials, equipment and plant; and, foreign consultants must enlist the support
of local designers. Possible markets are identified.
Wilkins identified different types of joint venture relationships that are likely to occur when contracting with the Chinese.
This complements the paper of Walsh. He discusses the high risks
involved which is important as joint ventures are the only way of
entering the Chinese market.
Mohan and Sofat provide a statistical analysis comparing lump
sum contracting with measurement contracts for housing projects in
India. This is a valuable study which would have been even better
with more measurement of other variables such as buildability
analysis, degree of co-ordination and complexity of projects.
More studies of this type are reqired.
Yong elaborated on the advantages of turnkey as a contractual
form in Malaysia; a measured comparison with other contractual
arrangements would have been valuable. Yong concludes that, if
properly managed, turnkey will lead to better results than other
forms. He recommends that a standard form of contract is
required.
Wahab gave a detailed description of the problems of project
organisations in Nigeria. He showed how the use of extensive
committees assisted the process. It would probably be generally
accepted that the greater use of committees would not be favoured
in the developed countries. A greater use of comparisons would
assist.
While papers such as these are necessarily descriptive they do
serve a very useful purpose in proving insights for later more
rigorous work.

Choice of a contractual arrangement (procurement form)

Numerous papers were presented on this topic and a number of
issues arise. Of fundamental importance is the range of definitions or, more accurately, impressions which exist with regard to
what is included in a contractual arrangement. These diferences
in views cause a waste of effort due to the problems of communication. It would be a great service to the Working Party if scales

were developed to measure exactly what is occuring on each of a number of variables such that whenever a contractual arrangement is mentioned the scales are used. Exmples of the parameters relevant to contractual arrangement include : degree of contractor involvement in design, overlap of design and construction, extent of competition, extent of cost reimbursement versus lump sum, relationships between specialists, conditions of contract, etc.

Bentil and Herbsman questioned whether Construction Management had fulfilled its objectives, concluding that it has performed both poorly and well. A greater use of statistical techniques would have improved the value of the paper. Rowlinson, while primarily comparing Design and Construction with the Traditional projects, concluded that Management Fee projects (Construction Management in US terms) were good performers; Management Fee projects were faster to start on site than either Traditional or Design Build. No difference was shown in construction time for any of the three forms. Finally Naoum and Langford found that Management Fee contracting did have a shorter construction time than Traditional projects. This conflict in results shows that more study should be made of effects of using different contractual arrangements. However it is the rapporteur's view that individual variables require measurement in addition to the overall contractual arrangement. If construction management leads to reduced construction time it may be because there is a greater degree of buildability analysis, better relationship between design and construction, less complex building forms produced, etc. If this is so these variables, and others, should be measured.

Ireland compared the practice of Construction Management in the USA and Australia based on case studies in both countries. It was found that designers in the USA have a reduced role by comparison with Australia providing only conceptual details which are completed by the contractors through shop drawings, thus introducing buildability analysis. In Australia much greater time was spent on analysing the design to produce forms of construction which were faster to construct. Speed of construction for high rise offices was modelled in terms of area and number of storeys, the former contributing to faster construction and the latter inhibiting speed.

Hauptfleish, examining the building process in South Africa, and reflecting changes that have already occurred in some developed countries, concluded that the role of the architect will diminish to design only, the quantity surveyor will take on value engineering, the proprietor will become more involved in the process and the main contractor will take on more of a role of providing management services.

Suite described a series of construction and legal models, developed to assist the mobilisation of scarce resources for the development of public projects in Trinidad and Tobago, which ended in failure. He suggests that the cause may have been too much freedom to propose any form of contract in combination with the lack of the necessary skills in government offices. A lesson is that the newer contractual forms need to be well documented so that all participants understand their roles and responsibilities. This would be a useful project for the Working Party.

Walker and Hughes, describing a sophisticated systems based case study, using linear responsibility analysis, on government building in the UK, showed that the deficiences of the organisation structure could not cope with the prevailing environmental conditions. Development of the tool, such that it can predict the appropriate structure for a particular environment, would be worthwile.

Davidson and Mohsini are also seeking the best organisational design however they use organisational conflict as a means of evaluating alternative organisational forms. This was based on the notion that the various organisations involved in a project have to resolve disparities between the temporary objectives of the project and their permanent objectives as an on-going organisation. By careful measurement on projects it was found that inter-organisational conflict can be used as a measure of a project organisation's performance. Availability and access to information proved to be the greatest source of conflict which lends support to Walker and Hughes' ideas.

Specific projects

Giritli, Sozen and Galin provided a brief description of the construction of the second bridge over the Bosphorus which involved co-operation between international construction firms.

Estimating

Taylor and Bowen suggest a modelling technique, based on a Pareto approach, by which frequency distributions for the quantities of labour and materials are established for various building types and an estimate is based on only 20% of such items. The authors point and a principle that the mechanics of cost gene-tation should be able to be traced through all inter-relationships to be of use to designers. Further work is proceeding.

Number of tenderers

Wilson, Atkins, Sharpe and Kenley examined the optimum number of bidders upon the outcome of the tendering process accepting that bidding must be paid for by the clients of the industry while at the same time greater number of bids may produce lower prices. It was concluded that open tendering is no more competitive and four select tenders provide the best results.

Barriers to entry

Bishop provided a long-term perspective by pointing out some changes to the industry that have occurred in the last fifteen years. These include procurement practices, reduced workload, decline in direct employment, technological innovation and increased competition. The responses by contractors include less research and development and less training of skilled and semi-skilled workers. Bishop suggests that increasing financial barriers to the entry of contractors, through increased intervals between interim or progress payments, and well defined objectives for quality assurance. The area deserved further research on the optimal interval between payments and whether this varies with project size; another aspect is whether the type of procurement method under which contractors usually operate has an effect on the degree of training and research and development that will be undertaken.

Management of the firm

A number of papers analysed the management of the firm. Eastham assessed the factor influencing tender prices by analysing the content of interviews. Peer analysed the allocation of over-heads on bidding strategy and concluded that is is more correct to allocate overheads to the production cost, that is the sum of the labour, plant, and general site costs, rather than the expected sales turnover, or construction cost. Birrell discussed the different methods in use by contractors to gather information about the performance of sub-contractors with whom they co-operate or will co-operate in future. It was concluded that the contractor's office staff are responsible for the majority of information gathering. Similar methods might be used to assess the competi-tive strength of fellow builders in the same market. Finally, Skitmore outlines the basis of a model by which firms reflect the major areas of cost. Because of the uncertainty of the variables he proposes that computer models be used to provide certainty for the whole process where certainty did not exist for its parts. Further development will be interesting as the manager-computer interface is developed. Kangari and Farid provided a comprehensive analysis of the various risks faced by a construction firm. The results from field tests will be valuable in due course.

CONCLUSIONS

The presentations of the papers show that even greater rigour is required of authors and referees in writing and assessing papers. Some aspects became apparent in a number of the papers including : the need to further develop and especially use common definitions; the need to be more rigorous in the use of statistical techniques; and the need to develop common measuring scales.
No conclusion has reached on the appropriateness of the title

of the Workshop. Many authors show interest in the activities at pre-construction especially as these impinge on construction.

It was concluded that the management of sub-contracting could have received more attention.

Communications with practitioners was seen to be essential and it was concluded that the research community must take the initiative.

A number of conclusions come from individual papers most the which are included. It is finally concluded that the authors who contributed papers made the workshop both stimulating and interesting.

PLANNING AND CONTROL

Rapporteurs : Professor John Christian and Jan Berny

The University of New Brunswick, Canada. Polytechnic of the South
Bank, UK.

INTRODUCTION

The theme "Planning and Control" was divided into 5 workshops
as follows :

2a.   Planning for industrial development.
2b.   Planning and scheduling.
2c.   Planning and controlling resources, especially finance.
2d.   The search for quality.
2e.   The future : where do we go from here?

PLANNING FOR INDUSTRIAL DEVELOPMENT

M A Al-Mufti and S R Cochrane, in their paper, showed that the
challenging task of planning national construction programmes, at
the policy making level, can be augmented through the study of
available data, reflecting past economic trends using a
hierarchical time plan base and sectoral trends on a world scale.
The data are used to derive linear functions based on strongly
correlated variables, which then form the basis of a simulation
model linking economic growth (GDP) to construction investment.
This leads to future detailed estimates.
In discussion S R Cochrane stated that it was less economic to
invest money in construction projects in 1970's than the 1960's.
The cost benefits in civil engineering, non-residential buildings
and residential buildings could be compared by the proposed method
of planning.
Sten Bengtsson's and Hans Bjornsson's paper described the
simulation of the consequences of differences of permanent/
temporary employment in the construction industry.
Results of the simulations which were interactive with
industrialist responses indicated that permanent instead of
temporary employment for a particular project may well encourage a
positive development of the construction firm.   The results
indicated that a permanent employment arrangement would not
necessarily be inconsistent with the goals of construction
companies.   An important example was the potential expansion and
reliability of sub-contractor work.
Ignatius Imbert's paper examined the nature of the construction
process.   The need for assessment of resource requirements and
availability was stressed and resource allocation and uncertainty
was discussed, including human resources.   His major emphasis was
to stress skilled human resource limitations as without their

113

assessment feasability was not even worthy of consideration.

What emanated from the discussion was the need for increased research into the subject of resource management. Valuation was required at both the quantitative level with respect to labour, fiscal and political issues, and the examination of allocation and physical utilisation considerations.

Further research was required into the effects of the turnover of manpower.

Dr Juraj Marusic, Mirko Oreskovic, Mladen M Bandic, in their paper, presented the organisation and technical solutions to a recreational and sports center project for the programme of the Universiade '87 - Zagreb. It was hoped that lessons for similar work could be learnt from the detailed exposition.

J L Meikle and Dr P M Hillebrandt stressed the need for construction resource planning, to avoid non-completion of, or delays to, projects and potential damage to an economy by trying to undertake programs for which resources were not available. The problems of transferability of data from one country to another were also considered.

The authors suggested the setting up of a focal point for the collection of data and a clearing house for its use. It was possible now to make a reasonable best estimate, together with a range of possibilities of resource requirements, of any major development plan anywhere in the world which would enable its feasibility to be assessed. However, the data needs to be refined to improve accuracy and make the process of estimation simple and cheaper, eg from sums expendable being known estimates of labour could be made and thence potential feasibility assessed.

Several speakers in the discussion recommended that more const-ruction resource planning was required.

Dr K N Ramamurthy's paper, entitled 'Project Management for Maintenance and Rehabilitation Works', discussed design materials, function, workmanship, use and their inter-relationships, noting that these factors determined the amount and nature of maintenance required during the lifetime of a building.

In the discussion the advantages of maintenance feedback was emphasised; it was often possible to derive general conclusions about maintenance which could then be applied to a new job.

Xu Shengmo and his colleagues in their paper discussed the application of a specific method of input-output analysis in a local authority. A series of direct and indirect coefficients of products and outside resources were considered. Results showed the latent potential of this method in the industry and expansion to other industrial spheres. A precedent might be set for western analysts as this technique had been out of fashion for some time - a case for serious reconsideration should be carefully assessed.

In the discussion it was stated that the paper showed the benefits of basic organisation.

Marcelo Zalcberg's paper reviewed current activities and char-acteristics of the Brazilian construction industry, including a brief analysis of the con-straints and implementations of the demands in the industry. Due to his absence from the Symposium there was no discussion of the paper.

In the general discussion following workshop 2A it was acknowledged that it was not necessary for construction resource planning to be very sophisticated in order to improve planning. Other topics which were discussed were as follows :

(i)   sometimes major construction projects have created huge debts from international loans in developing countries and sometimes large expenditures have been spent on inappro- priate schemes to make matters worse;

(ii)   in resource planning the forward and backward linkages of information were very important;

(iii)   the cyclical nature of the construction industry often creates a situation where governments generally exacerbate the situation rather than assist the industry. It was noted that caution should be observed if economic figures are used which may give the average over a decade whereby the cyclical nature is not shown;

(iv)   it is possible to apply data which have been obtained generally in the areas of time and resource management and maintenance and rehabilitation providing that extreme care is exercised. Divergencies should be considered and parameters altered with reference to geophysical conditions and learning curves.

PLANNING AND SCHEDULING

Brian Atkin's paper highlighted deficiencies in current cost planning practice. The value of introducing construction planning during early design was discussed. Decision CPM and deterministic dynamic programming were selected as the basis for a simplified technique to solve the optimisation problem.

The proposed technique represented a breakthrough in the evaluation of both construction costs and construction time of possible design options. It was demonstrated that the relation- ships between costs and time can be incorporated within a single technique which could guide the architect to feasible designs early in the design process.

The speaker clarified that by networks he meant 'flow-charts' as the decision and feedback criteria can be supported. The methodology has also a time/cost trade off algorithm which he stressed was of practical importance. Restrictions of construction data was an issue which would have to be considered in the future.

George Birrell's paper presented a description of the factors which should be considered when scheduling construction work and which of these factors should be included in the schedule. The factors, forming the foundation of the paper, came from senior executives in general contractors or construction mangement

115

organisations. These factors were classified into sub-groups and a systematic model was derived from their meanings.

The factors fall into four categories of overt/input, overt/output, covert/input and covert/output. It was concluded that scheduling of future construction processes could move forward from the mechanistic sequence of putting together the end product towards wisely producing a high quality datum. Further conclusions indicated that expert construction scheduling requires many more items of information than just lists of construction work tasks. There was potential for further research advances along this direction.

Discussion of the 'macro' view of planning and scheduling was viewed by one of the participants as revolutionary but this was subsequently toned down. An important point made was that more stress should be paid to the factors resulting from interviews taken than Professor Birrell's model. However, he did state that the next phase would aid in some quantification namely from discussions with sub-contractors and operatives.

In the paper by Shyzou Furusaka and Nai-Yuan Chi a method of construction planning was presented using the 'Line Balancing' technique. The purpose of this method was to determine the optimum construction planning by logically minimizing the amount of ideal time of labourers and machines, and levelling each production process. The major areas of concern were highly repetitive construction tasks.

The paper examined the applicability of line balancing to construction planning through a multiple activity chart approach.

The chairman applauded this advance in optimising recurring tasks to improve efficiency. Subsequent discussion showed that the operational research technique of machine scheduling could achieve a further step in giving a better 'automated situation'

Dr Juval Marusic et al in their paper presented the method of management of the complex heterogeneous programme of construction for the 14th International Sports Games Universiade '87 - Zagreb.

It was shown that even the biggest projects can be successfully executed with the appropriate organisation of management and the maintaining of good quality relationships between the employer and the other numerous participants in construction.

Surprise was expressed in regard to the fact that no time overrun occurred, despite many variations which occured during the const-ruction period.

David Morris' paper discussed electronic spreadsheet formats and macro language commands in order to carry out the critical path method and the programme evaluation and review technique, showing the benefits for project planners and managers.

It was concluded that the use of electronic spreadsheets and macro programming on microcomputers offered several possible advantages over menu selection and information retrieval programs written for large scale project management and scheduling packages.

116

A lively discussion arose from the practicability that spread-sheets could be used for CPM. This was carefully examined and while the pilot study was only for five activities, expansion was quite feasible but severe limitations were envisaged in the generation of new equations (scratch pad). This tool was possibly seen more in the light of showing the power of a spreadsheet within the educational ambit.

A few leading issues were raised in the general discussion. The importance of understanding the contractors scheduling problems in a global sense was stressed. The validity of CPM was questioned in particular with the difference between 'Client' and 'Builder' planning. However, the most important point made in this context was by Mr Bandic : CPM was a powerful tool for clarifying the logic required in analysing the planning issues.

PLANNING AND CONTROLLING RESOURCES, ESPECIALLY FINANCE

Lansford C Bell's paper stated that carefully designed computer systems were required to perform certain management functions on complex industrial construction projects, which were characterized by large volumes of piping, electrical and instrumentation materials.

The paper concluded that materials management computer systems were being utilized on large industrial construction projects to provide a valuable means of integrating the materials management functions of project planning, material take-off, vendor inquiry and evaluation, purchasing, expediting, field material control, warehousing and material distribution.

J Berny's and R Howes' paper demonstrated a method, aided by graphics, that had created a simple means of generating financial plans, monitoring, and contingency evaluation. It was based on a model evolved from new concepts in growth curve (commonly known as S-curves) forecasting.

Further developments were suggested on three fronts : first, a continual appraisal, improvement and expansion of software supported by industrial feedback. Second, the work described had raised many new areas of research which should be explored. For instance, the testing of alternative models and expanding the use of interpretive parameters. Third, and most important, the further extension of the development in risk/contigency analysis. This would require good and extensive collaboration with industry. The proposal provided a corporate and project financial planning aid in a comprehensive and quantitive manner and an analytical basis not provided by previous systems.

Robert I Carr's paper was presented by R B Harris. It compared the differences between the British cost practices, based on professional quantity surveyors preparing bills of quantities for owners, which contractors use to prepare competitive unit price bids for buildings, and American cost practices of cost engineers based on each contractor performing a quantity take-off from contract documents to prepare lump sum bids for buildings.

He concluded that construction in the UK did not move as quickly toward completion as in the USA, and it took about twice as long to accomplish. Society attitudes, labour laws and relations, and architectural engineering practices impact and mold the construction environment and make their own contributions to the more lengthy time of construction and its attendant cost.

However, the most immediately evident difference in the UK and US practices were in the area of cost engineering or quantity surveying. The comparison might well have also considered three other factors; namely quality, life and maintenance, as well as the two considered, that is construction time and construction costs. Nevertheless, the issues raised were valid, although other speakers disagreed on some points particularly quantitatively. The differences between a "team project management" and the "unbiased consultant" approach were briefly considered, particularly the harmonious versus confrontational difference.

R S Fellows', in his paper entitled 'Management of Escalation on UK Building Projects', stated that predicting price and cost indices accuracy might be improved considerably by using regression methods to modify published forecasts but, more significantly by using stochastic time series models.

One of the conclusions reached in the paper was that the stochastic time series forecasts of building cost indices and of tender price indices gave good results over a three year trial period.

The paper by John G Lowe attempted to analyse the reasons for variations in the cash flow profile of construction projects so as to assess the likely efficiency of predictive formulae.

He concluded that while such an estimate of cash flow pattern was useful, it was clearly limited in scope because of the range of possible solutions. However, there was little purpose in building models of ever increasing complexity in order to increase the precision of the estimate, since it was unlikely that the user would have sufficient knowledge about the variable factors to make use of any additional features. He did, however, point out that statistical analysis with a view to generate cost envelopes would be of value.

The aspects of front end loading of contracts was discussed and there was a divergence of views on whether this system was used by contractors.

The paper by Surinder Singh used mathematical models to establish envelopes which were utilized in developing a computer model for cash flow planning, based on the past historical records of numerous building projects in Singapore. Value-time envelopes were established for different types of highrise buildings.

The paper concluded that while it could not be claimed that the computer programs developed could invariably be used in all countries because of varying construction practices, the methods adopted in establishing the mathematical models, and subsequently the algorithm used in developing the computer model, could both be useful in other research work.

In the general discussion it was stated that cash flow profiles have different characteristics which depended on the type of projects. One speaker said that theoretical S-curves could predict the actual curves well but it was also noted that the theoretical curves could be imprecise in some circumstances, particularly for reasons of geography and type of project.

The question of the relevence and practical nature of research was also discussed. The value of refining complicated theoretical research in relation to the inherent vagaries of the construction industry was considered. The value of research would be improved if the aims were more industry driven, market driven, and wealth producing.

THE SEARCH FOR QUALITY

In the paper by Donald Bishop entitled 'A Search for a Better Solution to the Overall Management of the Aftermath of Latent Defects in Buildings', the participants of the construction process were identified before outlining the character of building defects and the principal features of current procedures for clients to obtain redress. Additionally, the concurrent effect on insurance was highlighted. This led to the major proposal that project-based damage insurance without recourse to subrogation was a practical possibility that could benefit clients and the industry alike and could reinforce improved quality of building.

The current status was that several options existed; in particular project-based insurance and liability insurance of building rather than producer-based. The question of improving quality assurance statutes was still under discussion.

John Dalton's paper described the scale of the problem of managing and maintaining quality on the Crown Estate. It defined the Property Services Agency's expectations on the performance of buildings and products alike : quality, durability and reliability. The paper described the management of quality policy in three distinct areas : in the specification of building components, in building design and construction process and in estate maintenance, and goes on to discuss the particular problems and developments in each. In particular stress was attached to the uniqueness of individual projects.

The paper concluded that when effective quality systems were operating in every stage in the building process - that is the design, construction, final evaluation, premature failure, maintenance and feedback, some major benefits would be realised.

K E Fletcher's and C F Scivyer's paper considered the application of formal quality assurance to the UK building industry. As a background to the implementation for quality assurance, various groups of building products were examined from manufacturer through to installation to consider what problems occured.

It was concluded that products which are claimed to conform to standards do not always do so and that the quality assurance of building materials and components was a step forward. However, the achievement of quality in the building process also depends on, for instance, the work of various designers; the performance of main and sub-contractors, who may also be involved in supplying various elements of design; the quality of complex 'one-off' products which were not always covered by standards.

An additional point made was that insufficient prototype testing was made. He further identified the need for a rigorous look both at practical situations and research.

J G Gunning's paper examined the present and potential roles of quality assurance in construction, particularly with quality assurance assessments of ready-mixed concrete producers and materials testing laboratories. He advocated this as an example of good QA practice pointing out the benefits the attention to detail has generated, namely improved semi-skilled sub-contractor quality tightening due to better management control feedback. By the improvement of quality and efficiency, one achieves conservation of resources and levelling up of standards therefore giving greater client security.

He concluded with the reminder that there are, in addition to the maintenance and assurance of materials, also client, user, contractor and designer elements which are inadequately stressed in assurance studies.

Robin Osborne's paper described investigations of concrete technology capability in the local Barbados construction industry, particularly as regards to specification production and testing with stress given to severe elemental risk. The study recommended staff training, new equipment, specification revisions with due regard to porosity of local materials, accreditation type requirements for producers and the requirement of further examination. These factors had to be particularly reviewed in the light of everyday needs. In the human resource case it was proposed that out of the research effort it should be possible to distil broad and well founded viable generalities.

Angus Wilson's paper on quality assurance by insuring quality considered the application of monitoring techniques to ensure functional and physical building adequacy. He selected three primary areas of concern, namely workmanship, maintenance with specific concern for roofs and paint, and communication or the fear of : when detrimental findings may be made. He suggested improvements to the current (1987) UK ten year guarantee. These should reflect allowance for anticipated 'wear and tear' defects as he recommended that investigation should be made into allowances for future costs supported by more accurate risk assessments countered by reducing inherent structural defects being reduced to acceptable levels. All the above should also be better interfaced with professional indemnity. The exposition was

120

usefully supported by practical quality assurance examples demonstrating the international nature of the issues.

The subsequent discussion drew attention to several particular points :
(i)   most defects and damages were caused by ignoring inside knowledge;
(ii)   analysis of surveyed data may have a greater role than pure research - eg bio-degredation rather than chemical, and their counteraction;
(iii) the international nature of assurance, in particular legal and code of practice issues, eg lessons from EEC countries were currently undervalued. The latter led to the concern with a shortfall of QA certificated persons. Currently this was only found in specific areas such as electrical work or welding. This focussed on the fact that most commonly tightening of legislation normally only arose as a result of latent defect disasters.

THE FUTURE OF PLANNING AND CONTROL

The final workshop proved to be a stimulating and worthwhile session. The pith of each of the four themes were presented and the floor was then passed to the delegates for what transpired to be an animated debate with a positive thrust. The essence, which was presented in the final conference session, was, we believe, in accordance with aims of future planning.

Planning for industrial development

The value of returns on investment was observed to vary according to the time period (eg. 1960's or 1970's) and also the type of construction, namely general civil engineering, non-residential and residential buildings.

Importance was attached to human resources, particularly the skilled resources were emphasised. Stress was given to future research into the effects of the turnover of manpower. Another area of concern was a shortfall in planned preventative maintenance.

Attention was then given to mega construction projects. These can create huge debts in developing countries, thus they create rather than solve a problem. Governments often exacerbate the cyclical nature of the construction industry by under-funding or overheating the economies at inappropriate times.

Turning to more specific issues it was noted that extreme care should be exercised when parameters, evaluated in a general construction activity, were used in specific cases, particularly with respect to the geophysical conditions and the learning curve effects required by adjustment to the 'particular'.

Planning and scheduling

The main thrust of this workshop may be paralleled with the economists' breakdown of his disciplines into MACRO and MICRO. The macro view was presented in terms of top management broad brush appraisal of the effectiveness of current planning and control methods. The micro view was seen as the supportive technologies.

The macro aspects showed that more attention should be paid to specific management reactions - less emphasis being paid to their structuring, ie, generating of a specific model. However it was seen that there was a need to form a bridge between the micro and macro view. To this end the programme of research required appraisal of lower management echelons.

On the specific technologies interest was shown in the development of the types of spreadsheets at one extreme decision network planning utilisations. This was seen as a potentially useful expansion of dynamic programming. At the other extreme, from the educational standpoint, a critical path package with crash programme was presented. However the most pertinent point about CPM made was that its major pragmatic use was a guide to logical planning and hence a means of enhancing efficiency.

Two new directions were specifically indicated. Professor Harris pin-pointed the need to expand work on line-based rather than network-based scheduling and Professor Bishop the exploration of related psychology - instancing the motivation to efficiency by sub-contractors who rent the road they are developing.

Planning and controlling resources, especially finance

This area proved to be somewhat controversial in the specific area of cash flow (S-curve) technology. However, the more general points made are enumerated below :-
1. The "team approach" in the US was compared to the "unbiased consultant approach" in the UK where perhaps more confrontational attitudes occur. Further research into delays.
2. Mixed opinions on the use and value of contractors front-end loading contracts (not discussed were the efforts of the International Lending Agencies who are attempting to eliminate this practice).
3. Cash flow profiles (S-curves) may have different characteristics which depend on the type of project and geophysical factors.
4. Re-examination of research results, eg, data today compared with 20 years ago.

Search for Quality

This subject area had so many ramifications and ingredients that it was seen as appropriate to, in the first instance, focus on the spread of the 'mixture' : legislation, insurance, to documentation control, avoidance of risks. The user, client, producer, manufacturer, designer. The project in its totality.

These diverse areas warrant much further study but a distillation of the information was seen to be of prime importance.

Greater emphasis on the testing of prototypes, evaluation of human limitations in the context of 'secure quality'. Attention to localised risks, a good example in the West Indies being hurricanes, as typical elemental extremes. By better observation, design and communication, risks may be reduced. It was noted that documentation could be simplified as the format was very similar at the design, contractor and sub-contractor levels. Thus both greater efficiency and clarity could be achieved amongst many other factors. However two key statements of wide-reaching value were made :

Professor Sebestyen suggested the imperative need to minimize defects and damages which are not caused by lack of knowledge but by ignoring our knowledge.

The second issue was crystalized by Robin Osborne who suggested that a ranking of the research issues should be made to establish and efficient programme "with a minimum of risk" and that it be unified with an emphasis on the "clarification of language".

In summary the areas of suggested further research are given below :

More work into construction resource planning and the degree of sophistification.

The supply, training and managing of skilled construction personnel in developing countries, also the effects on manpower turnover.

The causes and cost benefits of appropriate mega-projects in developing countries to avoid severe debt problems.

Contrast of preventive maintenance versus maintenance in appropriate circumstances.

Checking the validity of conclusions obtained years ago in today's context.

Investigation of the relevance and practical nature of research. The value of research would be improved if it were industry and market driven also wealth producing.

Problems investigation in planning and scheduling as seen by middle management and their bridge with relevant technologies.

Decision based networking was under-explored.

Line-based network methodologies should be given primary attention rather than the pure network scheduling.

The effects of psychological attitudes and their effect on schedule implementation.

Improvements in prototype testing.

Setting up a hierarchy of quality assurance problems with emphasis on communication and to reflect localized attributes.

Find a means of fully utilising known risk knowledge in

establishing quality assurance.

Investigate the means of simplifying quality assurance documentation by utilising the common grounds of the relevant disciplines.

The need to investigate means of establishing qualifications in quality assurance.

MANAGEMENT INFORMATION SYSTEMS AND EXPERT SYSTEMS

Rapporteurs : Professor Geoffrey Trimble BSc CEng FICE MIMechEng MIStructEng and Professor Abraham Warszawski

Loughborough University of Technology, Leicestershire, England.
Building Research Station, Israel Institute of Technology, Israel.

PREAMBLE

This review is presented in two parts. Part 1 by Professor A Warszawski reviews the papers submitted in this stream. Part 2 by Professor E G Trimble reports on the deliberations of the workshops.

PART I

INTRODUCTION

Over the recent years computers have had a growing effect on the performance of various managerial tasks in construction. Computers are routinely used today in most construction enterprises for accounting, office work, and various clerical tasks involved with administration of contracted and subcontracted work. More recently they have been used for cost estimating, the control of cost and schedules, preparation of tender documentation, evaluation of bid proposals, storage and processing of data on past performance.

The future uses of computers for construction include storage of comprehensive databases, employment of intelligent planning systems, real-time processing of data collected on site for modification of plans, and extensive use of graphical information for management use. In fact most of these future uses are already in a well advanced conceptual development stage. Their transformation into effective application tools is slowed down by the reluctance of construction enterprises to commit themselves to the considerable investment and organisational changes required and due to difficulties in realistic modelling of the construction decision process.

Most of the papers submitted to this workshop deal with the evaluation and improvement of the prevailing applications or with the development of novel techniques as enumerated above. The following report will briefly review the contents of these papers and then summarise their conclusions. For this purpose they will be classified arbitrarily into the following groups :

- <u>Management Information Systems</u>, which includes applications of computers to managerial control and project administration.
- <u>Expert Systems</u> and their possible applications as management

125

decision tools.
- <u>Other advanced decision tools</u> not included in the former categories.

MANAGEMENT INFORMATION SYSTEMS

As noted, this section deals with application of computers to information processing for the purpose of project control and contract administration.

Several papers offer general advice with regard to information systems which are to serve the construction process on site.

General requirements for an information system on site are described in a paper by Tyrvainen et at based on a survey conducted in Finland. The systems are classified by the authors into three generations - the first one, prevalent now, serves routine clerical and control activities, and the third one - to be in use at the end of the century, will employ advanced AT and CAD aids to decision making.

Cusack reviews the various conditions necessary to make an information system effective and reliable, and discusses the problems associated with the definition of the functions the system is to perform, and the selection of appropriate hardware and software.

Holes proposes a method for estimating of construction re-sources and progress time from simplified information about usable spaces in a building and their adjacent building components. This information could be subsequently used for control purposes, based on the reported progress rate of the project.

Suckarieh suggests a simple but effective control system for construction on site which can be run on a microcomputer with an aid of readily available "off shelf" DEMS and spreadsheet tools.

Several papers describe application cases involving large information systems employed in contracts administration by public authorities.

Shaeffer and Ferdman describe a development process of a contract administration system for a large public authoriy in Israel. The system, which is being developed in stages, is intended to prepare tended documents, evaluate proposals, control work progress and cost and perform all associated clerical opera-tions.

Antanavichius describes a system employed in Lithuania which assists in planning and control of projects. The planning function is assisted by a data file about past performances. The system may be adapted to the level of detail suitable to each particular user.

Carter presents a methodology of analysis of data flows which he applied to a information system employed by a public authority in the UK. The integration and re-routing of information flows as a result of the contractor, quality surveyor and various levels of owner's officers.

Finally, a survey reported by Sidwell and Cole in Australia reveals that at present about 80% of computer applications in construction are associated with financial and administration functions and only a minority are used for construction planning and estimating. In general the computers did not save labour but did enhance the quality and reliability of the processed information. These findings seem to be in agreement with the reported situation in other countries.

EXPERT SYSTEMS

Expert systems are often defined as interactive computer programs with a special structure intended to solve problems which usually require human expertise.

Several papers offer general comments about expert systems used in construction, based on the particular experience of the authors.

Trimble stresses goals definition of knowledge acquisition as more important functions of an expert system building process. He illustrates some other useful points while describing an expert system for diagnosis of dampness in building, and brings out the behavioural aspects which constrain knowledge acquisition.

Brandon emphasizes the advantage of expert systems as compared with the traditional decision models, but points out the difficulties in formalization of decision rules. He descibes in general terms the development of a system for strategic project planning. The system is intended to set a budgetary and time framework for the project execution, to determine its profitability and recommend an appropriate procurement method.

Chin suggests a procedure for construction of an expert system and reviews several systems recently developed. He stresses the value of teaching expert systems within the regular curricula of civil engineering studies.

A development of expert systems for specific tasks is the subject of other papers in this group.

Tommelein et al describes some problems involved in the development of a system for location of temporary facilities on a building site. Some aspects of knowledge acquisition and representation are discussed, and the formulation process of location rules is illustrated in the paper.

Several expert systems developed by CSTB in France and based on prevailing norms are described in a paper by Delcambre and Halleux. The systems have been developed in LISP and PROLOG for the following problems : selection of windows, thermal evaluation of a building, and the choice of its exterior facade.

De la Garza and Ibbs describe the structure of a knowledge base for an expert system for construction scheduling. The knowledge is represented in an ART environment by means of frames and semantic networks. The authors find the object oriented method of knowledge representation a valuable tool for modelling of the construction process.

A decision supporting system for construction time estimating is presented by Schaefer and Erkelens. The estimate draws from a hierarchical representation of the execution process in four levels and takes into account the production speed, site conditions and other factors.

Manesero and Chapman present general considerations in the development of an advisory system for construction. They describe a possible application to reinforced concrete work which includes a selection of an appropriate formwork method.

SPECIAL DECISION SUPPORTING TOOLS

This group of papers describes various computerised decision tools for specific construction problems.

Two papers discuss an automated site data acquisition system for real time decision making. Bengtsson and Bjornsson describe a system which takes video pictures of a desired construction activity, analyses its features and provides real time information to decision makers. Paulson and Sutoodeh-Khoo present development principles of a system which collects with the aid of sensors, the performance data of earth-moving scrapers, and determines in real time their optimal loading cycle based on the analysis of this data.

Halpin presents and interactive minicomputer system which assist in calculation and optimisation of earth work, and in fill allocation. He also describes a MICROCYCLONE simulation system for the analysis of repetitive activities. Another system for analysis of repetitive activities with an aid of their iconic representation is described by Lewis.

Atkin reviews the various possible uses of CAD in construction management. He also describes an experimental system which can graphically present desired work packages of their predefined attributes.

Wager reviews the technological innovations which can assist in the decision making process such as video discs, 3D graphical systems, artifical intelligence tools, and others.

CONCLUSIONS

a Although the use of computers in construction has considerably increased over the last years it seems that only a small part of their full potential has been realised in practice.
b The most prevailing applications of computers today are for contract administration and project management. This includes preparation of contract documents, cost estimating, control of cost, work progress and procurement, dissemination of project information and various associated clerical operations. Computer systems for these applications are readily available today and can be adapted to each particular user needs.

c An information system for any purpose should be carefully planned in view of the required information flows between all involved parties. It should use reliable software and hardware, especially suited to these needs.
d Expert systems have a considerable application potential in construction with its volatile environment and ill structured decision making process.
e The most intellectually challenging potential of expert systems is their use for modelling of comprehensive construction planning processes. This is however still unattainable at present due to difficulties with realistic recapturing of decision rules and complete domain knowledge essential for this purpose. Expert systems may be advantageously employed in the meantime for the solution of constrained problems using mainly factual or normative knowledge.
f Computers can play a useful role in simulation and analysis of repetitive activities which involve interdependence of work teams, stores and equipment.
g A promising area of decision supports is the possibility to capture relevant site information by means of sensors or video photography and its real time processing for immediate decisions.
h Another area of great future potential is the use of graphical CAD which allows storage and exposition of managerial information in user friendly and realistic manner.

PART II

WORKSHOPS 1 TO 4

In the notes that follow, IT (information technology) is used as a convenient shorthand for management information systems and expert systems.
The papers are their presentation identified the following uses of IT in construction :

- Accounting and related applications
- Scheduling and project control
- Aids to decision-making, notably simulation
- Aids to design
- Potential links between CAD and the information needed for management purposes
- Knowledge based systems (the expression expert system was widely used to describe such systems). The abbreviation KBS is used in the following notes.
- Capturing site data by video and sensors
- Robotics

Points that arose during discussion included the following :

- There are some important bahavioural problems that deserve attention. For example, people resist change unless new methods are skilfully introduced; they fear that they may be made to look foolish if they don't understand the technology; they may feel that their jobs are threatened by the development of KBS; site workers dislike video equipment which may record mistakes and malpractices.
- There is far greater use of accounting packages than of packages for scheduling and control. We can speculate about the reasons but there is little firm evidence about them.
- Although design is a knowledge based process, so far KBS for design will only select from pre-defined solutions or evaluate humanly devised trial solutions. The work of Iris Tommelein and her co-authors is a notable exception. Her approach is the nearest to design so far witnessed by the rapporteurs.
- Simulation is seen as an aid to the understanding of problems rather than to the generation of precise solutions. Nevertheless their structure needs to be verified. It was suggested that size of a model should not be equated with goodness. Some of the more helpful models are quite small.
- While robotics may be seen as something for mid to long-term application there are some real benefits available already. Professor Paulson quoted an example of a grader whose productivity was increased six times by the use of laser beacons and associated followers. Professor Warszawski described some developments notably of robots for internal finishes that may achieve pay-off in the medium term.
- Regarding KBS, the knowledge acquisition process is most effectively achieved by a combination of techniques. Rule induction is of limited value. Systems initiated by a client who knows how he or she wants them to be used will have greater success than those initiated by enthusiastic domain experts. Problem-orientation is more fruitful than technique-orientation; this may prove to be a crucial point in the explotation of KBS.

WORKSHOP 5

Before the symposium started Professor Trimble sent the following letter to authors in this stream. Its purpose was to provide a structure for the last very important workshop.

To authors of papers on Management Information Systems

Dear Author

CIB W-65 Symposium 1987

I believe that a very important aspect of the forthcoming symposium is the formulation of reasonable projections about the future. As one of the rapporteurs for the stream on "Management Information Systems" I shall be trying to co-ordinate the relevant points that arise from your paper and others in the stream.

If you would give some advance thought to this we shall all benefit. Some of the sub-headings that occur to me are :-

- How should information technology be used by the industry in the future?
- Where shall we have the biggest pay-offs? (eg, in dealing more efficiently with fairly mundane applications, in quantum leaps in understanding, in improved decision making, etc).
- Who will have the greatest influence in bringing about beneficial changes?
- Is it likely that the most influential people have sufficient understanding of the developing techniques to ensure that the benefits are realized?
- If not, how can we get new ideas across to such people and theirs to us?

If you would care to write to me in advance this would be much appreciated. If this proved to be impractical, any ideas you can put forward to Dr Warszawski and myself during the symposium will still be most welcome.

I look forward to seeing you in September.

Yours sincerely

GEOFFREY TRIMBLE

In the event the listed points proved helpful but were not adopted rigorously. Some of the points that emerged duplicate those reported above and the following record only the new issues.

- KBS can be used to capture and convey information. When used in this way they are no more a threat to the user than a well-written text book.
- Exciting developments in KBS should not divert attention from valuable schemes based on less esoteric technology such as data base programs.
- There were divergent views about the choice between stand-alone computers and centralised computing systems. However there was a clear consensus as to the need to respect the site manager's wish to operate with substantial autonomy.
- It would be of great benefit to undertake a systematic study of the needs of IT in construction and to publish a 10 year look-ahead. This would help not only in identifying needs but also in putting new projects into context. Such a study is likely to endorse the view that academics can be particularly useful in long-term issues while industry-based projects may be short-term. The plan should include proposals for achieving compatibility between these aims.
- In considering Dr Shaffer's objectives of increased effectiveness of research and development serveral issues emerged. The following are principally the views of the rapporteur.
- It should be made easier or industrial organisations to become members of CIB even where they have no track-record of research. Even quite modest companies can act as very effective "laboratories" for well-designed practical studies.
- CIB should lobby governments to introduce tax incentives to companies to send their young managers on post-graduate courses. The original rules of CITB, the (British) Construction Industry Training Board, provided effective financial incentives. Experience under these rules showed that the company-supported course student learns research techniques, helps to identify real issues for research, contributes constructively in seminars, and derives greater benefit from the course than the other students.
- Clients of the construction industry have the most to gain from improved efficiency. The initiative of the Business Round Table in the US in supporting relevant research is seen as a model that should be copied by other countries. In Britain approaches should be made by CIOB or CIB to the British Property Federation to lobby its support. The commercial interests of clients should ensure a practical orientation of the work supported and hence promote effective links between academics and industry.
- The influence of IT companies should not be over-looked. It can be beneficial but the over-selling of techniques can be counter-productive. Initiatives to promote liaison between CIB and the IT companies could be valuable in harnessing this substantial

commercial force.

PRODUCTIVITY : RAPPORTEUR'S REPORT

D. W. Cheetham Rapporteur

School of Architecture and Building Engineering
University of Liverpool. ENGLAND.

INTRODUCTION

The primary purposes of the symposium were for researchers to record progress in research and to expose their work to criticism. The papers assigned to the Productivity theme were considered in four workshop sessions 4A - Factors influencing productivity. 4B - New tools for productivity. 4C - The state of the art and new concepts. 4D - Productivity on site. Most of the papers were concerned with labour productivity or with techniques of site production analysis. A small group with off site production of precast concrete housing units in Eastern Europe and a few with productivity in developing countries.

The contributions of economists from Scotland and the West Indies caused many to think more critically about the problem of 'total' productivity rather than 'labour' productivity. Many authors recognised the limited framework within which they are conducting their studies and the need for consideration to be given to the total costs of production. Workshop session 4E provided an opportunity for participants to review the achievements of the research reported and the directions for future work. The question of how industry can become more closely involved in planning future research and implementing results was also considered.

Worthwhile discussion was conducted within a necessarily constrained timetable. Symposium participants contributed fully to the discussion throughout. The many positive contributions eased the rapporteurs task during the symposium but have added to the difficulties of producing an unbiased account of the proceeding. The author must accept responsibility for any inadvertent misrepresentation of others views. The presentation and discussion are reviewed across a number of workshop sessions rather than in strict sequence of presentation.

FACTORS AFFECTING LABOUR PRODUCTIVTY

Management Control

Horner presented a strong case for increasing labour productivity in the United Kingdom and suggested that this may be achieved by increasing the number of trade supervisors and management staff on site. Some 32 factors that are thought to influence labour productivity were identified and of these two considered in detail. A management control index defined as the ratio of the amount of management divided by the number of operatives. An assessment of the effectiveness of financial incentive schemes was made by questioning the management team.

Output data was obtained from 12 sites of mainly reinforced concrete framed buildings for concreting (cubic metres), steel rod reinforced fixing (tons) framework and brickwork (sq. metres). Productivity defined as output divided by available operative time. Available time is total paid time less unavoidable delays such as weather and meal breaks. Using techniques of regression analysis the authors conclude that productivity is strongly and positively related to the degree of management control. Perhaps more controversially incentive schemes appear to have little effect on productivity.

Activity sampling studies on 6 sites produced an unexpected result; there was no correlation between unit output and activity sampling and the authors suggest that measures of productivity based on activity sampling may give an erroneous impression of the scope for productivity improvement.

Barakat and Handa also considered that productivity can be improved by improving the effectiveness of site (field) management control. Studies of the techniques used for reporting progress and cost on 31 multi storey tower buildings in Ontario showed that irrespective of the size of the company, the value of the contract or the type of the building, the majority of the contractors prepared cost accounting reports and used bar chart schedules. These provide the main control tools. Some of the contractors were working on more than one project included in the study. Although stated company policies are applicable to all projects the authors were surprised to find no consistency in their implementation by site (field) management.

Site management can be the only source of data for completion of reports yet the authors noted that many reports were produced in head office by head office personnel. This often leads to a long turn around time (normally one month) for the preparation of progress reports and their feed back to site. This combined with an absence of regular monitoring and updating of work schedules (short term planning) indicates that present reporting procedures are failing to provide control of site activities.

There is limited authority vested in site staff and direct involvement of head office in daily operations. The fact that a certain company is making money does not mean that the job is run effectively and efficiently. A system of short term planning and cost control along with an increase of authority and responsibility of the field management staff is recommended to increase the direct involvement of the concerned parties in decision making. Awareness of the financial status of the project will reduce delays in taking action. This should increase site efficiency.

Unlike Horner, Barakat and Handa found insignificant correlation between the number of managers studied, the number of workers, the contract value and the efficiency of the site. On the other hand the number of workers was proportional to the contract value. The authors suggest however that consideration of the 11 sites having efficiency ratings greater than 76 percent "somehow" proves the basic argument that the number of managers and their input is directly proportional to efficiency.

Although computers were found on some 80 percent of sites they were regarded only as fast printing machines. The contractors are unable to take advantage of the potential benefits of computer application. The authors suggest that micro computer based systems for short term planning and cost control should be developed for site use to enable control to be exercised at daily and weekly intervals. During the presentation of the paper Handa observed that most sites are very badly organised, have poor materials management and emphasised that many companies give little responsibility to site personnel. He posed the question "If people know about CPM why don't they use it?"

During the subsequent discussion many contributors suggested that 30 and 40 percent activity rates (time men are observed to be working by activity sampling) were commonplace but agreed that 70 percent rates can be achieved by careful organisation and management of the work.

Repetition and learning curves

The learning or improvement phenomenon in a production process is defined as the acquisition of knowledge and/or skill which results in a reduction of operation time for successive completion of identical units.

Two papers considered this factor. Duff presented the paper written with Pilcher and Leach whilst Thomas presented that written by himself and Yiakoumis. The first based on studies undertaken in the U.K., the other in the U.S.A. Duff concluded that the cumulative learning curve is most applicable to construction planning and control. The factors affecting deviation from the theoretical curve include duration of the cycle of repetition, levels of experience of members of a gang of the activity and the introduction of a measured incentive scheme. Comprehensive statistical analysis and discussion of this analysis supports these conclusions which were based upon data gathered on two sites.

The activities studied during the refurbishment of two storey semi detached houses and flats were the fixing of timber framework to support new cladding, fixing small precast concrete simulated brick cladding units, fixing pre-cut panelling of simulated rendering material to reclad upper floors and replacing old timber window frames with new PVC frames. A 32 unit retail shopping development enabled data to be collected on the repetitive activities of concreting the ground floor slabs and laying partition blockwork.

Incentives

The contractor studied by Duff paid a 'standing bonus' at the commencement of these unfamiliar activities. A relatively small amount of learning resulted in slowly improving output taking place before the incentive scheme was introduced. Output improved considerably after the incentive scheme was introduced. Although the authors attribute this improved output to a change in the rate of learning it may be considered that the operatives expressed views quoted in the paper

"We're only coasting at the moment - just watch us when the bonus starts" suggests that financial incentives are important.

This of course differs from the conclusion reached by Horner who was unable to establish a connection between incentive schemes and output. There are however considerable differences in the types of operation considered in these two studies. It could be that incentives have no effect on well understood repetitive processes but are essential when introducing new processes.

Weather

The study reported by Thomas was similar in approach to Horner. Thomas also describes the first stages of development of a model which aims to take into account all the factors affecting labour productivity. This particular study takes into account the combined effects of weather and learning for the operations of constructing concrete block walls, wall forms and steel erection on 3 multi-storey sites in Pennsylvania. Some of the U.K. delegates were surprised that the U.S. concern with weather did not relate to rainfall but to high and low temperatures and high humidity.

The statistical approach adopted used a technique known as the Richardson Rapid Estimating system combined with assumed learning rates to derive expected productivity curves. Regression analysis was used to relate the actual productivity rates recorded on sites to departures from the expected productivity rates and air temperature and relative humidity at 1.0 pm. The most efficient productivity was found to be when the temperature is around $55^{\circ}F$ provided the relative humidity is not above 80 percent. Relative humidity only influences the equation when it is above 80 percent.

An interesting example is given of the application of the techniques to the development of a claim for extra compensation by a steelwork contractor when working methods are changed as a result of changes to the floor decking system. The first block permitted steel frame erection without interruption, concrete decking being installed later by other crews. The redesign involved interruption to the steel erection while the placing of precast concrete planks was phased into the production cycle.

Mechanisation and Equipment Policy

Efficiency in on site production requires the effective balancing of all resources, manpower, machinery, money and management. Management decisions as to the optimum level of investment into equipment and machinery for a particular economic/social cultural situation is important. Sozen describes the Turkish situation of declining productivity and economic crisis - high inflation and unemployment and suggests that equipment policies are needed. The reported low level of hiring and leasing seem to be peculiar to the Turkish situation. As would be found worldwide there are considerable differences in responses to the questions posed by firms of varying size. Her studies may be interpreted as indicating a large potential market for plant and equipment hire companies. However the monetary value of mechanical equipment used is a crucial prequalification for bidding in Turkey which requires ownership. This deters the development of a hire industry. Clearly there is a need for international comparison of the variations in extent to which equipment is used, its availability and the legal and government regulations concerning bids.

Hand held power tools are the aspect of mechanisation considered by Cheetham. His paper showed that the usage of such tools on U.K. housing construction sites has been found to be variable. Although generators were used on half the sites visited no temporary electrical distribution systems were found. Regrettably power tools are often regarded solely as an aid for performing tasks that might otherwise be unduly hard work rather than as an integral part of the production process. Many barriers to the greater use of hand power tools are identified. The most important action that tool manufacturers can take being to provide data on comparative studies of the same operations being undertaken by hand and with power tool assistance. The employment of individuals and small gangs of labour only subcontractors removes from contractors the incentive to improve working methods.

During the subsequent discussion delegates from USA and Australia expressed astonishment at the apparent backwardness of the UK house building industry whilst a delegate from a UK international contracting company expressed total disbelief. On being challenged he admitted to having no involvement with his company's house building subsidiary.

Buildability

Design with production in mind, provided the focus for the paper by Griffith presented by the rapporteur in the authors absence. Examples of alternative designs for foundations, service entry boxes, co-ordinated wall designs and flat roof design details illustrated the advantages of adopting an 'operational' rather than 'elemental' approach to design formulation. To reduce the number of operations, number of trades involved, and the number of repeat visits to a particular workplace reduces the complexity of the site management task and may increase the time operatives spend positively adding to the building rather than moving, of necessity, between work places on site.

None of the alternatives were costed and this was regretted by delegates during the subsequent discussions. It may well be that the cost of the increased concrete used in the trench fill foundation and the more expensive material in the single layer roofing felt is greater than the labour saving. The paper expressed the hope that a book of more buildable details will be produced. M.J.V. Powell of the Construction Industry Research and Information Association (CIRIA) outlined work commissioned by CIRIA which would shortly result in such a publication. The CIRIA work had approached buildability from a desire to improve quality rather than productivity and would not contain cost information.

This concern with advice to designers had also been the motivation for activity supplying studies undertaken by the Building Research Establishment reported by Stevens. The paper contains much data and suggests that operatives on house construction spend only about half their time on site directly 'making the building grow'. Stevens suggests that large amounts of time spent 'handling' or 'not working at the workplace' may indicate that the organisation of the work on site was inefficient. Innovatory design details associated with each of the schemes are assessed in relation to the labour expenditure required to construct the equivalent design details adopted by the other schemes for the same functional element. Single leaf block under-building and single service entry core showed labour savings of the order of 50 percent compared to conventional brick-block work up to dpc. Similarly single leaf block work external walls showed substantial savings on the more conventional brick and block work. Unfortunately the absence of data on plastering and drylining prevents a full comparison of this functional element. Surprisingly self finished insitu concrete slabs showed no labour advantage over insitu concrete plus screed.

The paper reports that single visit electrical installations using a harness wiring system and preplanned access ways failed to demonstrate that the single visit concept is more efficient. The studies on the single visit site showed however noticeable improvement curves in labour expended as electricians became familiar with the required tasks whereas on the multi-visit schemes there was not a significant learning curve.

Again the total cost of producing the element was not available. There was speculation that the cost of off site preparations of the wiring harness could well be considerable. Clearly there is much more data available than could be reported in a necessarily brief paper and the view expressed that the Building Research Establishment should publish a full National Building Study report on this work.

OFF SITE PRODUCTION/PREFABRICATION
The manufacture of prefabricated concrete panels is a technique which aims to reduce on site labour. Mrs Vukovic in a late paper described work and time studies in the factory production of concrete panels in Yugoslavia. Her paper is part of a larger study which aimed to improve the factory efficiency of the MONTASTAN system for producing reinforced concrete panels with a hollow ceramic block core. Continuous observation work study techniques were used to gather data which enabled improvements (not given) to be made to the production process. The results show that time distributions do not follow the normal distribution. As normal distributions are often assumed by those undertaking simulation exercises of repetitive operations the data in the paper could have application in such simulation studies.

This concern for delays is also showed by Beran and Hajek as a minor component in their theoretical application of reliability theory to the total building process. Their model endeavours to embrace all factors both on and off site, and assign mathematical values to each. In this regard it is more ambitious than the approach shared by Horner and Thomas but of less immediate application by contractors. Hajek when presenting the paper conceded that the techniques described do not solve the problems of increasing productivity but formulate the problem.

TECHNIQUES FOR PRODUCTION ANALYSIS
Activity Sampling
Activity sampling is a well established work study technique. Techniques described by Stevens speed up the processing and analysis of the data. The Building Research Establishment used an optical mark reader to record data and transcribe it accurately to a computer file. Analysis of the data is quickly undertaken using computer package operating on a Vax computer. During his presentation Stevens regretted that the package is not currently portable to other computer systems. He explained that the motivation behind its development had been to assess the extent to which particular design objectives had been realised during construction and how they affected the practicability, interrelationships and efficiency of site operations. They were not primarily concerned with operatives productivity.

There was general agreement that activity sampling unrelated to records of production output is of little use to either the contractor or researcher. Thomas supported Benjamin in the view that increasing operative work rates does not necessarily increase productivity. This supported the conclusion reached by Horner. The potential benefits of activity sampling in assisting site management decision making in specific problem areas was generally accepted.

Work Sampling
Rather than attempting to study all activities on a site a simpler work sampling technique relying only on paper and pencil techniques was described by Baxendale. Examples of studies on housing sites for drainlaying, brickwork, concreting floor slabs and fixing plasterboard were given which showed both good and bad site organisation practice. Inefficiencies in site operation often exist because site management is too close to the work and too busy to see them. Though the studies were conducted to develop and prove the technique it is the author's intention that its use in practice should be a response to particularly low outputs. This may be identified when weekly measurement is made for piecework payment purposes.

The studies had been conducted on sites where all operatives were labour-only subcontractors and site managements had apparently abdicated any responsibility for giving detailed instructions to those undertaking the work. The author had found that the tally counts could be analysed within half an hour at the end of each day and should give information on which site management could quickly act. Indeed he hoped that site foremen would undertake their own studies. Often a low level of productive work resulted from simple organisational errors such as materials being deposited a long way from the workplace, extended teabreaks and late starts and early finishing. The range of productive work found varied from 37 to 76 percent. During discussion Stoneman of Sheffield City Polytechnic observed that he had satisfactorily used similar techniques to identify areas of inefficiency in a joinery shop.

Validity of Work Study and Work Sampling Questioned
Benjamin presented a late paper by Neal, Benjamin and Hize which

concluded that work sampling studies do not yield valid results as to the efficiency with which a site is organised and the productive effort expended by operatives. Examples based on nuclear power plant construction showed a general trend to a reduction in direct activity as a project moves towards completion (complexity increases). Typically it fell from 60 to 30 percent. Comparisons between several sites showed variation of between 32 and 60 percent direct activity having little effect on the cost of the finished plant. This confirmed the observations made by Horner and similar views were contained in the paper presented by Lewis.

Lewis suggests that the problems that result from a time and motion type of study is that they always indicate a sizeable proportion of the total time spent on a job as categorised as non-productive. This leads managers to attempt to reduce it and by focusing on labour productivity they fail to consider all other factors affecting productivity. He recognised that the detailed analysis of activities by work study techniques to improve the way a job is done can be of benefit to individual workers but suggests they are concerned with the ergonomics of production, not with its economics, with performance rather than with productivity and logistics rather than profit. Verschuren informed delegates that the Japanese were undertaking work studies of manual methods as a prerequisite to robotics.

Lewis argued that overall efficiency in the use of all resources in the construction process is more important than labour productivity. The view that large variations in apparent labour productivity could have little effect on product cost proved controversial. Coates, chairman of session 4, a major employer stated that although directly employed labour accounted for only 10 percent of his companies turnover it had the greatest effect on profitability. Clearly this is an area requiring further consideration.

There was general agreement among delegates that non-productive time could be reduced to 20-30 percent by more careful management and that management organisation of work produced greater results than exhortation to individuals to work harder or faster. Some individuals can work hard but ineffectively. There was also agreement that on many U.K. housing sites being built by labour only subcontractors the management needs to organise the work as though the operatives were hourly paid employees. Too many site managers have abdicated responsibility because, by definition, the labour costs of labour only subcontractors are fixed.

Video linked computer analysis

Recent developments in video recording linked to computers described by Wijesundera aimed to ease the task of convincing site managers that they have a problem and can take action. Microcomputers are programmed to store and analyse the information contained in the video recording. Computerised multiple activity charts were then used to reconstruct the sequence of tasks to enable managements to eliminate these operations deemed inefficient and unnecessary. As most managers cannot accept they have a problem, generally caused by poor planning, video pictures of inefficient working methods have proved

141

useful in convincing managers that problems exist. The techniques had been mainly applied to plant intensive operations such as earth moving. The reported involvement of major contractors encouraged Stevens who observed that BRE attempts to record site operations from distant video cameras had created so much hostility that the study was abandoned.

Earth moving also provided the example for the development of a microcomputer based expert system being developed by Christian. Christian was concerned to emphasise the low expenditure on research and development in construction. The next stage of his research is to gather data in order to validate his model.

During discussion of these two papers other experiences of using videos were described. Stoneman observed that operatives like to see themselves. They will always co-operate providing that they are involved in the studies and do not consider that 'spy' pictures are being recorded. Such videos had been most satisfactorily used for method studies which avoided the need to rate the speed of working. There was general agreement that video film allows examples of poor site organisation to be shown to the responsible site managements.

Curwell cited Australian examples of the use of video for recording project history. Time lapse video recording 1 shot per second enabled 4 days progress to be recorded on a 4 hr tape. The motivation had been to obtain a record in case of litigation rather than productivity improvement. Verschuren mentioned the use of a hand held recorder which enabled data to be entered by the observer and fed directly to a computer for analysis. This had enabled his organisation to abandon the intermediate stage of video recording with subsequent analysis. This reduced both the time taken to obtain data and the cost of the investigation.

Computer linked predetermined motion time systems

The micro computer speeds up the data assembly and calculation aspects of the application of the Maynard Operation Sequence Technique (MOST) described by Minkarah in the paper by Suckarieh, Minkarah and Ahmad. This system has been developed for manufacturing industry and involves the summation of engineered time standard for the movement of objects between co-ordinates rather than the small movements of the body and limbs as found in conventional predetermined motion time systems. Examples are given which show that similar operation times result from calculation by the MOST system and the more traditional method time measurements but the MOST system is quicker to use.

Clearly this is a construction application of a sophisticated manufacturing engineering technique. Concern was expressed that the construction industry did not have the equivalent of work study engineers. Who is responsible for advising on working method? Who is responsible for organising sites to aid individual operatives improve their personal performance? Despite many views that management in general shared responsibility the main concern of delegates was that only too often it was not one individual's primary responsibility. Examples were cited of U.K. contractors recently closing their work study departments while many contractors had never had such productivity support services.

Ergonomic design of site tasks

Concern for operative health and wellbeing is shown by Verschuren and Spekkink in their paper describing the development of a workload data system. The aim of this ergonomic based system is the prevention of losses due to absenteeism arising from physical overexertion. The recently developed technique combines the energy expended on physical tasks with the time taken on these tasks from basic work study data produced by the Dutch Research Institute for Labour Economy in the Building Trade. The degree of exertion can be calculated and if found to be between "moderately severe" and "severe" improvement in materials, equipment and working methods can be sought.

The technique is a further development of ideas first presented at the W65 Dublin symposium. In response to questions Verschuren explained that their motive was to increase the useful working life of operatives. The data was based on Dutch experience and appropriate primarily to that climate. Similar calculations ought to be possible for different climates if the basic data is available.

PRODUCTIVITY IN DEVELOPING COUNTRIES

Low and decreasing productivity have been a source of debate in Trinidad and Tobago. The functions and experiences of a National Productivity Council are described by Suite. His paper focuses on the common error of equalling "labour productivity" with "total productivity" and the assumption that workers are the sole cause of low productivity. In this respect his argument is similar to that proposed by Lowe. A generalised definition of total productivity is derived and five strategies for improving productivity considered, four of which do not require workers to change their behaviour and none of which involve individuals working harder. The view is expressed that we need to define productivity at four levels:

   i) the building sector as a totality;
  ii) the design or construction company;
 iii) the site level - comparison between sites within the same firm;
  iv) the activity or the task comparison between gangs and individuals.

Suite concludes that in developing countries the question of measurement of productivity must be preceeded by the definition of the concept in such a way as to permit quantitative and qualitative evaluation. The central task in developing countries will then be the systematic collection of data based on measured levels of output of different workers performing similar tasks, across sectors, as well as within a particular sector. This exercise will facilitate the establishment of norms or average output rates such as those produced by the SAOB in Holland for Dutch working method. On each specific construction site measurements should continue and achieved rates should be compared with norm rates.

Attempts must be made to drive up the output of the individual worker, of gangs, of subsector and of sector nearer to the corresponding norm values. Together with this there should be a broader sectoral and national thrust to increase the output of the norms for each unit. Management must be conscious of technological innovations worldwide and constantly seek to adapt as well as motivate within im-

143

proved management systems. This would mean that there must be a constant study of international norms. This is the sequence of the tasks which today faces developing countries particularly in their effort to industrialise their construction industries.

A detailed account of such studies concentrating on labour productivity in Tanzania is provided by Parker et al. Unfortunately he was unable to be present and introduce his account of the establishment of a schedule of rates for standard bill of quantity items. These schedules being derived from activity sampling studies. The authors point out that the implications of the labour productivity study are not related to any consequent decrease in the direct costs of construction. Labour in Tanzania constitutes an extremely small percentage of cost compared to materials. For example the labour component of concreting is only 3 to 4 per cent of the base rate. The real implications of their studies being that a reduction in activity times would enable management to reduce indirect costs through reduction in total time of construction and reduction in time based escalation of direct costs stemming from volatile increases in material costs.

TOTAL PRODUCTIVITY

A broad economic overview is also provided by Lowe who proposes a classification of approach to improvements in total productivity. After a full discussion of factors influencing both productivity improvement and decline the paper concludes that the labour intensive mode of production represents a rational response to the economic situation faced by the industry in the U.K. During discussions considerable doubt was cast on the validity of the international comparisons contained in the paper, fluctuations in rates of exchange, balance of activities between sectors and a failure to identify plant and equipment costs being those of the difficulties experienced by others. A decline in the U.K. construction productivity in tables derived from Bennett's work might be simply explained by the increasing proportions of total output of the U.K. industry being devoted to repair, refurbishment and rennovation and less to highways, dams and new building.

There was broad similarity between Lowe's view and those of Lewis who also commented on the changing balance between capital investment and labour and the effects of inflation. During discussion Lewis observed that if general inflation is greater than wage inflation and productivity is defined as output in £ divided by labour input (number of men or man hours) then productivity rises without any action being taken by management (at all levels) in the industry. Conversely general deflation may lead to an apparent fall in productivity.

Clearly the problem of definition is crucial to further research, particularly when making international comparisons. Those authors concerned with site studies of labour productivity generally used measures of such as Output (sq.m. or cubic metres of material fixed) divided by Input (total man hours or available man hours) but rarely mentioned the supporting plant or power tools or availability of artificial light to provide adequate illumination over the working day.

Those authors concerned with comparisons over time used variations of the output/input model which relate output by value (of total construction output or by a particular sector) or by number (number of dwellings etc) to the total number of persons employed in the industry or the number of operatives or similar. No doubt these ratios are used because statistics on output and on the labour input are more readily available than other statistics. Unfortunately change in the value of the ratio value of output/number of operatives employed are often interpreted as measuring changes in labour efficiency when in fact, some other factors such as mechanisation, prefabrication, change in demand may well have influenced the equation. Changes in proportion of activity between various sectors can make aggregated values of construction output almost meaningless.

There was general agreement that many international comparisons do not compare like with like and produce meaningless results. Problems of inclusion/exclusion of equipment costs, balance of activity by sector and even definition of the scope of the industry were mentioned. The value of output will also change within a country with demand, contractors charge what the market will bear rather than the cost to themselves of undertaking the work.

Jacobsson, in discussion pointed out that while Japan was increasing manufacturing output at 15 percent compound per annum construction output was remaining constant and suggested this is because it is actually very difficult to improve productivity in construction. The nature of the process, based on changing site location with different product types, different design teams, different combinations of subcontractors on successive projects precludes the significant gain possible in manufacturing. There was almost universal agreement that productivity cannot be increased in a declining market.

DISCUSSION

The papers considered ranged from description of techniques which could be readily applied by industry such as those by Baxendale and Wijesundera and Harris to descriptions of the early stages of development of potentially powerful tools such as those by Beran and Hajek and Christian. The symposium clearly reported progress made since the Waterloo 4th International Symposium. Typically that by Cheetham reported an extension of his work on small scale site mechanisation while Verschuren and Spekkink described a workload data system foreshadowed by an overview of ergonomics in the construction industry presented at the 3rd Symposium in Dublin.

These proceedings will, along with those from previous symposia, form a useful source of reference for recording research and pointing the directions for future work. There is unfortunately evidence to suggest that some studies are being undertaken without the necessary preliminary literature searches. All researchers are recommended to examine previous symposia proceedings.

There was less reference to the problems of the management of construction firms than expected. How do they adopt and survive in changing markets? The management of firms is a potential growth area for research currently receiving modest attention in the W65 subgroup of that name. Who is responsible for improving productivity? Is there a connection between productivity and profitability? Are companies made more profitable as a result of marketing and aggresive work valuations?

Few of the papers actively involved themselves with cost or evaluated the effects of alternative balances of input resources to the building process. We simply do not know whether or not more "buildable" designs are cheaper. The outcome is influenced by the relative balance of labour and material prices. Evidence from Tanzania showed labour to be so cheap that it has a marginal affect on price. The proposed linking of W55 - on Building Economics with W65 for a joint symposium in Australia in 1990 is welcomed.

None of the papers were concerned with the capital investment in a project by a contractor and upon the return on that investment. During discussions figures of 1 to 2 percent of contract sum were quoted by UK and US delegates, viz on $100M, project the contractor would invest $1 to 2 M. The suggestion was made that the Labour/Capital balance varied 2:1 in USA, 1:1 in UK and 1:3 in Japan. The source of these figures was not known but the possibility that greater investment by contractors might produce cheaper buildings is worthy of future research.

The workshops successfully permitted exchange of information, ideas and exposure of papers to criticism. There was a general concern for making research relevant to the needs of industry. Before research can be communicated to industry it must be expressed in a manner capable of ready comprehension by the industrialists present. Researchers should be hardly surprised if some sentences are not readily understood. "The application of sensitivity analyses and the use of artificial intelligence are being incorporated in the computer models, using an integrated package program, interfaced with a shell program, so that the examination of the construction process under consideration will possess diagnostic capabilities and be able to handle fuzzy sets of data." This is overfull of buzz words!!

Some researchers were disappointed at the limited attendance of industrialists and some industrialists disappointed at what they considered to be a lack of immediately applicable research. There is clearly a problem here. Many management researchers had experiences similar to those reported by Pilcher in plenary session. Construction companies are anxious to involve researchers in technical issues which involve short term problem solving but do not recognise the possibility that their management performance might be capable of improvement. Unless researchers can expose their ideas to comment they cannot respond to the criticism or sensibly plan the development of future investigations.

CONCLUSIONS
Research funding is a problem in all countries. If contractors and other industrialists wish to influence the direction of future research they should fund it. Two papers from the UK, Horner and Cheetham, independently propose a National Centre for Construction Productivity Improvement and a Power Tools Institute. Such proposals

are capable of consolidation. Clearly researchers will respond to advice from funding bodies. Contractors all know the "golden rule" - he who has the gold makes the rules. Contractors within the U.K. are generally unaware of the influence they can exert on the direction of research as a result of modest levels of funding to supplement government funds available through the Science and Engineering Research Council CASE and Co-operative Awards Schemes.

An implicit conclusion of examples given from U.S.A., Canada and England of the low status of site management is that continuing Professional Development (CPD) for mid-career managers is essential. There was general agreement in discussion that an increase in the quantity and quality of management to organise and control work would improve labour productivity. The aim of such increased provision of management staff being to enable individuals to work more effectively by improving working methods and reducing double handling of materials.

The main point of agreement arising from the Workshops was that labour productivity is a management organisational issue and is not concerned with making individuals perspire. Indeed perspiration and rapid energy consumption do not improve long term productivity if operatives are so overstrained, injured or acquire medical conditions such as arthritis such that they are unable to work beyond the age of 50.

The current level of financial awareness of site managers is considered to be low and delays of a month in preparation of cost reports by head office staff common place. These delays preclude the possibility of site staff taking speedy corrective control action. They simply do not know of the problems. The development of linked micro computer system with both site and head office input ought to be developed. Such developments would not only provide information and improve the quality of decisions taken but also improve job image There is a view that it ought not to be necessary for head office staff to be involved in day to day site matters. The most appropriate location for control, site or head office, requires further research.

In the U.K. the considerable growth in self employment and labour subcontracting has led many firms to ignore the basic management of site activity, particularly on housing sites. The men are simply left to sort it out themselves. This point was made by both Baxendale and Cheetham.

It is essential that site managements accept responsibility for improving work methods, organising sites and reporting to head office Evidence worldwide suggests that on many occasions the responsibility is not accepted.

DIRECTIONS FOR FUTURE WORK
Many factors are thought to influence labour productivity and papers explored the effects of some of these variables. Contradictory conclusions may be attributed to differences in definitions and techniques used by researchers, nature of tasks studied and cultural differences. There is a need for international comparisons of similar tasks and operations. As a first step Productivity needs definition. Agreement as to appropriate measurement systems and the development

147

of mutually acceptable techniques will be necessary before international comparisons can be made. As monetary comparisons are influenced by fluctuations in exchange rates methodologies will have to be developed which consider all inputs, manpower, materials used, money, working methods/techniques, support technology and level of management supervision. To establish such international comparisons will be a major challenge to the worldwide construction research community. It is to be hoped that an appropriate task group can flourish under the auspices of the W65 commission.

The major input to construction activity are capital investment, materials, machinery, manpower and management. Changes in the balance of these inputs can affect the output of the industry. The 'ideal' or best combination of resources to maximise output will vary in different parts of the world depending upon the relative cost of each. In economic analysis all resources can only be compared in terms of their cost. If the machinery and materials used are expensive whilst manpower is cheap then management resources must be devoted to optimising the use of machinery and minimising materials wastage. If management is expensive whilst other inputs relatively cheap then apparently wasteful methods of production may well be the 'best' solution for that particular socioeconomic system.

This view negated a suggested definition of productivity - the avoidance of wastage of resources and points to some of the difficulties to be overcome when making international comparisons. The broader view of considering all inputs strongly suggests that too much research is concerned with detail work study analysis. Management researchers ought to be concerned with the total process of conversion of raw materials to finally positioned components in buildings. Why can the Danes buy Finish and Swedish timber and convert it to high performance windows for use in England more cheaply than the English? Why has the UK curtain walling industry collapsed under foreign competition?

It will only be through the creation of an industry funded National Centre for Building Productivity Studies charged with the task of investigating working practices and disseminating details of good practice that co-ordinated progress will be made in the U.K. Such an organisation could usefully be based upon the Dutch Research Institute for Labour Economy in the Building Trade (SAOB). Without such a U.K. input it will be difficult for us to make a contribution to solving the problem of the Year 2010 posed by Dick Shaffer, the W65 Co-ordinator in his plenary address.

The major landmarks of the workshop sessions have been agreement on the need for:
1. Concern with total productivity, not simply labour productivity.
2. Valid international comparisons.
3. Establishment of national norms and improved working methods.
4. Consideration of integration of off site production with on site production.
5. Examples of GOOD practice rather than BAD.

ACKNOWLEDGEMENTS
Thanks are due to the Workshop Chairman, Brian Hall and Alan Stevens

of the Buiding Research Establishment, Watford, and Brian Coates,
Managing Director of Ashby and Horner for their careful preparations
for the Workshop Sessions and the skill with which they conducted
them. C Peter Verschuren, joint rapporteur and Director of the Dutch
Research Institute for Labour Economy in the Building Trade (SAOB)
for the stimulus he provided to the discussion throughout the symposium and for comments which have been incorporated in this report.

HUMAN FACTORS

RAPPORTEURS: Dr. Zeyned Sozen and Professor V.B.Torrance

Teknik Universite, Turkey and Heriot-Watt University, Edinburgh

SESSION 5A

ORGANISATION AND ENVIRONMENT: THE COMPANY

At long last, more attention is being devoted by research groups to the performance of organisations within the markets and business environments in which they operate. Seven papers were presented which contained the results of investigations into various aspects of the organisational performance of companies within the construction industry.

The authors focused upon two broad areas:

a) The internal organisation of the companies and how they behaved.

b) The relationship of the companies with their markets and their operational strategies.

The papers are summarised in the order in which they were presented. Authors were in attendance to present all seven papers in this workshop.

A study of the productivity of five U.K. chartered building surveying firms were presented by P.S. Barrett. A systems model had been adopted and tested by the contingency approach. A series of factors which can be changed were charted. The performance of the firms had been assessed and their performance measured against appropriateness. Specifically, profit and turnover were examined and the success of the firms in profit maximisation was examined.

A further postal questionnaire survey of the senior partners was carried out. Their job maturity was graphed against their experience and used to give a test of the appropriateness of their leadership style. Finally, each firm was given an "Organisational Asset Account" which showed their Overall Organisational Score.

Strategic planning within small and medium sized companies in the Canadian construction industry had been the subject of research by M.W. Prince. Sixty four contractors and sub-contractors were investigated and their planning processes identified. In particular, the characteristics of the planning executives in the companies were studied, together with attitudes to strategic planning.

Factor analysis was validated and used to identify the underlying structure of the companies in terms of strategic planning. Analysis of variance was used to determine key relationships between factor scales and attributable company or executive characteristics. Four factors were analysed for interpretability. Results were presented which reflected the progression in the planning systems from reactive to proactive future oriented patterns of strategic planning.

The author intends to carry out further empirical work in order to extend the preliminary model and to provide companies with a planning structure to assist their future operations.

J. Carlisle provided a paper in which the results of his studies of fifteen small construction companies in Northern Ireland were discussed in terms of the company strategies employed and the levels of success achieved. These results were further compared with the performance of five companies outside Northern Ireland. In particular, the objectives and strategies of the companies were compared in terms of growth, status and survival ability.

The internal strategies of the companies were assessed and related to the external strategies associated with market conditions. The performance range over two time periods, of 5 and 10 years duration was compared. Performance, in terms of growth in turnover, was measured and presented as below, average or above. These rates of success against stated objectives were compared to those achieved by the five outside companies and found to be poor.

One of the most interesting findings was that the extent of leadership and involvement by top management correlated with degrees of success. It was also shown that where strategic awareness had increased the performance of the company had improved. Companies had been most successful when they combined the features of flexibility within their established market, the founder had certain leadership and entrepreneurial skills and had remained heavily involved in the company.

Corporate culture as a basis for organisation and management was presented by G. Dressel. This paper provoked much interest both at the time of its presentation and during discussion sessions. The system of attitudes, beliefs and goals within a company was discussed, together with its influence on the organisation and management. The idea of a "Silent Revolution" of value concepts was explored and survey methods which can be used to give a profile of corporate culture were presented. The aim being to deduce the extent to which corporate culture coincides with the corporate strategies actually employed.

151

Maturation and creativity reinforce or challenge personal initiative. Corporate culture can be promoted to these ends and applied to strategic and operative planning in the company. This, together with a participative style of management, ensures that employees at all levels are involved in the relevant aspects of management.

Dr. Patricia Hillebrandt presented the achievements of the first stage in a three year programme which is attempting to make three links; i.e., the theory of the firm with the various disciplines brought together and combined for the purpose of examining how best to improve the body of management theory applicable to construction firms. The object of the paper was to describe the U.K. Science and Engineering Research Council support for the investigation into the extent to which economic and management theory is relevant to large firms in the construction industry.

During the first stage of the programme nine knowledgable authors were invited to collaborate in the preparation of a book, combining their knowledge of the construction industry and of existing theory. For the second stage, lengthy structured interviews with senior management in large, internationally oriented construction companies were being carried out. The programme had coincided with an interesting set of conditions in the market but was already showing the relevance and applicability of theory to practice, although contracting has shown some special characteristics not highlighted in the theory.

The third stage of analysis, writing and publication will take until 1989 to complete, when a two volume book will be published.

A paper was presented by H. Embiyauglu, Z. Sozen and V. Usdiken which reported an exploratory study of contextual and structural correlates and performance implications of the use of advanced management systems in construction firms in Turkey. A cross-sectional study of twenty four Turkish general contractors had been carried out in which the relationships between organisational, contextual and structural attributes and the use of management systems were investigated. After giving a useful historical background to this area of research the authors provide a clear explanation of the research methodology employed together with tables of the correlations and partial correlations obtained.

The research findings are interesting and well expressed. Generally, the contractors studied operated in international markets but did not appear to make use of sophisticated management systems (contrary to the findings of Khandwalla). The authors also found that the development of sophisticated construction techniques led to decentralisation within the organisation. There was also a strong positive association between the use of management systems and the perception by management of their organisational performance. Finally, in addition to pointing to the need for longitudinal studies, other possible streams of highly significant research were suggested.

Singapore was the location of the final study reported, in which C. Wheeler and P.M. Woon had investigated the marketing practices of building contractors. An audit of marketing effectiveness had been carried out in 1984 involving 50 companies, of which forty one were local and nine were of foreign origin. Thirty three of the companies were surveyed by questionnaire and seventeen by interview. Eight facets of the Singapore contractors' marketing philosophy were analysed. Only around one quarter of the whole sample were found to have satisfactorily defined marketing.

Other factors analysed were pricing strategy, communication strategy, strategic orientation, operational efficiency and the costing of marketing effectiveness. These performance measures were then compared with those existing in the U.K. The means of improving marketing practices in Singapore were identified and explored. Finally, the need was shown to examine the international approach to marketing by the companies.

SESSION 5B

ORGANISATION AND ENVIRONMENT: THE PROJECT

Six papers were included in this workshop, although only five authors were able to present their papers.

The paper by D.A. Langford, R. Newcombe and R.F. Fellows began by emphasising the need for further fundamental research into the nature of the building process, with a specific focus on the need for further investigation of the range of procurement systems available to clients. The authors addressed themselves to the problem of structuring a general model for the building project process. Particular emphases were given to:
a) The information flow through a project
b) Decision making during the life of a project.

Previous models were considered, with the authors stressing during their presentations Mintzberg's Model and Checkland's Law of Conceptualisation. Emphasis was given to three key aspects of decision making; the decision, the decision maker and the decision process.

The generalised model being developed was presented and the attempts which had been made to clarify and improve it were discussed, with particular reference to the application of systems theory.

The next paper presented had not been made available in advance. In the verbal presentation G.T. Dreger discussed a case study of Managing Building Construction Costs During the Design Phase. This outlined the practical applications of systems developed for the project studied. The paper focused on resource control systems and the methods used to develop and refine the systems and controls were discussed. The owner's definition of the consultant's requirements concerning cost, time, quantity and quality were described.

A diagrammatic description of the relationship between the design and construction groups together with the consultant's services allowed the various functions to be defined. The means of controlling the schedules was described, within the organisational framework. The cost control model was presented as an example of the control systems.

During the discussion session, the author further explained that the study had mainly been concerned with the design phase of the project. Another important concern had been constructability, which was seen to be the application of construction management controls to design influences on the construction process. It was further explained that construction management skills had been used during the design phase, at an early stage, when establishing the budget, the project conceptual phase, producing the probable cost and the contract documentation. This approach was additionally valuable when relating the contractor's bids with the budget and in negotiating with the lowest bidder to obtain a cost breakdown.

An interim report was presented by J. Bennett of a continuing project aimed at Simulating Construction Project Management. The paper emphasised that contractors' management relies on differentiation and co-ordination and that it was on these two main influences that the research project focused. Models were being developed of the processes of differentiation and co-ordination in project management. Co-ordination devices used in practice were identified and a technique used for measuring their use in practice was developed. The process of differentiation was discussed, whereby essential work is divided into separate roles each occupied by a team.

Much detailed information was provided concerning the use of questionnaires to measure the use of co-ordination devices during the construction of a series of office buildings. The author expects that the usage of patterns of co-ordination devices will fall into distinct groupings related to degrees of project difficulty. Once the links between co-ordination devices on specific projects have been established the results will be related to models. The object being to establish more detailed links to

154

provide project managers with advice on choice of co-ordination devices.

C.P. Imbert discussed his professional experiences in a paper dealing with Aspects of Project Management for Building Projects, with particular attention to multi-disciplined specialist sub-contractors. The structure of contracts employing separate trades was considered and potential areas of conflict were identified. Possible time savings by overlapping of the design and the building processes were considered. The paper mainly dealt with contracts in which separate trades sub-contractors predominated.

Through the evidence from two case studies, the project management function was examined and the need for continuous and active on-site management was shown. The viability of separate trades contracting was shown and the advantages highlighted. However, serious disadvantages were also identified and discussed.

The paper by D. Weiller and J. Piona was presented by Miss Weiller. A very helpful summary of the main points contained in the paper, in english, was provided for all present in the workshop session and is given below:

1) A sociological study of relations between a large construction company and its sub-contractors: the application of the CBC partnership policy (discussion-based survey of a 25 firm sample).

2) Partnership: a new approach in the building industry. It is in keeping with the new strategies of large companies aimed at acquiring a leadership position with clients and the various firms involved in production. This policy aims at ensuring the collaboration of sub-contracting firms at the earliest stages so as to be able to offer a product which is better adapted to demand and optimize quality/price ratio.

3) The sub-contracting market is expanding. Firms swing between two extreme situations: 'suicidal' and 'controlled' sub-contracting. Will partnership relations, based on co-operative relations rather than relations based on strength, lead to the establishment of new-style sub-contracting?

4) The principles of partnership according to CBC: a) create loyalty of sub-contractors, but without exclusive relations: one partner per lot is sought on the basis of a pre-fixed budget and flexible specifications. b) involve sub-contractors in preparations for the job by organising joint consultations between all the partners.

5) The conception of partnership by sub-contracting firms is different. In an ideal situation it would be a 'marriage', with sharing of risks. More realistically, the aim should be to form a 'team' to execute the main contractor's project.

6) The application of the partnership approach varies. The consultation procedure (1 partner per lot) comes to grief over the reality of prices: the budgets proposed by the main contractor are considered insufficient. Moreover, the principle (1 partner per lot) is applied especially to those trades with a high degree of technicity. The most usual practice is limited call for tender.

7) Consultation between partners is solely bilateral between CBC and the sub-contractor. There are no contacts with the client, architect or the other firms. Such joint consultation is held especially with the technical trades, in whose view it does not take place sufficiently earlier in the project and is restricted to minor matters.

8) Partnership is a positive approach, but is unfinished. In its application there exists a disparity between the different types of firms, which disparity is liable to increase. For those possessing a high level of technical skills, with a structured organisation and negotiation power, partnership relations could possibly lead to a new-style of sub-contracting. For the others only to privileged relations as performers.

G. Winch was not available to present his paper on The Construction Firm and the Construction Process: the Allocation of Resources to the Construction Project. This paper set out to show the limitations of the systems and contingency approach. It covered misconceptions concerning the nature of project organisation. It states that projects organisation is a coalition whose viability is dependent upon the project meeting the goals of the individual organisations involved. Each member is most concerned with their own parent organisation. Secondly, the systems and contingency approach is derived from literature developed for the analysis of the internal working of organisations. But project relationships depend upon contractual and informal links between organisations.

The origins of uncertainty are discussed. The bounded rationality generated by project uncertainties are compounded by those generated by project complexity. The total cost of construction is the sum of transaction costs and production costs. Transaction costs have not been a focus of concern since they are borne by the client. The paper advances the argument for the 'constructor' tendering on a design and build basis. This seeks to minimise both the construction and the transaction costs. Also the hierarchy would provide economies and ease the transfer of expertise from one project to another, thereby enhancing performance.

Factors such as professional autonomy and bureaucratic inertia can be seen to be preventing change, with independent practice being favoured by many professionals. The paper claims that project management fails to tackle problems of contracting uncertainty and organisational uncertainty. Contingency analysis has shown that management contracting does not allow project management to be used to its full potential. The author calls for further critical evaluation of new contracting forms and for the wider use of design and build contracting.

SESSION 5C

THE INDIVIDUAL AND THE GROUP

The topic of the individual and the group has become increasingly important in organisational research. Individual and interpersonal processes are inputs into the organisational system were the theme of Session 5C.

There were basically two issues that were emphasised by the authors of the papers:
. personality and organisation
. cognitive bases of individual behaviour

Personality was emphasised in terms of integration of the individual and the organisation. "Personality Characteristics of First Line Managers" by Torrance and Suiter summarised the results of research into personality types and their influence on career choice and development. The central theme in this paper was the problem of matching skills to jobs.

The paper has implications about individual and group performance and reduction of stress. Matching of jobs and personality implies job satisfaction, which may have a positive relationship to individual productivity.

Dodd and McDermott's paper is on the impact of a) each individual, b) the dynamics of the group on the incidence of variations (change orders). As a result, the authors conclude that variations appear to be related to personalities and human relations rather than time and cost variables.

The study attempts to use a personality inventory and to measure originator-compatibility, defined in the text as the degree to which one person's excess of a need expressed or received in a given area is balanced by the other person's excess in the reverse direction. The results were interesting for the frequency of variations was found related to the individual personality of the architect and his/her relationship with the contracts manager.

The paper is a successful combination of quantitative and qualitative assessments.

The second major theme that emerged was the cognitive basis of individual behaviour. In other words, the theme was the translation of the environmental factors into human action.

The cognitive processes emphasised in this session were perception and problem solving behaviour.

Koehn and Cook's paper attempts to probe into the perceptions of different work levels. The results of the study indicate that there are fundamental differences between upper and middle management's and tradesmen's perceptions of each other and of themselves.

The study has implications for the causes of communication gaps between levels. These gaps might be due to differences in perceptions.

Lansley's paper titled Managerial Skills and Corporate Performance in the Construction Industry emphasises the relationships of problem-solving behaviour and team performance. The paper also touches issues of team build-up and team compatibility.

The management implications of this particular paper centre on team build up as an effective motivational tool. The paper is valuable in the sense that it examines one of the core cognitive processes and its significance to organisational behaviour.

Substance Abuse: A Construction Industry Response by J.L. Rounds was not presented. The paper does not directly relate to the basic themes mentioned above. However, it is interesting to note that the paper touches upon a defense mechanism, called upon to reduce anxiety produced by conflicts.

SESSION 5D

DEVELOPING THE INDIVIDUAL: EDUCATION AND TECHNOLOGY TRANSFER

The papers grouped in this session touched upon the following questions:
. conditions affecting innovations
  (including institutional relationships and roles within which innovation is possible)

. education
  (directed towards problem solving and action alternatives)

Dressel and Diepeveen's paper argues that the process of innovation
in the building industry is slow. The authors stress the need for
all research to lead to innovation in building practice. According
to the authors, the flow of information between the research world
and building practice is actually a two-sided flow, whereas it is
usually regarded as a one-sided flow. There seem to be problems in
the transfer of information as well such as problems of language,
media, message and the level of the target group.

The authors emphasise the necessity for the establishment of an
intermediary organisation, a 'linking pin' between the world of
research and that of building practice.

Neale and Austen's paper on Development of Construction Management
Skills stresses the view that international experiences of agencies
provide evidence of the need to develop local construction
management skills. The authors also argue that the nature of the
construction industry is such that it often requires the creation
of a unique institution which can have a practical and pragmatic
approach to industry problems.

Rau's paper describes the foundation and functions of the National
Institute of Construction Management and Research as a privately
founded institution and stresses the importance of the contract
conditions and the contract document as a research question.

The papers mentioned above all relate to the organisation and use
of innovation in the building industry. All of the papers suggest
that the link between the world of research and the world of
practice is a necessary interdependence and that the establishment
of intermediary organisations might be useful to facilitate the
flow of information between the two worlds.

The role of basic management education is stressed by John Andrews
in his paper titled Education and Training for the Management of
Construction in Indonesia. Andrews criticises the teaching of
management techniques as if they were management and emphasises the
importance of a sound theoretical basis for economics and
management.

Imbert's paper on Human Issues Affecting Construction in Developing
Countries also relates to the issue of teaching management as a
basic course and stresses the extra investment needed in developing
countries for education. Imbert examines the issue of
underdevelopment within this context, as a factor inhibiting
effective planning and implementation of construction projects.

Austen and Neale also refer to the issue of underdevelopment. The authors stress the importance of a sound institutional basis for the development of construction management skills and for performance improvement.

One common thread that is easily seen in all the papers is the concern with the social context of invention and education. Underlying this is the assumption that social context has a potentially important role in these issues.

SESSION 5E

GENERAL DISCUSSION ON RESEARCH

The following are some general observations concerning relevant issues which emerged from the discussion session.

Some criticism was directed at academics and research works as being too theoretical and somewhat removed from practical reality. Academics, on the other hand, tend to be critical of industrialists, perceiving them to be too interested in short-term issues, as being too preoccupied with the immediate technical and financial issues involved in running their companies and not being sufficiently aware of the development of new knowledge. There is a danger of a credibility gap developing between these two important groups of people. Therefore, communication between those involved remains a problem to be tackled.

It was felt that more building contractors should involve themselves in research and should participate more in research conferences and forums. Researchers should be encouraged to work less in isolation and should identify how to engage in longer term collaborative projects. Company development and consultancy practice should feed on research. Continuing professional development (C.P.D) activities were seen as one mechanism for feeding back information to where it could be applied. Industrialists should be less concerned with the immediate applicability of research and more conscious of the length of time required to obtain and test sound research conclusions and then translate them into applicable forms.

Approaches that were considered to be of potential assistance were; more short-term applied research, oriented by industry's immediate needs, and more partnership in medium-range research between industrial and research organisations. Professional practices were perceived as being better at collaborating with sources of research. It was also pointed out that the professional institutions could do much more to facilitate research and to integrate research and practice.

More needs to be done to encourage the building industry to take a longer term vision, to define its own research needs and how to meet them. A good deal of time was spent in discussing how research is funded in various countries. A number of problems in funding research in the U.K. were considered, together their effects on staffing and organising research.

Turning to consider the future direction of research, there was a general agreement that further research into skill development in the management of human resources is required. Specific areas mentioned were leadership, better human relationships within the industry, more effective management of human resources together with a greater understanding of the attitudes of both the management and the labour force.

A need was seen to change attitudes among those engaged in research for it was considered that academics and industrialists alike tended to find techniques easier to deal with and human factors more difficult. There was a call for the development of greater knowledge, skill and involvement in human management issues. This was seen as starting from a need for more behavioural factors to be included in undergraduate courses, to greater levels of skill development in industry and on to better applications of knowledge in the working environment. Quality assurance was taken as an example, in which there had been too much focus on procedures and not enough on the human issues.

Finally, the needs caused by the growing international nature of the market for building contracts was raised. From this it was seen that more research into the cultural aspects in the management of international contracts is necessary.

It can be seen from the five workshop sessions considered that much is being done to ensure that construction management begins to reach those levels of development in the management of human resources already being achieved in other industries. Clearer concepts of the performance of companies are being developed, greater emphasis is being given to the concepts of strategy and the problems of fit between strategic and organisational variables. Consideration is also being given to the effects of these on organisational behaviour.

But much still remains to be done, in the labour intensive building industry, to develop and apply a greater knowledge of both individual behaviour and organisational performance.

Part X
Late papers

EDUCATION AND TRAINING FOR THE MANAGEMENT OF CONSTRUCTION IN INDONESIA

John Andrews

Construction Industry Development Unit, University College London.

Summary

An account is given of introducing a course in construction project management into a post graduate engineering degree programme and presenting short training seminars in the subject to post-experience audiences; then providing for the continuation and extension of this work by planning the establishment of a construction management centre in a technological university, thus contributing to the achievement of the long term aims of the government agency responsible for improving the performance of the domestic construction industry in Indonesia. From this and considerable earlier experience some propositions are generalised and practical first steps suggested for other countries devising strategies for the education and training of the management of construction.

Resume

L'introduction d'un cours de gestion d'un projet de construction dans un programme de diplôme universitaire supérieur de la science de l'ingénieur et la présentation d'un séminaire d'instruction rapide destiné à une assistance déjà formée dans la matière, sont expliquées. La continuation et l'extension de ce travail seront facilitées par le projet d'établir un centre de Gestion de l'Industrie de Construction au sein d'une université téchnologique. Ceci contribuera également à la réalisation des buts à long-terme de l'Agence Gouvernementale responsable de l'amélioration de la performance de l'industrie de construction domestique Indonésienne. A partir de ceci et avec les connaissances considérables déjà acquises dans ce domaine, certaines propositions sont schématisées et les premières actions à mettre en pratique sont suggerées a l'intention d'autres pays qui développent des stratégies pour l'éducation et la formation de la gestion de construction.

Key Words

Construction management, developing countries, education and training, government/industry/university co-operation, research and development, technology transfer.

INTRODUCTION

In another paper, some strategic aspects of the organisation and management of a major academic project for the Ministry of Works in Indonesia were considered; concluding that greater care in design, timing, direction and control of such projects was needed.[1] The paper, which should preferably, but not necessarily be read first, provides some background for this present account of introducing a course on construction project management into a post graduate educational programme in the Institute of Technology Bandung (ITB); and mounting short training seminars for post experience audiences in Jakarta. Then drawing upon other experience in the UK and overseas, outlines permanent arrangements proposed for continuing this work, by establishing a Construction Management Centre (CMC) in ITB, contributing to the work of the Construction Industry Development Bureau (BSP) of the Ministry of Public Works (MPW).

It will be helpful to bear in mind that 'Education and training are complementary aspects of a single learning and teaching process for the acquisition of knowledge and skill. Each contains an element of the other, both must be related to experience if their purpose is to be achieved: preparing people to do the right things well at the right time. Education helps us to know, to understand; training prepares us to act, to perform roles'.[2]

Selected strategic issues about providing education and training for the management of construction are summarised and commented upon in this short paper but are fully documented in other papers and publications noted in the references.

POST GRADUATE COURSE IN CONSTRUCTION PROJECT MANAGEMENT IN ITB

The aim of the course was 'to complement the students' engineering knowledge with an introduction to the management of construction contracts and to assist students to make an effective contribution to inter-disciplinary teams, working at development/design/construction stages of capital investment projects, and with further experience and training to lead and manage projects'. After a short introduction to the structure and operation of the construction industry and its place in the economy, principles of management and organisation were outlined, then the application of these principles to practical matters during the stages of the construction process, drawing attention to the use of appropriate management techniques, especially for planning and control of time, cost and quality.

The mandatory 2 credit course was taught in the 3rd of 4 semesters in a 48 credit, 2 year, MSc (S2) degree programme. It is documented in 2 substantial manuals [3] & [4] from which the foreword and a teaching note are reproduced below:

Foreword

This document[3] collects together reference and other material used by me when teaching the course 'Project management and contract administration' in the Graduate (S2) Programme in Highway Engineering and Development in the Institute of Technology Bandung. I designed the syllabus and taught the course unaided three times. First as a visiting teacher in late 1983, then on two further occasions when I became Director of the UCL project in ITB from February 1984 to September 1986.

I wish to acknowledge the use of 'Managing construction projects - a guide to process and procedures' as the basic introductory text. I contributed to the writing of this document when working with ILO Geneva and tested it in pilot programmes in many 'English speaking' countries in Africa. Since then I have used it consistently and thoroughly recommend it to a wider audience of managers and officials concerned with construction.

I found in Indonesia, as in the African region and many other countries in which I have worked, that the students had no earlier formal knowledge of the subject. It was necessary first to teach principles of the management process - in the context of construction - with a reduced time spent upon other matters. Long experience of developing academic courses at first degree and post graduate level, and post experience training courses for managers and officials has convinced me that without laying this ground the teaching of procedures and techniques is counter-productive. 'You cannot' as Nehru said, or rather should not, 'get hold of a modern tool with an ancient mind'.

Some thirty years ago I started to gain an understanding of management, then to help others to do so. A selection of my papers since those early days with a preface, study guide and newly written introduction 'Thinking about Management for Development' have been collected and are presented in a companion volume 'Management Notebook'.(4) Taken together they may encourage students to learn about this topic. Of greater consequence in Indonesia at this stage of development is that staff of construction disciplines in academic and training institutions may recognise the importance of this subject and commit themselves to research and teaching it. They will find a most stimulating field of work awaiting them; intellectually demanding and significant in its contribution to national development.

Teaching note

No attempt has been made to present a detailed syllabus and package of support material in a structured format. The essence of management teaching, in contrast to teaching technical courses, is that teacher and students together explore the subject field afresh each time the course is offered. Demanding alike for students and teachers. They both must read widely in the copious but uneven literature, to absorb a range of points of view, enabling them to tolerate alternatives and make rational decisions. This is especially necessary when teaching scientists and engineers since their early education does not fit them easily to deal with conflicting opinions about complex human situations and the exercise of subjective judgement. The objective is to open the mind of students to the distinctive set of skills or process of management. To lay a foundation of principle (since as yet we have no rounded theory) which will provide a frame of reference for the student to continue his studies throughout his professional working life, so to deal with management situations.

Students and their sponsors clamour for techniques and procedures. This should be resisted by teachers since great dangers arise from the presumption that techniques are management and from attempts to apply techniques without prior knowledge of the context in which they will be used. Like a knife in the hands of a surgeon without knowledge of the physiology of the human anatomy; not to mention the psychological disposition of his patients. This means that teachers of this topic must first be taught themselves, not only the state of their art and the tools of the trade, but have been immersed deeply over many years in the practice of management and continue in consultancy in an appropriate context. Although students, even at post graduate level, often have no prior formal knowledge of management ideas; many have experience of managing, or being managed, or mismanaged by others.

The teacher must gain the confidence of his students by his grasp of practical affairs before offering principles which do not -always- accord with their own experience or will be challenged when students attempt to put them to use. To this end I have included a number of papers about management teaching, and teaching management teachers. There is no need to repeat in Indonesia the hard lessons learned over the past twentyfive years developing a cadre of management teachers in Europe, USA and Japan, with all the waste and frustration which will surely follow.

POST EXPERIENCE TRAINING SEMINARS

A number of one day seminars were given in Jakarta for officials of MPW on topics of current concern selected from the curriculum of the project management course being taught in ITB. In addition were two seminars, specially designed for members of the Indonesian Contractors' Association (AKI). 'Contractors strategy in a declining construction market'[5] and 'A case study of rapid growth and diversification'. All these occasions used the classic format of introductory presentations followed by questions, discussion and framing recommendations, taking local needs and constraints into account. An unusual feature perhaps, was using the overhead projector to display headlines current in the local newspapers and journals, to stimulate discussion of contentious issues.

It was evident from the responses that very few of those attending had received any formal management education or training, most were interested in the material presented and saw an urgent need for more such events, especially to bring together mixed audiences of clients, officials, consultants and contractors, to discuss issues of common interest and concern.

CONSTRUCTION MANAGEMENT CENTRE (CMC) IN ITB

During the time of the UCL project, ITB were beginning to think about how the subject of construction management could be introduced into the curriculum of SI(BSc) and later S2(MSc) degree courses in the construction disciplines: planning, architecture and engineering. But this was being attempted piecemeal, without institutional focus and no members of ITB staff had been educated formally in the subject. The Ministry of Public Works (MPW) had requested ITB to give greater emphasis to this subject, but although ITB wished to do so, could not, for lack of properly skilled teaching staff and other resources. Since it would take many years to acquire qualified staff, or select and send others overseas to study the subject at post-graduate level, it would be wise to concentrate this absolutely limiting resource, once available, in one Centre initially, to service all other interested departments. Later, departments could develop their own additional specialist management teaching and research capability.

Interest was further stimulated by circulation of an invited paper 'A Management Centre in ITB'[6] setting out the objectives of the Centre: 'to develop in each student an awareness of the impact of technology and industrialisation upon a developing society; to encourage a positive attitude to solving economic and social problems and to provide an understanding of the management process'. The establishment of a Centre rather than an additional academic department was proposed: 'implying a focus, as between all the major technological departments in ITB and the industry they serve. It also implies the central and unifying role of management in all technological and industrial activity' - and would help recognition by and collaboration with industry-an essential condition of success. The Centre would have two components, academic and industrial, with experienced teachers, active in consultancy, conducting both academic and post experience training programmes; and research 'specially relating to the particular needs of local industry and development programmes'. The Centre should be boldly conceived to make an initial impact 'not only advocating good management-but-evidently being well managed'.

Discussions were held with staff concerned, to explore possible working relationships between the proposed Centre and other Departments which would draw upon the expertise of the Centre, to develop courses and provide management teaching in degree programmes offered by them. Finally to dispel possible misconceptions about the idea and purpose of a Centre; and the academic philosophy, content and scope of this unfamiliar subject matter; a paper was presented at a senior staff seminar in ITB.[7]

Concurrently, with the approval and support of MPW, a proposal was submitted to the Overseas Development Administration (ODA) through the British Embassy in Jakarta for pump-priming financial support.[8]

CONSTRUCTION INDUSTRY DEVELOPMENT

Attention to the importance of the construction sector in influencing, determining even, the rate of general economic development was first drawn by Turin in 1969. There has since been a growing flow of papers on aspects of the subject. It is self evident, whatever the precise economic relationship between investment in, and growth of, the construction sector and that of the economy as a whole, that almost any improvement of the performance in the construction industry, in all countries at every stage of development, is desirable.

To be effective this requires 'a comprehensive programme to ensure that the domestic construction industry is itself developed, so that it may play its full part in providing the construction component of development plans'.[9] A pre-requisite for this is a greater understanding of the nature, organisation and management of the whole construction process by clients, government agencies and firms in the industry. This understanding flows from the establishment or expansion of appropriate education and training facilities in the countries concerned. In turn this requires the provision of a national cadre of teachers, trainers and researchers; of necessity receiving their own first introduction to the subject of the management of construction and how it might be researched and taught, in other countries where apropriate institutions already exist.[10]

CONSTRUCTION INDUSTRY DEVELOPMENT BUREAU IN THE MINISTRY OF PUBLIC WORKS, JAKARTA

The Government of Indonesia had recognised and become increasingly concerned about weaknesses in its construction industry which delayed the implementation, or led to the abondonment of projects. A Construction Industry Development Bureau, Biro Bina Sarana Perusahaan, (BSP) was established in

(MPW) in 1975 with the assistance of the World Bank. Following a detailed study by consultants in 1981, BSP was acting upon recommendations contained in their report to effect improvements. The World Bank are currently supporting the further strengthening of BSP in MPW.

The establishment of a CMC in ITB is seen as contributing to the work of BSP in four major ways:

1. ensuring that all graduates from ITB entering the Ministry, consultancy or contracting firms have received an introduction to the management of construction at under-graduate (S1) level;

2. undertaking research projects in the management ofconstruction of special interest to BSP/MPW;

3. assisting development of short training courses and seminars and teaching aids e.g. research papers, books, video films etc. in translation and Bahasa Indonesia, for use in education and practical training events;

4. developing a post-graduate (S2) course in the management of construction.

The work of CMC in ITB should be closely co-ordinated with BSP so that this work contributes to the policy needs of BSP; especially to ensure that the services of the very few experienced individuals, as they are educated formally in the management of construction and return to Indonesia, may be most effectively utilised in teaching, research and consultancy.

PROVIDING QUALIFIED STAFF FOR STARTING UP A NEW FIELD OF STUDY

An earlier paper [10] addressed the general problem: 'How may otherwise qualified nationals of developing countries receive a sufficient education in the management and economics of construction, to enable them to contribute meaningfully to construction industry development as teachers or researchers'; and described a MSc (S.2) programme in University College London, which has met the needs of students from some 30 countries during the past 18 years. On this experience and evidence 'it may be said that it is possible to gather together groups of graduates in quite separate technological and professional disciplines, from widely different international, experiential and cultural backgrounds, without prior formal knowledge of management or economics; and in one year provide them with an understanding of these subjects. And help them to adopt inter-disciplinary attitudes towards influencing the solution of construction industry problems at varying levels of general development, as teachers or researchers'.

Attention was drawn to developing a teaching and research cadre in ITB.[11] One experienced civil engineer from MPW Jakarta took the course in 1984-5; two nominees regrettably did not achieve an adequate proficiency in English language to enter the course in 1985; two members of the architectural staff of ITB will graduate in September 1987 and a fourth nominee from Indonesia will attend during the coming academic year. Thus by the end of 1988, there should be four experienced people in Indonesia, qualified to Masters level in construction economics and management, enough to form a nucleus of staff available to contribute to the work of CMC.

Despite the urgency for creating a small group of people, properly qualified to launch a new subject, it must be recognised that in most developing countries a PhD degree is a pre-requisite for obtaining, or achieving promotion in, a tenured university appointment. Apart from losing members of staff for three to four years to obtain PhD degrees overseas (thus delaying the start of any new initiative) greater benefit might accrue from staff carrying out research into management topics in their own countries.

An alternative programme, for qualifying staff might be:

Year 1   take MSc degree in overseas institution, submitting PhD proposal with literature review in place of a Report;
Year 2 & 3 complete literature review and undertake field work in own country, meanwhile monitoring, or contributing if only marginally to, the work of home institution;
Year 4   return to overseas institution to write up PhD thesis and present for examination.

Depending upon many factors the programme might need to be extended over an additional year or two. The operation of such a strategy elaborated in a paper[12] could lead to staff exchanges, curriculum development, joint supervision and other fruitful associations between home and overseas institutions, with benefit to both.

PROPOSITIONS AND PRACTICAL FIRST STEPS

The sum of UK and international experience during the past 30 years, amply confirmed and strengthened by this most recent work in Indonesia, leads to a generalised set of propositions and practical first steps, which, taking account of some mistakes and missed opportunities, may assist others in countries now beginning to shape their own strategies for education and training for the management of construction (and development).

Propositions
1.   The construction sector holds considerable potential for influencing the general rate of economic and social development.
2.   Very rarely is this potential fully realised.
3.   This arises from lack of understanding of the complex nature of the construction process and structure of the industry.
4.   There is emerging an underlying body of knowledge, stronger conceptual tools for investigation and analysis of complex processes; and a growing experience of how this may be applied in a changing industry.
5.   Higher management capability is required to introduce a more rational process of construction and structure of the industry and to ensure its continued effective operation.
6.   There is a massive need, world wide, for improved management performance of the construction (and development) process.
7.   Because the quality of existing management regulates the amount of new management which can be absorbed, this limits absolutely the amount and rate of construction (and development) a country can undertake at any time.
8.   This calls for management training for existing managers up to the highest levels; and management education for those likely to become the new managers.
9.   The concepts and skills of management are often misunderstood, but can be taught.
10.   Unless a foundation of sound principle is laid and an open minded attitude encouraged in earlier educational courses, much subsequent management training effort is remedial or wasted.

11. Every national development plan should make provision for management development - which starts with management education and training.
12. So, first teach the teachers of the management of construction (and development).

Practical first steps
1. As part of policy for strengthening its domestic construction industry, government, through the responsible ministry or agency, decides to establish or upgrade a national capability for teaching the management of construction; identifies an academic institution in its own country with well established technological courses in the construction disciplines.
2. Government and the national academic institution jointly identify and approach a similar institution overseas, with international reputation based upon long experience in researching and teaching the management of construction.
3. Government provides pump-priming finance enabling the two academic institutions to arrange exchange visits and prepare a plan and budget; then select national staff for qualifying at higher degree level overseas.
4. The overseas institution provides staff to design and teach courses in the national institution until their own staff are qualified and back in post; thereafter maintaining close links through staff exchanges, external examining, joint curriculum development and research projects.
5. Such a national research and teaching capability, once established, could be regarded as a centre of excellence upon which other centres could be modelled in turn.

Whatever approach is decided upon, the key factor is to draw together with continued government support, a small nucleus of experienced and qualified staff, with institutional identity eg. CMC within a reputable university, committed to the further development of the research and teaching of the management of construction. They could then be expected to produce a discernible effect within a decade.

REFERENCES

1. ANDREWS. John, The organisation and management of a major academic project for the Ministry of Works in Indonesia. Proceedings CIB W-65 Fifth Symposium 1987 pp.9
2. ANDREWS. John, Education and training for a construction profession and Education for the management of construction: the way ahead from a long way behind. Proceedings joint IAAS/CIOB seminars 1982/3 pp.13
3. ANDREWS. John, Project management and contract administration. Teaching Manual for ITB Part I pp 314 1986
4. ANDREWS. John, Management notebook. Collected papers. Teaching Manual for ITB Part II pp 175 1986
5. ANDREWS. John, Contractors strategy in a declining construction market. Proceedings, Indonesian Contractors Association (AKI) Seminar, Jakarta, May 1986 pp.15
6. ANDREWS. John, A management centre in ITB. Unpublished seminar paper, ITB, 1984 pp.4
7. ANDREWS. John, Thinking about management for development. Unpublished seminar paper, 1986, pp.12

8. ANDREWS. John, Construction management centre in ITB. Unpublished proposal to ODA, 1985 pp4

9. ANDREWS. John, Construction industry development: a comprehensive programme for strengthening the construction industry in developing countries. Proceedings CIB Mini-Symposium 1982. pp.16.

10. ANDREWS. John, Education and training for the management of construction in developing countries: First - teach the teachers. CIB Mini-Symposium 1982 17pp NB: Not included in Proceedings.

11. ANDREWS. John, The management of construction: developing a teaching and research cadre in ITB. Unpublished 1983 pp5

12. ANDREWS. John, Higher degrees for teachers of technology in developing countries - the doctoral dilemma. Unpublished 1985 pp5

POLITICAL CHANGE AND CONSTRUCTION ACTIVITY IN GIBRALTAR

Daniel   Barton, B.Sc.(Hons)
24/2 Scud Hill, Gibraltar

Summary
This paper describes the changes which have occurred in construction
in Gibraltar during a period of negotiations between Britain and Spain
on the contentious issue of sovereignty of the territory. It presents
an overview of construction activity before and after the recent agreement against a general backcloth of politial, economic and social
change. The paper then presents hypotheses on construction activity
derived from the Gibraltar study and links these with the political
question of sovereignty. It concludes by emphasizing the difficulty
of extrapolating events in Gibraltar to situations of larger magnitude.

Sommaire
Ce document cherche a descrive les nouveaux developpements apparus
dans l'industrie de la construction a Gibraltar, depuis l'accord
hispano-britanique sur la question contentieuse de la souverainete du
territoire. Il presente un expose de l'activite dans la construction
avant et apres l'accord, vue contre un fond d'evolution politique,
economique et sociale. Le document puis presente de hypotheses sur
l'activite dans l'industrie derivees de l'etude sur Gibraltar, et il
essaie d'etablir un bien entre ces hypoteses et l'issue politique.
Les conclusions soulignent la difficulte d'extapoler les evenements a
Gibraltar a des situations d'une plus grande importance.

Keywords
Gibraltar, political change, construction supply characteristics.

GIBRALTAR AND THE PROBLEM OF SOVEREIGNTY
Gibraltar is a British colony situated at the confluence of the
Atlantic and the Mediterranean, at the southernmost tip of Spain. Its
geographical position makes this small land mass highly valuable in
military and commercial terms as it commands control of the Straits of
Gibraltar. This value has been recognised by many nations and several
military confrontations have occurred in attempts to gain control of
the territory.

The struggle for Gibraltar continues today. Sovereignty of the
territory was obtained by Britain from Spain in 1711 with the signing
of the Treaty of Utrecht after it was captured by the British in 1704

during the War of the Spanish Succession. Spain however challenges Britain's sovereignty of the land and claims that Gibraltar is Spanish.

Spain has attempted to establish its alleged "territorial integrity" and has taken measures at coercing the Gibraltarian community into accepting Spanish sovereignty. These measures have been varied, the most important occurring during the period 1969 to 1982 when an "economic seige" was placed on Gibraltar. This resulted in the total ceasure of communications with Spain.

The impact of the economic seige was considerable as Gibraltar depended heavily on imports from Spain. However, it was the advantages which Spain gained from its economic interaction with Gibraltar that gave it effective, albeit non-sovereign influence over the Rock.

The economic implications of the 1969-1982 seige on Gibraltar were tremendous. The small size of Gibraltar has prevented the development of a self-contained resource base to support its community and virtually all goods and labour were imported before 1969, primarily from Spain. The severance of communications imposed an additional economic burden as these resources had to be imported from further afield, mainly from the United Kingdom. As a result, economic dependence and interaction shifted from Spain to Britain.

Spain re-established communications with Gibraltar in 1982. Since that time the Colony has experienced an almost total reversal towards the economic situation which existed in the sixties, augmented by the changes resulting from the economic and social development of Spain in more recent years. The cycle of events, economic interaction with Spain followed by seige followed by interaction, has had severe effects on all facets of life in the Colony and in particular on political thinking. The construction industry was not exempt from the changing environment and construction activity has reflected the changes in the political scene of Gibraltar. The remainder of the paper describes the effects of the 1969-1982 seige conditions on construction activity and the links between construction activity and political issues.

THE CONSTRUCTION INDUSTRY AND THE CHANGING ENVIRONMENT IN GIBRALTAR
The economic impacts which Gibraltar underwent via the series of political events described also led to many changes in the construction environment and thus in the nature of construction activity. This section of the paper qualitatively illustrates the supply of construction activity through the 1969-1982 time period.

The Pre-Seige Years
The construction industry in Gibraltar was virtually an extension of the Spanish construction industry. With the exception of some electromechanical equipment which did not comply with the Gibraltar Building Regulations, all materials were imported from Spain. Similarly, all labour was Spanish although resident in nearby Spain. Construction organisations were Spanish, Gibraltarian and British, the latter mainly operating for the MOD/PSA.

The construction technologies employed by the industry varied with the three main typed of Client which required construction. The southern Spanish model of concrete skeletons with hollow pot flat slab flooring and infill walling dominated the private sector. This work often used a system of sub-contract packages under a form of management contract predominant in southern Spain. On the other hand the British approach dominated the work of the MOD/PSA, tending towards traditional British construction managed by general contractors. Finally a hybrid system operated for the Gibraltar Government with the emphasis on Spanish or British approaches varying according to many factors ranging from funding sources to the number of British expatriate professionals within the local Governments in-house design office.

The Seige Years
The industry underwent a dramatic transformation following the start of the economic seige. The Spanish influence and dependence ceased overnight and the colony became more dependant on the United Kingdom and Morocco. During this period all materials for the industry origi- nated from the UK and most of the labour came from Morocco. All Spanish contractors withdrew to be substituted by medium sized British firms. In all respects the industry modelled itself on Britain.

Post 1982
The end of the seige started a process of de-Anglicisation of the industry and an almost complete reversal to the pre-1969 character- istics. The industry's linkages formed during the seige years quickly became re-aligned towards Spain.
The economic advantage of Spain began to be felt again and to determine the selection of materials. Spanish materials began to be imported in large quantities substituting many of British origin. See Table 1. Similarly Spanish labour began to replace Moroccan labour. The process continues and EEC labour reciprocity which will be fully operational in 1993 will eventually break the Moroccan hold so that Spanish labour will pre-dominate.
For contracting organisations an almost full reversal to the pre- 1969 period has occurred. Spanish contractors have been able to take a large share of the private sector market whilst British contractors still operate for the MOD/PSA and local contractors for the Gibraltar Government. There has also been a full reversal of construction technologies to the pre-1969 situation. Again the Spanish approach mainly operates for the private sector, the contemporary British model for the MOD/PSA and a hybrid British/Spanish model for the Gibraltar Government.

Table 1.   Imports of Major Building Materials for 1985

Material	Spain (£)	United Kingdom (£)
Bricks, Blocks and Tiles	281,000	99,000
Woods in the rough	33,000	62,000
Cement	248,000	16,000
Aggregate	289,000	minimal

Source: Economic Planning and Statistics Office, Gibraltar

CONSTRUCTION DEMAND IN GIBRALTAR (1969-1986)
Construction demand underwent dramatic changes during the three
periods. In the pre-seige and post-seige years demand in all markets
was high relative to the seige years (Annual construction demand -
estimates pre-seige £20m; seige £6m; post-seige £30m at current
prices).
    The explanations of the cyclical effect in construction demand are
easy to explain. In the pre-seige years the general economic activity
of Gibraltar rose with that of the neighbouring Costa del Sol which
was growing rapidly as Northern Europeans flooded south in search of
the sun. Many of the large hotels in Gibraltar were built during this
period. Additionally the UK was financing large housing schemes in
Gibraltar out of its development aid budget. The compounded effect
of both resulted in a situation of high demand for construction work
in Gibraltar.
    The seige years conversely brought economic decline. The advan-
tages which Gibraltar gained from Spain were severed with the cessation
of communications and virtually all private sector economic activity
slid into recession. Construction demand was limited to Gibraltar
Government spending from UK Overseas Development Administration aid
packages and some MOD/PSA spending on military facilities. The
1969-1982 period proved to be leanest years for contracting organisations. Many large expatriate firms dis-assembled their operations
on the Rock and some firms went bankrupt.
    The post 1982 years however have seen a revival of construction
activity. Construction projects worth £142 million are expected
between 1985 and 1987. Much of the demand is composed of large
marina type luxury developments with some speculative housing schemes.
Much of this demand is tourist oriented, with Gibraltar rapidly
becoming an extention of the Spanish Costa de Sol. As the economic
machine of Gibraltar gathers momentum with the opening of the border,
so there has been visible sign of urban regeneration. The repair
and refurbishment market has grown particular well in the commercial
sector as a result of increase number of tourists visiting Gibraltar

177

from Spain.

CONSTRUCTION SUPPLY HYPOTHESES AND THE TOTAL ENVIRONMENT IN GIBRALTAR
This section of the paper presents a number of hypothoses about the
way in which patterns of construction activity change in relation to
political and economic influences, based on observation of the
construction industry in Gibraltar.

The main observation is the existence of apparently stable types
of "construction industries" within the pre-seige, seige and post-
seige years time periods. This leads to a general hypothesis that
there exists a particular industry configuration, or what may be
termed as a construction supply system, associated with a political/
economic environment which is optimal, in a form depending on the
market in question and on the constraints operating therein. It has
also been seen that it is possible for an industry configuration to
change from one form to another through definable relationships.
This is the second general hypothesis.

The industry configuration or construction supply system can be
defined as a set of basic resources (labour, material and plant)
operating in the industry described in both qualitative and quantitative terms and in terms of particular methodologies which describe
both qualitatively and quantitatively the processed through which these
resources may be combined to achieve construction output. Aspects
like the nationality of resources can be considered within the qualitative dimension.

These configurations can be viewed as industry "anatomies". Comparing these with the environment of the industry more specific hypotheses can be developed.

In two of the three major markets for construction in Gibraltar,
the private sector and MOD/PSA, in the post-seige years the observed
extent, and hence rate, of change of the construction supply system
operating for them have been different. The industry operating for
the private sector has sought to exploit the advantages to be gained
from the new environment by importing both resources and techniques
from Spain. Clearly, in this case criteria affecting the supply of
construction are purely economic and the aim to maximize return on
investment. This is evident, as within a year the construction supply
systems operating for the private sector after the re-establishment
of communications with Spain showed a strong level of Hispanisation.
For the MOD/PSA on the other hand the decision making crieria include
economic and military considerations. These latter impose severe
constraints to change. The difference in optimal systems appears not
to have been very great between the new post-seige environment and
the seige years. the changes consequently noted in the construction
supply systems for this market for construction within the year after
the re-establishment of communications have been marginal and limited
to material and plant imports and some specialist sub-contract labour
from Spain where these have become competitive with direct importation
from the United Kingdom keeping in mind adherence to UK building codes

Thus, despite being able to achieve ends via more economically oriented construction supply systems the procurement criteria point towards another system which is optimal in this market for construction.

Table 2.   Markets: Divergence and Change

	Divergence in optimality post-seige relative to seige	Extent of Change	Rate of Change
Private Sector	LARGE	LARGE	RAPID
MOD/PSA	SMALL	SMALL	SLOW

These observations lead to the following hypothesis. That the extent and rate of change from one construction supply system to another is related to the difference between the optimal systems determined by the markets.

The "effort" (time, organisation, expenses, etc) required to effect change is the next observation made from the Gibraltar study. If price per unit of output of construction (quality and speed is assumed to remain constant) is considered as the main dimension measuring the level of effectiveness with which an industry can meet requirements, then in the pre-seige and post-seige period the level of effectiveness was clearly higher than in the seige years. Cost reductions of up to 50% for similar buildings were noted in construction output after the normalisation of relations with Spain compared with 100-150% increases in cost when the seige commenced. The cost changes reflect the effort and difficulties of driving the change in the construction supply systems in producing output. The "effort" in change as reflected in price changes is less from the seige to the post-seige years than vice-versa. This is corroborated in the descriptions given in section 2 where it was shown that a far more complicated and less efficient system existed in the seige years compared with the pre and post-seige years.

Table 3. Effort and Effectiveness

	"Effort" as measured by price changes	Effectiveness of construction supply system
Pre-Seige	High	High
Seige	Low	Low
Post-Seige		High

This leads to the hypothesis that the effort involved in change is less when the change in the supply system in operation is in the direction of being able to more effectively ssatisfy the requirements of the industry.

The last observation is the qualitative direction of change. Three major factors appear to operate in changing the qualitative aspects of the construction supply systems in a situation like Gibraltar which is totally dependent on construction resource imports. These are the size of the exporting countries, the number of exporting countries and the accessibility of the exporting country relative to the importing country. The first two factors are quantitative in nature but the last incorporates a number of qualitative and quantitative factors such as distance, cultural and language barriers, commercial infrastructure etc which all combine into the hybrid concept of the ease of flow of goods from one place to another.

In the Gibraltar case it is possible to observe two distinct qualitative directions of change in the construction supply system with the changing political environment. The change from the pre-seige to the post-seige years involved the change from an Anglicised to Spanish oritented system. This would suggest that the emphasis on the British or Spanish practice result from a direct relationship between the construction supply system characteristics and the relative accessibility and size of the exporting country. For example, Morocco and Portugal have exported materials and labour to Gibraltar but their influence has been small as both their relative size to other important sources and accessibility to Gibraltar are small. The third factor, the number of exporting countries, mitigates the emphasis of any given source on industry characteristics as alternative sources for resources reduces the influence of any one country from which the imports originate. This was the case with Moroccan labour imports during the seige years which reduced the total Anglicisation of the industry in

Gibraltar. Thus, the characteristics of the construction supply
system in Gibraltar relative to any exporting source appears to
follow the relationship described below. This would suggest that the
influence of an exporting source on a construction supply system is
directly related to its accessibility and size. The strength of the
influence of the source reduces with increases in the number of
alternative sources.

Table 4. Accessibility and Supply

	Highest Accessibility exporting Countries to Gibraltar	Largest exporting* Countries as measured by GNP	Construction Supply System characteristics
Pre-Seige	Spain	UK	Spanish
Seige	UK	UK	British
Post-Seige	Spain	UK	Spanish

* Major exporters to Gibraltar
  UK, Spain, Portugal, Morocco

CONSTRUCTION DEMAND AND THE TOTAL ENVIRONMENT IN GIBRALTAR
The previous section concentrated on construction supply systems and
construction supply markets and the respective effects which the
changing environment has had on them. The changing environment has
also altered demand behaviour under the period studied.

The private sector has shown the largest and most detectable signs
of change over the three periods. The other two large markets for
construction in Gibraltar - the local Government and the MOD/PSA -
have not shown the sensitivity of the private sector link with the
rest of economic activity, at least in the short term, as other criteria are involved in the decision making process. In the latter,
social and military considerations tend to dampen the response effect
of demand.

As described previously, the level of economic activity in Gibraltar
has varied almost cyclically over the three time periods under consideration, fundamentally being high in the pre-seige and post-seige
years, relative to the seige years. This supports macro-economic
theory which explains there is an approximate direct relationship
between the level of macro-economic activity and the level of construction demand.

Table 5. Dynamics of Demand

	Discounted Revenues	Construction Costs	Demand
Pre-Seige	High	Low	High
Seige	Low	High	Low
Post-Seige	High	Low	High

CONCLUSIONS
The changing political environment in Gibraltar has had enormous
effects on the economy of the Rock and in turn on the total environment within which the construction industry operates. The effects
have been felt on the supply side of construction activity. General
descriptive accounts of the changes have been given and used to form
specific hypotheses about construction supply and demand. In particular
the existence of stable construction supply systems with stable
political environments and the movement and mechanisms of these changes
have been described.

Currently, as part of a doctoral research programme, attempts are
being made to compare the experience of Gibraltar with those of other
countries affected by substantial changes in the political and
economic policies of their neighbours. However, Gibraltar's size
probably places it at an extreme position relative to other countries
in terms of the vulnerability of construction supply and demand to
changes in political and economic policies.

ACKNOWLEDGEMENTS
The work described in this paper is part of a doctoral research
programme being carried out through the Department of Construction
Management, University of Reading.

WORK SAMPLING STUDIES: DO THEY YIELD VALID RESULTS?

Neal B. H. Benjamin, PhD and Jimmie W. Hinze, PhD

University of Missouri-Columbia and University of Washington, USA

Summary
Results of a study of the use of work sampling in nuclear power
plant construction are presented. The literature pertaining to
mathematical basis of work sampling and its application as a work
improvement technique in construction is reviewed. Observations are
made of the use of work sampling in nuclear construction.
Violations of the assumptions that render the technique valid, the
use of work sampling to detect and correct causes of delays, and the
use of work sampling results to compare direct activity and
productivity of different projects are discussed and conclusions
drawn.

Sommaire
Les resultats d'une etude de l'emploi de "work sampling"
(l'observation de travail) dans la construction des centres
nucleaires sont presentes. On passes en revue la litterature qui a
rapport a la base mathematique de "work sampling" et son application
comme technique pour ameliorer les travaux de construction. Il y a
des observations au sujet de l'emploi de "work sampling" dams la
construction nucleaire. Il y a egalement une discussion des
violations des supportions qui rend la technique valide, des
rapports de l'emploi de "work sampling" pour trouver et corriger les
causes du delai et l'emploi de ces resultats pour comparer
l'activite de construction.

Keywords
Work sampling, Nuclear Power Plant Construction, Statistics

INTRODUCTION
Work sampling is an industrial engineering technique that is used to
find out how workers spend their time without having to perform
continuous time studies. The industrial engineering applications of
work sampling make observations of a worker's activity at randomly
selected times. These observations are used to estimate the
proportions of the time that he is active and that he is idle and to
estimate width of the confidence interval containing the true but
unknown value of the proportion. Properly executed, work sampling
should give reliable, valid, and timely information to identify

183

causes of idle time of delays. With a sufficiently large number of observations, it is claimed that the various percentages of direct activity, support activity, and delays computed from the observations are representative of the entire population of workers within stated limits of accuracy at some prescribed level of confidence.

The technique has been used in the construction industry as a production control tool to identify construction activities experiencing excessive delays. Indications of delays should trigger additional study of the causes of the delays, resulting in corrective action being taken to eliminate those causes.

Work sampling was used during the construction of many nuclear power plants in the United States to measure proportions of time spent on direct work, support work, and delays. Work sampling on some projects was done almost continuously for the duration of the project. On others it was done intermittently for 10 to 20 working days each quarter. And on others it was done perhaps twice a year. Some work sampling was performed by contractor industrial engineering departments. Some short-term work sampling studies were done by employees of the contractor, utility, and A-E, trained and supervised by consulting firms.

A study was undertaken by the University of Missouri at the request of the State Public Service Commission to compare the results of continuous work sampling studies made during the construction of the Callaway and Wolf Creek nuclear power plants with the results of similar studies made at other nuclear plants and with "industry averages" of direct craft activity. The purpose of the study was to provide the Public Service Commission information on which to base an opinion of the managerial effectiveness of the utilities and their contractor in relation to other utilities and contractors engaged in nuclear construction.

Three questions were addressed in conducting the Missouri study: (1) How did the direct activity at the Callaway and Wolf Creek plants compare with direct activity during the construction of other nuclear power plants? (2) Was work sampling used correctly and effectively as a production control tool during the construction of the Callaway and Wolf Creek plants? (3) Can the techniques of conducting work sampling studies and evaluating the results of those studies be applied correctly to the measurement of direct activity of workers at large, complex construction sites.

The results of the study were inconclusive and questioned the use of work sampling to compare labor utilization during the construction of different nuclear power plants or to indicate correctly the levels of direct activity, support activity, and delays at different stages of the construction.

STUDY PROCEDURE
The study began with a thorough review mainly of the industrial engineering and civil engineering literature relating to work sampling in the manufacturing industries and in construction. Reports to several public utility commissions of investigations into the costs of nuclear power plants and testimony filed with the New York State Public Service Commission regarding the Shoreham plant

were examined.

All public utilities that had built nuclear power plants since 1975 were asked to provide any available work sampling data, foreman-delay surveys, and manpower utilization reports. Many refused. Several provided data with the assurance that it would remain confidential. Some data was obtained by the Missouri Public Utility Commission by "discovery," and data for several plants was furnished by John Borcherding of the University of Texas.

The Missouri Public Service Commission provided work sampling, foreman-delay, and manpower utilization reports for the Callaway and Wolf Creek plants. Work sampling was performed at Callaway from March 1977 to December 1983 as the project progressed from about 4% to over 95% of completion. At Wolf Creek, work sampling was done from August 1979 to April 1981, 44% to 75% of completion. Reports were prepared by the industrial engineering departments at the job sites between four and twelve days after the end of the reporting periods. The typical report indicated the number of observations, the number of sampling rounds, the percentages of direct activity, support activity, and delays, the 95% confidence interval for the estimate of the percentage of direct activity, and the trend during the period. They contained a narrative description of the more significant changes of direct activity, support activities, and delays and suggested probable causes of these changes. The report tabulated by area, craft, and (sometimes) crew the percentages of observations of 16 categories of activity and inactivity. Some of the reports contained 200 pages or more of computer output.

The Missouri study was concerned mainly with levels of direct activity at various stages of construction. Percentages of direct activity were plotted against percentage of completion by job and by craft in each job. Linear regression analysis was used to fit curves to the data. Labor utilization factors were computed with various weights being given to support activity. These factors were also plotted against percentages of completion. Categories of contributory and ineffective work controllable by management were grouped as suggested by Thomas (11). The resulting values were also plotted against percentage of completion.

OBSERVATIONS

Work sampling apparently originated with Tippett's use of the "snap-reading method" in the 1920's to identify causes of stoppages of weaving and spinning machinery in British cotton mills (2:240-266). He modeled the percentages of the number of stoppages by the binomial distribution and stratified his sampling, in some instances, by the quality of cotton and by processes. Mostly, though, samples were taken from populations doing essentially the same kind of work with the same kind of machinery.

Barnes (2:41-50) showed the working time and idle time of a drill press operator measured by work sampling to compare favorably with results obtained by continuous time study. In addition to presenting several examples of industrial applications of work sampling, he also discussed the basis of work sampling in the laws of probability and the determination of appropriate sample sizes and confidence intervals.

185

Parker and Oglesby (8) suggested the use of work sampling in construction to provide timely indications of the effectiveness of management in managing the labor resource. More recently, Drewin (4) and Adrian (1) have given work sampling the textbook treatment. Drewin presents an interesting example of what might be considered to be cluster sampling in simultaneously observing at random times the activities of all the members of a crew, much the same as required in preparing a crew-balance chart. All of these authors list the criteria that must be satisfied for work sampling to give reliable and statistically valid measures of activity: the sample size is sufficiently large; the sample is a random sample--at any time all members of the population have an equally likely chance of being observed; and observations are independent and identically distributed--the probability of observing a worker working is unchanged from worker to worker.

Thomas (11, 12, 13, 14) identified systematic and sampling errors in the context of work sampling on large construction project. He compared sampling programs used by various contractors and consultants and showed a great variety of activity categories to exist in the sampling programs of different organizations. He observed that even the definition of direct activity varies from some sampling program to the next and that what is considered to be direct activity in one sampling program may be classified as a support activity in another.

Palmeter (7) and Strandell (10) presented figures that are considered to be representative of the percentages of time that construction workers on power plant projects are engaged in different work-related activities. Palmeter's figures are derived from 41 studies at nuclear plants and 16 at fossil fuel plants, involving 10 different projects and 8 different utilities. He found that workers on nuclear projects are, on the average, engaged in direct work 33% of the time, wait/delay 24%, transport 5%, travel empty 16%, tools and materials 4.5%, personal breaks 7%, late start/early quit 4.5%, and plan/instruct 6%. Strandell, whose figures are based on one nuclear job, found workers to be engaged in direct work 32%, tools/materials/transportation 7%, tavelling 13%, waitings, 29%, instruactions 8%, personal breaks 5%, and late start/early quit 6%. Her figures were used by Godfrey (6) in his article on productivity at the job site and by a large engineering and construction firm as a baseline for comparing initial sampling results.

Russell (9) collected direct activity measurement from 51 work sampling studies done at various nuclear power plants at different stages of construction. Using SAS, he fitted a third-order polynomial through these data points, claiming an R-square of 0.98. He observed that direct activity declined as the job progressed and concluded that it is not possible to compare direct craft activity at one stage of a project with that at another stage or to compare the activities of different crafts.

The staff of the New York State Public Service Commission and its consultants (5) used Shoreham Power Plant direct work percentages of 21%, 23%, and 22% at 62, 72, and 77 percent complete, respectively, and other assumptions to draw curves of direct activity as a function of the percentage of completion. They compared ordinates of these curves with (1) a regression line through six points derived from work sampling studies at seven different nuclear plants, with (2) a least–squares curve through the results of 26 studies conducted by TVA, and with (3) the work sampling results at the Clinton Nuclear Power Plant to recommend that the cost of 7.6 million craft manhours not be included in the utility's rate base. These curves are shown in Figure 1: the Shoreham 1 curve with the NY PSC Staff curve, Shoreham 2 with 26 nuclear plants, and Shoreham 3 with Clinton.

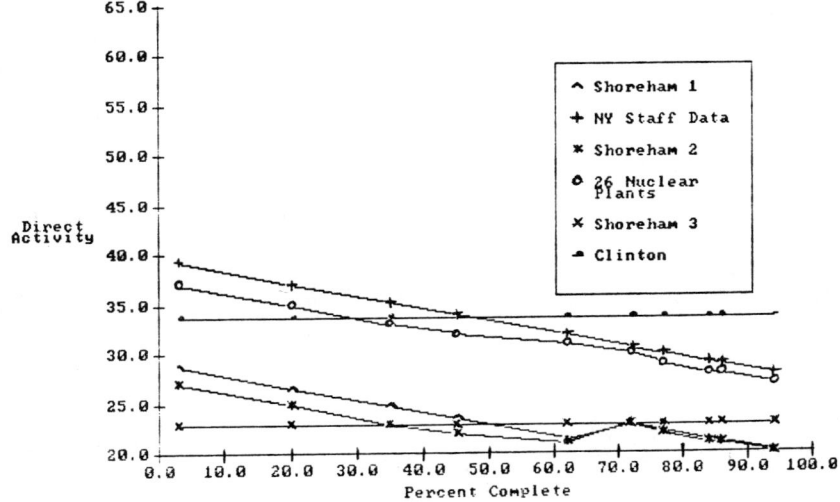

Figure 1 Work Sampling Comparisons
NY Public Service Commission

DATA ANALYSIS
Summary data contained in the Callaway and Wolf Creek work sampling reports were first compared to the figures reported by Palmeter and Standell. The activity categories used by the contractor's industrial engineering unit included direct activity. Getting equipment, equipment travel, getting material, material travel, and travel were grouped as support activities and equipment delay, material delay, crew delay same, crew delay other, supervision delay, miscellaneous delays, field personal activity, quality control, and break personal activity were grouped as delays. Strandell grouped activities into 7 categories and Palmeter grouped them into 9 categories. The only activity that could be compared directly was direct work, and there is some doubt that it is defined in the same way in the various sampling programs. On the average, direct work at Wolf Creek and Callaway was 39.9% and 45.2%, respectively. These are significantly different from the values of 32% and 33% reported by Standell and Palmeter. Average support

187

activity at Callaway was only 18.9%, but 33.3% at Wolf Creek. On the other hand, there were 34.7% delays at Callaway and 26.8% at Wolf Creek.

Direct activity at the Callaway and Wolf Creek plants was plotted against the percentage of completion. Similar plots using the data collected from the other plants were superimposed on the charts. Straight lines determined by linear regression analysis of the data were superimposed on the charts as were plots of data points obtained from other utilities. Typical plots are shown on Figures 2 and 3. Figure 2 shows the direct activity at Callaway and a Wolf Creek and trend lines generated by the Microsoft Chart program. Figure 3 compares the direct activity at Callaway with that at two other plants.

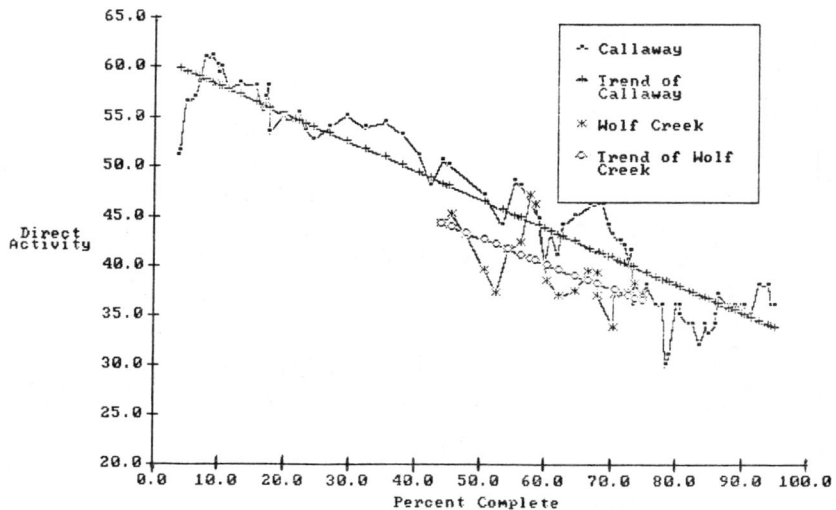

Figure 2   Direct Activity Comparisons
Callaway vs Wolf Creek

By and large, the direct activity measured by continuous sampling at Callaway, and Wolf Creek was greater than it was at most of the other plants for which data was obtained. Direct activity at Callaway was greater than at Wolf Creek, but the support activity at Wolf Creek was greater than at Callaway. Delays at Callaway were greater than at Wolf Creek. The final construction costs of the two plants were about the same, about $3.05 billion for Callaway and about $3.10 billion for Wolf Creek.

The direct activity at Callaway and Wolf Creek were greater than Plants 1 and 2 shown in Figure 3. But it is interesting to note that although Callaway and Wolf Creek, with relatively high direct activity, were completed at costs of about three and a half times the original construction cost estimates. Plant 2, with relatively low direct activity, was considered to be an extremely successful project.

188

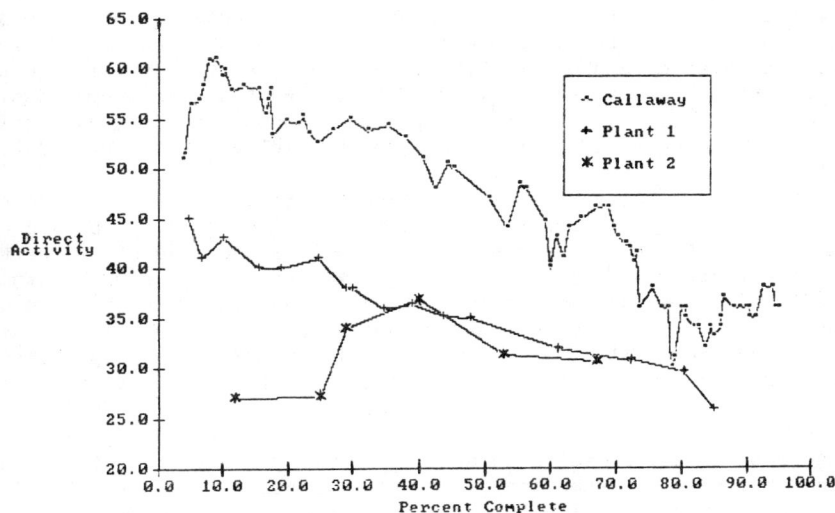

Figure 3   Direct Activity Comparisons
Callaway vs Plants 1 and 2

DISCUSSION
Statistical Validity
The mathematical basis for making statements about the category
proportions, limits of error, and confidence intervals is the
binomial probability distribution. The binomial distribution is the
distribution of the number of "successes" in a number of
replications of independent Bernoulli trials where the probabiltiy
of success does not change from trial to trial.   A Bernoulli trial
is an "experiment" in which there are only two possible outcomes,
i.e., success-failure, working-not working, etc. Independence is
assured by random selection of a sample from a population.

It seems that the assumption that the outcomes of successive
Bernoulli trials are independent and identically distributed is
violated in sampling from a population of workers at a job site.
The literature indicates that the probabilty that a worker in one
craft is working at any given time differs from the probability that
worker in another craft is working.   That is, direct activity
ratings differ from craft to craft.   This difference alone renders
the notion of a direct activity rating based on random sampling for
the total project rather meaningless.   Furthermore, work done by
members of a given craft varies with its location within the
project.   For example, laborers may be found placing concrete,
digging ditches, stripping or moving forms, operating certain kinds
of tools, etc.   Just as a difference in direct activity exists from

one craft to the next, so differences in direct activity of members of a given craft occur from one kind of work to the next. Crew-balance studies have shown workers in a given crew to work different percentages of the cycle time in repetitive construction operations. This results in a violation of the assumption of identical distribution even when the results of work sampling is stratified by craft.

Once the observer's starting time and tour route have been selected, the assumption of independence of the observations would seem to be violated. Successive observations are made of workers who are either working together or in proximity to each other. The activity of one worker may be influenced by the activities of those around him, i.e., observations are not independent. At any time during the tour, it is unlikely that all members of the population of workers are equally likely to be observed, i.e., the sample is not random.

While it cannot be disputed that work sampling gives an indication of the relative amounts of activity and inactivity on a given job site, it seems inappropriate to cloak the results of work sampling with any statistical precision or lack of precision. At best, the technique is capable of indicating where there are delays and potential problems on the job site. This should trigger the use of other work recording techniques to identify the causes of the delays or problems.

Production Control

Work sampling is a part of a production control system which collects, classifies, and records activities at the job site, compares them to norms or standards, and indicates those parts of the job that may require closer supervision, more careful planning and scheduling, and so forth. The real value of the use of work sampling and the analysis of the results is in timely indication of problems on the job site that should receive the attention of job-site management. Explanations of significant increases in delays should be sought using other work or activity measurement techniques such as timelapse photography, five-minute ratings, crew balance charts, foremen delay surveys, etc. And corrective action should be taken.

The Callaway and Wolf Creek work sampling reports and supporting documentation were examined to determine if information was provided in a timely manner, if the results were analyzed to detect potential delays and causes of delays, and if the reports were used by management to take corrective action. Reports were published four to twelve days after the end of the reporting periods which seems no more timely than the weekly cost reports that Parker and Oglesby objected to. Observations by industrial engineering such as

"The following crafts made significant gains in Direct Activity as well as reducing Personal Activity: Cement Finishers +22.8% to 72.4% DA, Boilermakers +29.5% to 68.8% DA. While many crafts made good improvement in reducing Personal Activity, the

190

following crafts show 9% or greater Personal Activity
Electricians 11.2% . . ."

seem to be meaningless in directing the attention of management to
the factors that caused the increase in direct activity or the root
causes of delays.

The standard or norm against which performance is to be
measured does not exist. Industry averages are of interest only in
a retrospective sense and cannot be used as a standard for
comparison. Examination of Figures 2 and 3 reveals that direct
activity, with some exceptions, tends to decrease as the job
progresses and that there is a more or less random variation about
the trend line. This can be explained by the increasing complexity
of the job, the increasing manpower loading, crowding of the work
space, etc. the target is a moving target, and the movement is
difficult to predict.

Comparisons

There is a tendency to try to compare the work sampling data
collected at different construction projects. This seems to be a
misapplication of the technique if, indeed, the technique may be
correctly applied at all to large construction projects. With few
exceptions, the condition of one plant at a reported percentage of
completion is not comparable to any other plant. They are
completely different entities.

The Callaway and Wolf Creek plants were the only plants in the
Standardized Nuclear Unit Power Plant System (SNUPPS) to be
constructed. They are similar in design. They were designed by the
same engineering firm, they were built by the same general
contracting firm in roughly the same section of the country at the
same time, and the work sampling programs were the same at both
plants. One plant was built by union labor under a project
agreement, the other was built open shop. One utility is the sole
owner of one plant and a part owner of the other. One plant lead
the other by three to six months during construction. It was
completed in September 1985 and the other in January 1986. The
final costs of both plants were roughly three and a half times the
original construction cost estimates.

It might be possible to compare the work activity of two crews
of the same craft performing similar tasks if the information has
been obtained by the same observer. However, when different crews
are involved on differing tasks, comparisons become less meaningful.
This is shown clearly in the comparison of the work sampling data of
Callaway with that of Wolf Creek. These projects are so very
similar, i.e., same design, same contractor, same designer, same
general geographic area, same work sampling plan, etc., that it
would be expected that the work sampling data collected at the two
plants would be comparable. But the results differ quite
noticeably. The contributory activity at Wolf Creek was
significantly greater than at Callaway. There is no rational
explanation why the activity of these two seemingly "identical"
projects, as measured by work sampling, should differ so greatly

while the total construction cost are about the same. It seems that measures of direct activity, or of support activity and delays, may not be good predictors of differences in construction costs.

When data is collected on a project such as Wolf Creek in a consistent and unbiased manner, the results are meaningful only to the management of that project. In the same way, data that is collected in a consistent and unbiased manner on another project, such as Callaway, is of value only to the management of that project.

CONCLUSIONS

Because of difference in work sampling programs, it is not possible, in general, to compare work sampling results of one plant with those of another. Direct activity, support activity, and delays are defined differently in the various sampling programs. And those programs with the same category definitions have different observers with different biases.

Because of differences in plants at various stages of completion, comparisons of work sampling results of one plant with those of another are meaningless. In particular, it is nonsensical to judge the effectiveness of management or the ineffectiveness of mismanagement on the basis of direct activity measurements derived from work sampling.

Because of changes in the nature and complexity of the work as the job progresses, it is not possible to compare direct craft activity at one stage of completion with that at another stage of completion. There are no standards with which to compare estimated values of direct activity, support activity, and delays.

Because of the ways work sampling observations are analyzed and reported, use of the technique does not provide job management with the information needed to detect and correct productivity problems. Reports are not timely, and analysis is superficial.

Because the technique as it is applied in the field violates the assumptions upon which it is based, the results do not have the statistical validity generally claimed. In particular, when a level of direct activity is determined for the entire job by observations made by touring the job site at random times on randomly selected routes, the sample is not really a random sample and the observations are not independent and identically distributed.

ACKNOWLEDGEMENTS

The authors wish to acknowledge the assistance of Chris R. Rogers, formerly Manager of Generating Facilities on the staff of the State of Missouri Public Utilities Commission, and Cameron Berkuti, Rob Morgan, Sanjay Raut, and Dr. Prapon Phasukyud, graduates of the Construction Engineering and Management Program, Department of Civil Engineering, University of Missouri-Columbia.

REFERENCES TO PREVIOUSLY PUBLISHED WORK

1. Adrian, James J., Construction Productivity Improvement, New York: Elsevier Science Publishing Co., Inc., 1987.

2. Barnes, Ralph M., Work Sampling, Second Edition, New York: John Wiley & Sons, Inc., 1957.

3. Benjamin, Jack R. and C. Allin Cornell, Probability Statistics, and Decision for Civil Engineers, New York: McGraw-Hill Book Company, 1970.

4. Drewin, F.J., Construction Productivity, New York: Elsevier Science Publishing Co., 1982.

5. Dvorsky, Thomas G., Kevin M. Broner, Bijoy K. Misra, Lee E. Burgess, and Dennis J. Schumaker, Quantitative Testimony and Exhibits filed with the New York State Department of Public service in the Investigation of the Shoreham Nuclear Power Station, Case 27563, February 1984.

6. Godfrey, Kneeland A., "Productivity on the Construction Site," Civil Engineering, American Society of Civil Engineers, Vol. 103, No. 1, January 1977, pp. 74-76.

7. Palmeter, Saxon B., "Work Sampling Studies, New Construction, 1982," personal correspondence with Saxon Palmeter.

8. Parker, Henry W. and Clarkson H. Oglesby, Methods Improvement for Construction Managers, New York: McGraw-Hill Book Company, 1972.

9. Russell, James R., "Work Measurement and Performance Goals in Major Power Plant Construction," Industrial Engineering Unit, TVA.

10. Strandell, Marjatta, "Productivity in Power Plant Construction," Transactions of the American Association of Cost Engineers, July 18-21, 1976, pp. 334-337.

11. Thomas, H. Randolph, Jr. and Mason P. Holland, "Work Sampling Programs: Comparative Analysis," Journal of the Construction Division, American Society of Civil Engineers, Vol. 106, No. C04, December 1980, pp. 519-534.

12. Thomas, H. Randolph, Jr., "Can Work Sampling Lower Construction Costs?," Journal of the Construction Division, American Society of Civil Engineers, Vol. 107, No. C02, June 1981, pp. 263-278.

13. Thomas H. Randolph, Jr. and Jeffrey Daily, "Crew Performance Measurement Via Work Sampling," Journal of Construction Engineering and Management, American Society of Civil Engineers, Vol. 109, No. 3, September 1983, pp. 309-320.

14. Thomas, H. Randolph, Jr., Mason P. Holland, and Carl T. Gustenhoven, "Games People Play with Work Sampling," Journal of the Construction Division, America. Society of Civil Engineers,

Vol. 108, N. C01, March 1982, pp. 13-22.

15. Thomas, H. Randolph, Jr., Quantification Rebuttal Testimony filed with the New York Public Service Commission in the Matter of Long Island Lighting Company Shoreham Nuclear Generating Facility, May 15, 1984.

MANAGING BUILDING CONSTRUCTION COST DURING THE DESIGN PHASE: A CASE STUDY

Garvin T. Dreger, AIA

Georgia Institute of Technology, USA

Summary

Management systems developed to plan and control building cost during the design phase are presented. Emphasis is on organization forms and the duties and responsibilities of the team members. The case study is used to focus on the management approaches applied in the design development processes of a major public office building in the USA. The project is an excellent example of how a construction consultant can be successfully integrated into the design development team. Modeling methods for planning and controlling cost and time resources are introduced. Processes for value analysis and constructability reviews are presented as viable management methods for use in the decision making process.

Sommaire

Cette communication présente divers moyens de contrôle des coûts de construction au moment de l'étude d'un batiment. L'accent est mis sur les responsabilités et les attributions des membres de l'équipe de concepteurs et sur les formulaires d'organisation de l'étude. Le cas particulier présenté a été choisit pour démontrer les différents moyens de contrôle lors de la conception d'un grand immeuble de bureaux aux Etats Unis. Le projet est un excellent exemple de l'intégration d'un expert en construction dans l'équipe de concepteurs. Différentes méthodes sont présentées pour la planification de la construction et le contrôle des coûts. Des procédés d'analyse de valeur et d'hypothèses de constructabilité du projet sont aussi présentés comme des méthodes valable de contrôle en vue de leur utilisation au moment des prises de décisions.

Keywords

Organization Forms, Management Systems, Team Responsibilities, Cost Modeling, Schedule Modeling, Constructability, Value Analysis, Life Cycle Cost.

INTRODUCTION

In the spring of 1983 the Building Authority of Fulton County, Georgia tendered a request for proposals (RFP) seeking the services of a "Construction Consultant" during the design development phase of a $45 million dollar, 450 thousand square foot office building complex and 1000 space parking garage. The facility was to be constructed in the middle of downtown Atlanta on a 3.6 acre site which is surrounded by busy city streets, and bounded on one side by the imposing edifice of an historical Superior Court Building.

The RFP stated that the project development strategy by the owner was for the Building Authority to act as owner and developer for the project, leasing the facility to the County government as a tenant. The Authority planned to retain a design team (Architect/Engineer) and a "Construction Consultant" to prepare construction documents for public bid by general contractors.

While most elements of the development strategy by the owner were common practice, the role of the "Construction Consultant" was unique. The Authority recognized the importance of cost estimating and scheduling to the design process and desired to establish a working framework which would result in an optimum benefit from services by the "Construction Consultant", (CC). The CC was to provide services under a direct contract with the Owner and have a working relationship with the Architect/Engineer (AE).

The Owner, Architect/Engineer, and Construction Consultant would perform as a team during the design - all working toward the goal of achieving a design solution to meet the program requirements which, in the owners words, would be "attractive, functional, efficient, and cost effective".

OBJECTIVES

The Owners' RFP described four major areas of primary services desired from the Construction Consultant:

1. Cost Estimating

Provide continual examination of project costs from the initial establishment of a Cost Model to detailed costs estimates of final documents prior to bid. The estimating function should be both pro-active and re-active. That is, designers should have the benefit of cost information as a decision-making tool before drawing the plans. Estimates of completed designs are therefore primarily a checking function.

Schedule regular project review meetings with the Design Team (bi-weekly) to provide the opportunity for budget updates and monitoring of the Cost Model by the Construction Consultant.

It was expected that the Construction Consultant would keep current with market conditions and prices.

2. Value Analysis

Assist the Architect and Owner in achieving the greatest value for the least cost. Rigorously inspect alternatives. Understand the Owner's definition of "value". Consider attributes of materials and systems that transcend first cost, i.e., useful life, maintainability, servicing, replacement, obsolescence, energy consumption, etc. As with cost estimating described previously, value analysis should occur before final design.

Working within the framework of a Cost Model, the Construction Consultant will identify items that warrant value analysis, usually concentrating in areas likely to have the biggest opportunity for cost savings.

The Construction Consultant will assist the Owner and Architect in preparing bid documents and alternates, and in reviewing the bids when received and the qualifications of the bidders.

3. Scheduling

Prepare detailed schedules to guide the design phase and project likely construction schedules.

At the beginning of the design phase, the Construction Consultant will conduct a planning exercise involving all members of the Design Team, Owner, tenant, regulatory agencies, etc. to develop a master design schedule. In this way, the project is "designed" before it gets to the drawing boards. More importantly, it allows all participants to think through their roles and responsibilities in the process and to clearly identify dependencies and constraints.

Again, regular project review meetigs will provide the opportunity to update and monitor progress against the schedule mode.

The Construction Consultant will also prepare and update a more general master project schedule that includes activities beyond design. The Construction Consultant will advise the Owner of antipated changes of long-lead items, separate bid packages, and other schedule impacting items.

4. Constructability Review

Provide critical appraisal of proposed materials, systems, and their combinations to identify "better" ways of putting the pieces together.

In this capacity the Construction Consultant will look at the design as a contractor would. Are the elements of the design arranged in logical sequence, and in accord with local practices? Are the drawings and specifications complete, accurate, clear and consistent?

DETAILS OF STUDY

The elements of this study of construction management control systems are provided in the following project proposal descriptions which were developed in response to the RFP. The format and examples presented and expanded in this presentation are designed for this specific project. These systems afford opportunity, however, for broad use applications in construction management systems for virtually any type of project where time, cost (initial and life cycle), quality, and quantity are precious resources and desired goals.

PROJECT PLANNING AND CONTROL

The project planning and control approach is based on the "modeling" theory of establishing initial levels of cost increments, time phases, quality levels, and quantity goals by developing rational, easily understood, and easily updated management models. As the design develops, the subsequent components of each of the building systems are tested against the original project model levels and adjustments made as required. The involvement of each team member in this process of project control establishes performance commitments by those responsible for the individual tasks.

The management approach is to apply "decision management" techniques involving the appropriate team members in the decision making process, to rationally evaluate pros and cons of each matter, and then to ensure that decisions are made in a timely fashion with the results communicated to all parties.

ORGANIZATION MODEL

The essence of competent management requires the establishment of an organization model to control the planning and control process. The organization model must have clear lines of authority for decision making, established communications procedures, and well defined work flow channels. The project development team organization model as shown in Figure 1 incorporates each of these elements through its organizational framework and staffing assignments and responsibilities.

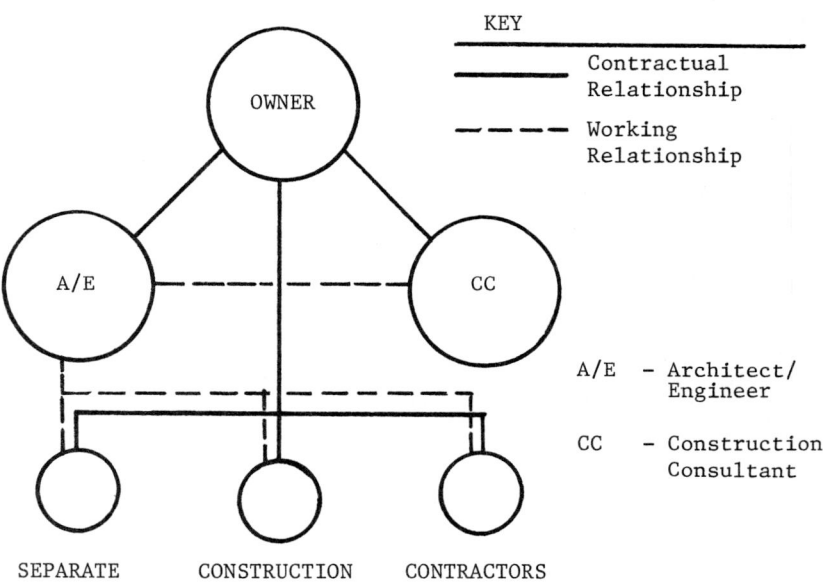

Figure 1. Project Development Organization

The Owner has unprecedented project authority and is responsible for the ultimate success of the project. The Architect/Engineer has the more traditional role of design development to satisfy the varied functional, cost, quality, and quantity parameters established by the owner. The Construction Consultant takes the lead role in monitoring the design to establish cost control and scheduling control management models and applications. The CC also provides rational value analysis applications and constructability reviews as the project design is developed.

CONSTRUCTION CONSULTANT ORGANIZATION MATRIX
The internal organization matrix of the Construction Consultant's
staff is dependent upon the specific project complexity and needs.
For the Fulton County office building complex, a vertical organizational matrix of multi-disciplined professionals was established as
depicted in Figure 2. The vertical matrix is utilized for two main
reasons. It provides a graphic pictorial of the levels or responsibility and identifies the major discipline coordinators by name and
hierarchal levels of responsibility.

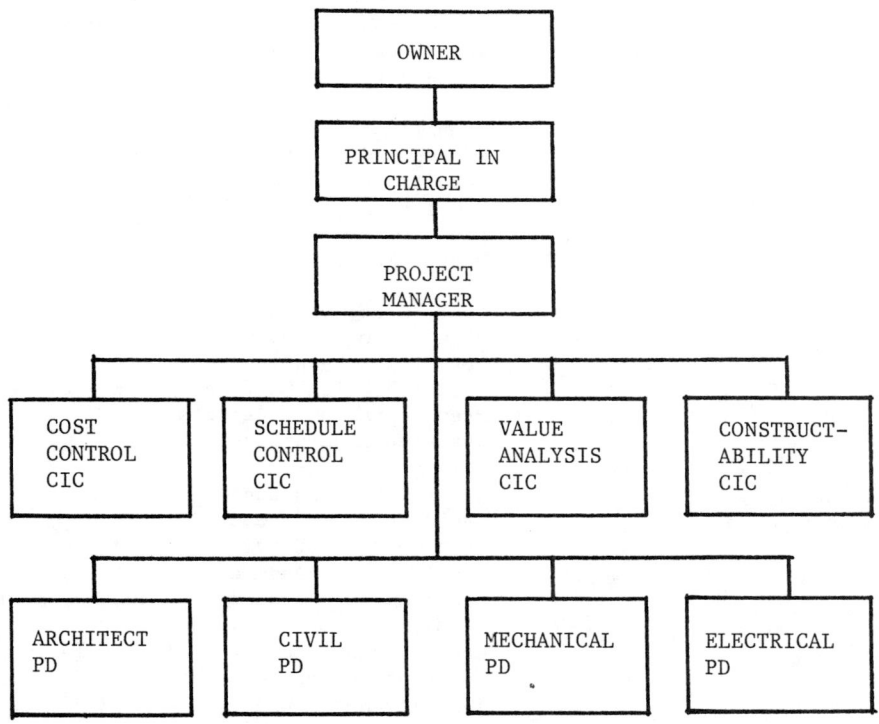

CIC = Coordinator in Charge
PD = Professionals in Design Disciplines

Figure 2. Construction Consultant Organization

Project Title	Duties and Responsibilities
Principal-In-Charge	Overall Project Administration Personnel Assignment/Management Financial Management Team Member Co-ordination Budget and Schedule Control Value Analysis
Project Manager	Overall Project Technical Direction Project Playning Coordinator Technical Input/Analysis Supervision of Technical Personnel Scheduling and Estimate Management Report Preparation Value Analysis
Cost Control Coordinator	Overall Cost Estimating Component Budget Establishment Detailed Estimates Sub-system Costing Alternatives Bid Analysis Market Surveys
Schedule Coordinator	Overall Project Scheduling Master Project Development Schedule Detailed Scheduling Activities Interface with Cost and Constructability Prepare Schedule Reports Evaluate Alternative Schedules
Constructability Coordinator	Overall Constructability Review Evaluate Sub-systems Recommend Construction Alternatives Provide Labor and Market Analysis Means and Methods of Construction Analysis General and Special Conditions in the Construction Contracts Identify and Evaluate Separate Bid Packs
Value Analysis Coordinator	Value Analysis Coordination Conduct VE Workshop Prepare VE Control Process Monitor all Sub-system Design Preparation of VE Reports Follow-up of VE Proposals Recommend VE Design Alternatives

Design Disciplines	Detailed Analysis of Design Submissions
Professionals	Review of Technical Design
	Preliminary Evaluations
	Consultation with Principle Coordinators
	Design impact Analysis
	Preparation of Work Products
	Value Analysis
	Document Coordination

PROJECT MANAGEMENT AND CONTROL WORK PLAN

The strategy in managing and controlling the successful development
of the project within the established cost and time resources and
stated levels of quality and quantity is a team approach working
with each member of the triumvirate of Owner, Architect, and Construction Consultant. The basic approach is to establish the time
and cost models at the beginning of the project and provide periodic
updates of the models as the design is developed. The management
models used are simple, effective, inclusive, and provide for fast
and accurate updating. The Management Systems are designed on the
basis that management tools should be clear and easily understood by
all parties responsible for the project production.

COST CONTROL MODEL

The basis of the cost model, as shown in Appendix A, is the development of a component budget estimate for each of the major project
sub-systems of the building prior to the start of design. The Component Budget Estimate (Level 1) will be used for comparative cost
analysis as the design is produced. It is important to understand
that the establishment of dollar levels of each sub-system also establishes quality levels. It is therefore recommended that representatives of the Owner, Architect, and Project User be involved in
the Component Budget Estimate development process. The Level 1 cost
figures are developed using historical cost data for a medium-to-high
cost office buildings recently constructed in the local area.

   Major progress milestone reviews for cost control evaluation will
be scheduled at three major design development stages: 1) The Schematic Stage, 2) Design Development Stage, and 3) Contract Document-
Pre Bid Stage. Incremental estimating control in the various sub-
systems should be accomplished on a much greater frequency as the
design is developed.

   The cost estimates will positively consider and quantify the following elements: 1) space analysis listing the program occupiable
areas, support areas, and the gross areas with comparisons to the design documents; 2) controlled net to gross ratio of not less than 80%;
3) a design analysis for each discrete phase discribing the proposed
systems and related cost in parametric and detailed formats; 4) site
analysis; 5) a market survey to determine material availability,
capabilities of fabricators and precast yards, labor craft availability, construction market glut or capacity, local cost escalation
trends, or other factors which might influence the bidding.

   Each estimate at the various levels of design development will be
compared to the project budget as projected in the cost model.

Necessary adjustments will be made to control the overall construction cost.

While performing the required estimating services, the Construction Consultant will perform a review of the designed work for potential cost savings. A specific portion of this effort shall be a design review by the Construction Consultant of the structural, mechanical and electrical systems to ensure that higher cost is not caused by: a) Providing excessive spare capacity; b) Providing unnecessary redundant systems/components; c) Designing for unnecessary expansion; d) Splitting systems/loads; e) Not designing for a degree of risk in lieu of peak conditions; f) Adding unwarranted factors of safety in sizing equipment systems.

SCHEDULE MODEL

The approach to be used for the project schedule control, like the cost control, is based on the modeling technique. The schedule model as depicted in Figure 3 will allow for the planning and control of the necessary time elements in the design, procurement, and construction phases of the project development.

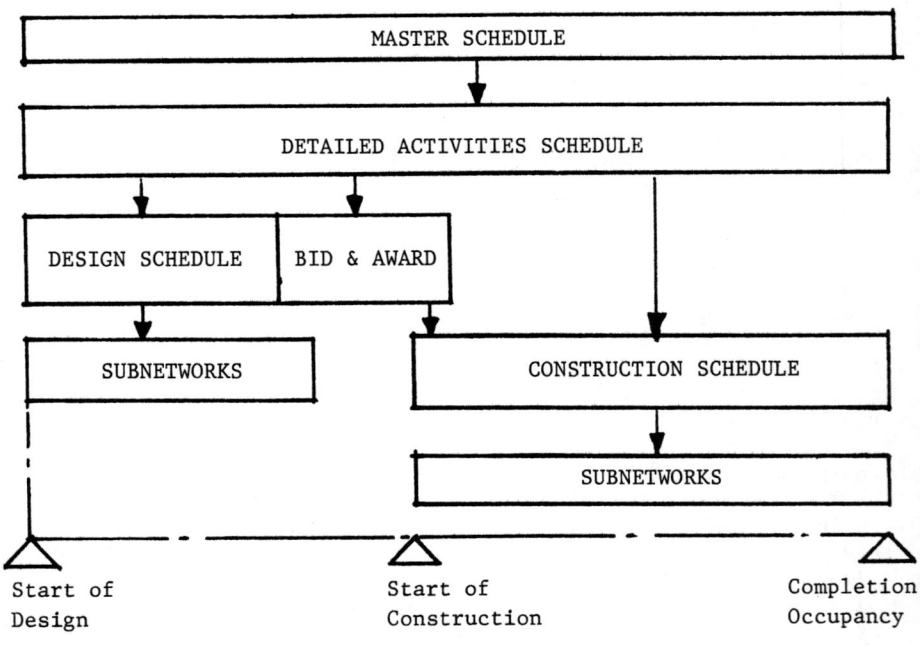

Figure 3. Schedule Model

202

The basic approach will be to develop a Project Master Schedule which will depict time frames to accomplish each major activity. Detailed design, bid and award, and construction phase schedules will be provided at stated periods of frequencies as the project is developed.

Master Schedule
The Master Schedule is made up of all the major activities in the project delivery process, i.e., major design phases, procurement phases and construction phases for each bid package. In order to obtain the necessary input for the development of the Master Schedule, The Construction Consultant will conduct a thorough site analysis, analyze the construction market, and in general, gain a thorough overview of the major tasks which must be accomplished in the total project development cycle.

Design Schedule
Working in close contact with the design Architect-Engineer and Owner, the Construction Consultant will develop the detailed design phase schedule based on the major design development phases: schematics, design development, and working drawings; the milestone cost estimating intervals; and the presentation and approval stages. The design development schedule matrix will be bi-weekly intervals with defined responsibility assignments by tasks. Bi-weekly schedule review and update meetings will provide tight control over the scheduling process. The schedule update report will be generated monthly as the design is developed.
The Design Development Schedule will be further broken down into sub-network assignments for each design professional discipline, i.e., architectural, civil, structural, mechanical, electrical, etc. The management of each dicipline on the design team will be the responsibility of the A-E with control monitoring by the CC. The frequency level of the sub-network by responsibility schedules will be in days with calendar deadline dates established.

Bid and Award Schedule
The procurement activities will be detailed in a Pre-Bid Schedule by task and responsibility. Dates will be established for each procurement activity including invitation to bid, bid document availability, Pre-Bid Conference, receipt of bids, evaluation of bid response, award date, and notice to proceed date.

Construction Schedule
The Construction Consultant will develop a simple, but effective construction schedule during the design phase to afford the means for a reasonable projection of construction cost escalated to the proper time period of construction. A detailed construction schedule will be subsequently developed by the successful General Contractor to the level of detail outlined in the bid documents. (Note: The construction phase and occupancy phase CC services are not a part of this study)

CONSTRUCTABILITY ANALYSIS

The constructability analysis will involve each of the Construction Consultant's team members including the principals and technical staff. The reviews will consider market availability, materials handing, site access, storage capacity and speed of erection. The constructability evaluation will be made in the context of possible input to the time and cost models as well as sensitivity of the concerns of the design team in the design development process. The historic nature of surrounding buildings, urban site location, pedestrian and vehicular access will be considered in the overall constructability review process. The constructability analysis will occur on a bi-weekly basis with reports generated monthly.

VALUE ANALYSIS

The application of the Value Analysis process will be an ongoing program throughout the design development phase. A short VA workshop will be developed prior to the start of design. The workshop will be specifically tailored to the management process employed on the project. Training will be provided in the methodology of value analysis, and all project development participants, including the Owner's representatives, will be required to attend.

A detailed Value Analysis evaluation will be performed at the end of the Schematic Design Phase and Design Development Phase with reports generated and disseminated to all team members. The value analysis application will be integral with the cost control, schedule and constructability review processes.

The Construction Consultant's technical staff of Architects and Engineers will propose alternative sub-system solutions to the A/E design team as the schematic designs are developed. The alternatives will be governed by the cost and schedule parameters and include detailed considerations of constructability and life cycle cost.

PROJECT:
LOCATION:

PROJECT NO:
ESTIMATOR:

BUILDING SUB-SYSTEMS	Level 1 BUDGET DATE:	Level 2 DESIGN DATE:	Level 3 DESIGN DATE:	Level 4 DESIGN DATE:	BID ANALYSIS DATE:
01 Foundations					
02 Substructure					
03 Superstructure					
04 Exterior Closure					
05 Roofing					
06 Interior Work					
07 Conveyors					
08 Mechanical					
09 Electrical					
10 Gen Conditions/Profit					
11 Equipment					
12 Sitework					
SCHEDULED CONTRACT DATE ☐					
DESIGN CONTINGENCY					
ESCALATION TO:					
PROGRESSIVE COST		$	$	$	$
TARGET COST		$	$	$	$
DIFFERENTIAL		$	$	$	$
COST PER SF	$/SF	$/SF	$/SF	$/SF	$/SF
GROSS FLOOR AREA	SF	SF	SF	SF	SF

REFERENCES
1. American Institute of Architects, Life Cycle Cost Analysis, Washington, D.C., 1977

2. Associated General Contractors of America, CM for the General Contractor, Washington, D.C.

3. Dell 'Isola, Alphonse J., Value Engineering in the Construction Industry, New York, Van Nostrand Reinhold Company, 1982

4. U.S. General Services Administration, Project Estimating Requirements, Washington, D.C., August 24, 1981

5. U.S. General Services Administration, The GSA System for Construction Management, Washington, D.C., April, 1975

THE LINE OF BALANCE CONCEPT FOR LOW-RISE FLATS CONSTRUCTION SITES
- A VIEW ON THE ALLOCATION OF LABOUR RESOURCES TO THE ACTIVITIES AND
THEIR DURATIONS ACCORDING TO THE "S" CURVES APPROACH

Dr. L.F. Heineck, PhD. - Lecturer, Pós-graduação em Engenharia Civil,
                         NORIE, UFRGS, Av. Osvaldo Aranha 99, 3º an-
                         dar, Porto Alegre, RGS, Brasil

Summary
    This research work deals with the systematic observation and anal-
ysis of the production characteristics (duration, resource consumption, intensity of work, etc.) on a number of house building sites in
the United Kingdom. The major aim is to investigate the possibilities
of supplying data according to the requirements of line of balance
programming techniques as applied to repetitive construction.
    Data was obtained through an improved method of activity sampling.
This method of data acquisition introduced several difficulties   for
the quantitative evaluation of the above characteristics. These diffi
culties and how they were overcome are discussed along the text.
    The randomness and lack of order in the observed progress of work
from housing unit to housing unit prevented the development of classi
cal "S" shaped curves relating the percentage resource consumption to
the percentage elapsed duration. Instead, boundary curves are proposed, setting the maximum and minimum possible allocations at any pe
riod of time.

Sommaire
    Cette recherche s'agit de l'observation et analyse systematique
des caracteristiques de produccion (dureé, consommattion de ressources, intensité de travail, etc.) d'un certain nombre de chantier pour
la construction de maisons au Royame-Uni. Les donneés etaient obtenu-
es par la methode des observations instantaneés: cela introduit plu-
sieurs difficultés pour l'evaluation des caracteristiques de produccion décrites au dessus. Cette difficultés et comment peuvent être
surmontés sont analyseés.
    Le confusion géneralle du progress du travail au chantier empêche
le development des courbes classiques "S". Au lieu de cela, courbes
limites sont proposés, pour determiner le maximum et le minimum d'allocations dans n'importe quel période de temps.

Keywords
    Line of Balance, "S" Curves, Labour Allocation, Housebuilding
Sites Programming, Duration of Activities, Activity Sampling, Production Data Acquisition, Control and Measurement of Productivity.

INTRODUCTION

Despite its crucial importance to the programming and control of housebuilding sites, the allocation of labour to the activities and their durations has not yet been the subject of systematic field observation. A small number of reports attest to the fact that the intensity of work (number of man-hours deployed per time period) is usually very low on building sites, leading, thus, to large durations of activities (1, 2 and 3).

This research work deals with the systematic observation of the production characteristics (duration, resource consumption, intensity of work, etc.) on 3 house building sites in the United Kingdom. Data was obtained through an improved method of activity sampling. While this method made it possible to collect quickly and inexpensively a huge amount of data, it introduced several difficulties for the quantitative evaluation of the above elements. These difficulties and how they were overcome are discussed throughout the text.

The intensity of work was variable and erratic: in a large number of weeks only 1, 2 or 5 man-hours were deployed: sometimes large allocations of 30, 50 man-hours/week were intermingled with them. No mathematical rule was found governing the allocation of manpower to the activities, week after week. Reference nº 4 discusses in greater depth how work was performed on the 3 sites. In the next section it can be found a discussion on the appropriatness of including weeks in which very low allocations were made (1, 2, up to, say, 5 man-hours/ /week) in the calculation of the duration of activities.

THE IDENTIFICATION OF WEEKLY SIGNIFICANT OCURRENCES OF WORK

The total number of hours allocated per stage per week was the information available for the calculation of durations. A straightforward measurement for this variable would be just count the number of weeks in which work had ocurred. It will be seen now why this oversimplification of the problem was not encouraging.

Due to the workings of the activity sampling package used in this research work, the amount of labour resources allocated weekly to each stage or operation represents an accumulation of man-hours deployed to the activity from Monday to Monday, with no indication of the exact timely ocurrence of work during the week, or on its continuity: a weekly allocation of 10 man-hours could have been obtained through the observation of one man working continuously during 10 hours, or sporadically visiting the work place 10 times during the week, or, finally, by the observation of a gang of 10 operatives instantaneously engaged in the activity. The duration of the activity would be taken as one week in all three cases, while according to the latter example it could have been almost instantaneous.

Even if if its apparently obvious that the activity was performed continuously during the week, some uncertainity still remains on the exact number of days represented by the first and last weeks of labour allocation. In the hypothetical example below, the specially high allocations (as it will be seen later) in the intermediate weeks are an indication that work was performed continuously during weeks nº 11 and 12: however, the actual duration can be anything between 2 and 4 weeks, depending on how far work spread to weeks nº 10 and 13.

```
weekly allocation (in man-hours)    -- -- 05 60 75 35 -- -- --
                        week nº    08 09 10 11 12 13 14 15 16
```

It should be borne in mind that the availability of information
aggregated on a daily basis would solve the problem only partially:
again, due to the nature of the package aggregation process, no infor
mation would be available on exactly when during the day the activity
started or finished. The same reasoning can be extended to all other
possible levels of data aggregation, that is, morning and afternoon
periods, hours, minutes, etc.

The use of activity sampling data do calculate durations will
always imply an inaccuracy of the same magnitude of the average inter
vals between the observation rounds. Thus, the above difficulty might
be taken as irrelevant, because activity sampling data could have
been obtained at any duration-related accuracy, as a function only of
the frequency of observation rounds. Observations were made in general at hourly intervals for the 3 sites under investigation: therefore
it would be possible to produce durations accurate at the level of
hours. However, the next paragraph will show that the frequency of
observation rounds is not the only factor influencing the identification of the duration of activities.

Scattergrams of the weekly allocation of man-hours to the activities showed a wide dispersion of the amount of resources deployed in
consecutive weeks. Figure 01 depicts a typical example of such scattergrams: no clear pattern of allocation is discernible; there was a
great number of interruptions of work and allocations of different
magnitude; the number of weeks without the ocurrence of work was of
the same order of the number of weeks in which work had taken place.
If anything, the cumulative plot of resources allocated vs. time
elapsed might produce an "S" shaped curve, but, certainly, the interruptions of work make it more difficult to find a meaningful and
representative fitting curve. If the objective is to draw "S" curves,
weeks without work could be removed, but it would still be necessary
to justify the inclusion of weeks with low allocations of man-hours.

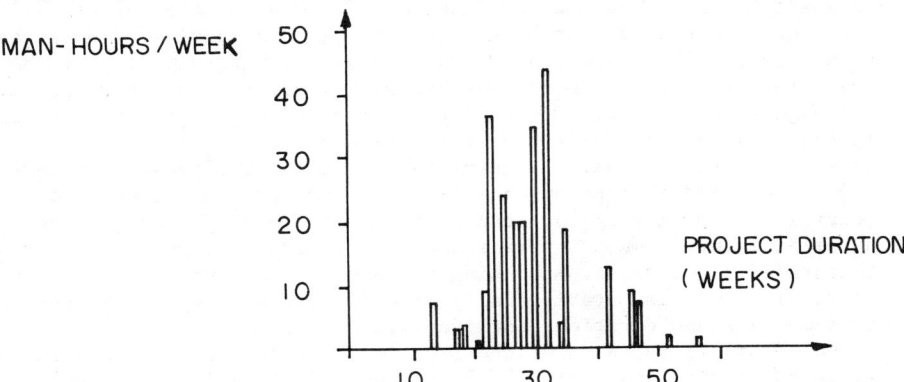

Figure 01. Weekly Allocation of Man-hours to the Plasterboard
Jointing Operation, Block nº 3, Ladygate Lane Site

209

The observation of the 2145 scattergrams similar to that one, respectively dealing with the 51 operations in 10 blocks of houses in the Ladygate Lane site, the 18 stages of work in 29 blocks of houses in the Pitcoudie 1 site, and the 21 stages of work in 53 blocks of houses and flats in the Pitcoudie 2 site suggested that it would not be possible to obtain the duration of activities just by counting the weeks in which work had taken place. Common sense dictates that the allocation of just 1, 2, or 3 man-hours per week to an activity is not an indication that work was undertaken seriously during that time period. Therefore, it is necessary to decide first on a minimum weekly allocation that would be a good indication that substantial effort was devoted to the activity during the time period, choosen for this research work as a week.

A reasonable approach is to count towards the total elapsed time only the weeks in which the allocation exceeded a given amount. Graphically this approach corresponds to drawing horizontal lines at specific "Y" values in figure 01 and counting the number of weeks with allocations that are at or above this line. This "Y" values will be called Minimum Significant Weekly Allocation of Resources (MISWAR) for short), throughout the rest of the paper.

MISWAR AND THE DURATION OF ACTIVITIES

The ultimate goal of this research work is to provide means of predicting the duration of activities. This can be achieved, for example, by relating the duration of activities to the respective labour consumption per block of houses: a regression model would be able to define such relationship. However, the inaccuracy in the measurement of both variables, labour consumption and durations, was large, making possible models unreliable. Thus data was aggregated at a still higher level of aggregation; stage labour consumption was not only totalled for the various houses comprising a block, but still further totalled for all blocks in a given site; likewise, durations were taken as the sum of durations in each individual block.

Information at the level of individual construction units (blocks) is lost. However, previous analyses of the data amassed for the 3 sites under consideration had indicated that overlapping of work was considerable; blocks were undertaken on a rolling group of units basis rather than on an individual basis. This fact allows the author to suggest that the production information for each individual block is not as important for the crews concerned as the total amount of work available on site, the permissible spreading of work to the various blocks and the approximate flow of work throughout the site. General information at tactical level should be sought before the detailed information at operational level. Moreover, the small architectural differences from housing type to housing type made it more difficult, and less statistically significant, to compare resource consumptions and durations for individual units.

No advantage is taken of the repetitive nature of housebuilding sites to provide statistical information. Construction industry projects are generally of a one-off nature: construction companies have very few opportunities to observe the repetition of experiments, that is, to build the same project again or to undertake the same set of

210

activities on different sites under controlled conditions. Housebuild ing sites provide the unique opportunity for replicated experiments; for example, the largest of the 3 sites, Pitcoudie 2, would make it possible to produce statistical inference based on 53 or 253 repetitions; there are 53 blocks of houses/flats with each block comprising a different mix of houses/flats, making a total of 253 dwellings. On the same account, Pitcoudie 1 would make it possible to analyse 29 or 108 pieces of information, while the smallest of the three sites, Ladygate Lane, would offer 10 or 71 variates.

The proposed aggregating procedure put forward by this research work reduces the 53 repetitions available for the Pitcoudie 2 site to just one pair of variates, that is, aggregate resource usage and aggregate duration for each particular stage of work or operation. Fortunately, as it will be seen later, the activities showed very similar production characteristics, which fact made it possible to explore statistically in a unique study the pair of variates produced by the 51 operations in the Ladygate Lane site, the 18 stages of work in the Pitcoudie 1 site, and the 21 stages of work in the Pitcoudie 2 site, giving a total of 90 activities to work with. It is worth mentioning that operation, in the case of this research work, corresponds to the notion normally used with PERT/CPM methodologies, while stage of work corresponds to a group of operations normally performed by the same trade. In this sense electrical instal lation corresponds to a stage of work, while wiring and conduits, sockets and switches, and fitting of electrical appliances are three operations within the latter stage.

The total duration for each stage of work was obtained by adding the total duration for the stage in each block: for each block, the stage was considered started once the MISWAR was exceeded and finished once all succeeding allocations were smaller than the MISWAR. Durations were calculated for every MISWAR taking into account the number of weeks with ocurrences of labour allocations greater or equal to the chosen parameter: weeks without work were not taken into consideration. The maximum duration for each activity was given by setting MISWAR to 1 man-hour: this duration was called D1 or Dt. The durations obtained by setting MISWAR to 2, 3, 4,..., n man-hours (D2, D3, D4, ..., Dn) can be expressed as a percentage of the above maximum duration.

The same procedure was used to quantify the allocation of resources associated with each MISWAR and its respective percentage in relation to the total resource consumption for each stage of work. Various relationships between duration and resource consumption are explored in the following sections.

THE RELATIONSHIP BETWEEN RESOURCE CONSUMPTION AND DURATION OF ACTIVITIES
Boundaries for "S" shaped Curves
The first set of models developed during the course of this research work consists of a relationship between cumulative percentage resource usage and cumulative percentage elapsed time (duration). Both percentage resource usage and percentage duration were ordered and accumulated along the "Y" and "X" axis respectively. Ordering

was given by increasing values of MISWARs. Figure 02 was obtained by plotting on the same graph the curves drawn for the 90 activities on the 3 sites.

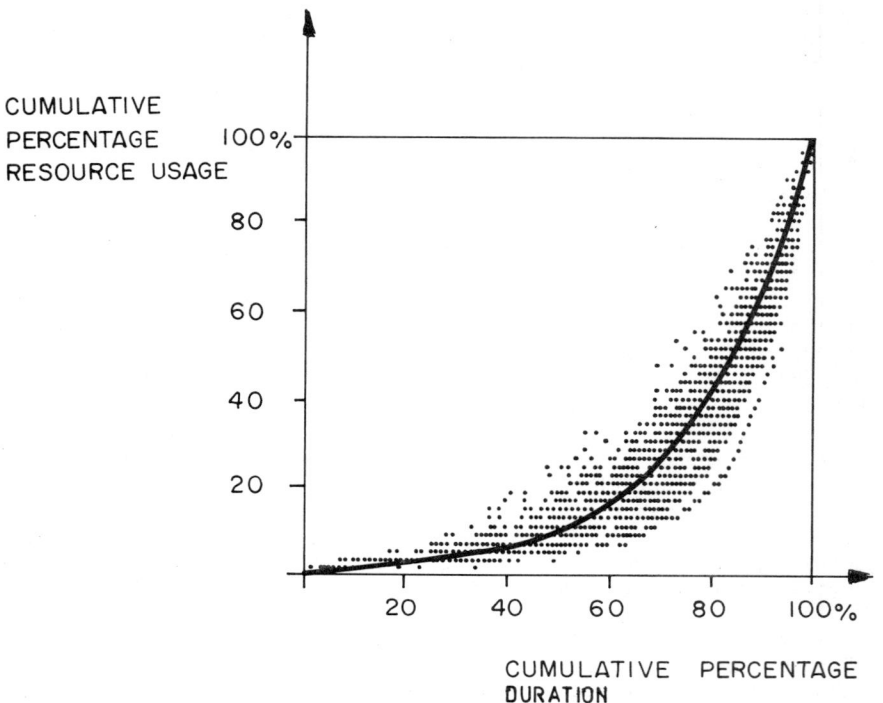

Figure 02. Cumulative Percentage Resource Usage vs. Cumulative Percentage Duration for 90 Activities on the 3 Sites

This figure shows that all activities had a similar pattern of relationship between cumulative percentage resource usage and cumulative percentage duration, despite the fact that they were performed on 3 different sites, had different labour contents, were defined at different hierarchy levels (operations on the Ladygate Lane site and stages of work on the Pitcoudie 1 and 2 sites), and referred to the work of different types, sizes and housing mix of blocks. Some blocks for example, contained only 2 small houses (for 2 dwellers), while other blocks contained as much as 10 medium-sized houses (for 4 and 5 dwellers).

In essence, the graph demonstrates that a large proportion of the total duration of activities (Dt) consists of weeks in which small allocations of man-hours were made. Figure 02 establishes that for 50% of the total duration, resource utilization as a percentage of the total labour resource used by the activity comprises only 10%; conversely, only a small proportion of the total duration was used in connection with significant allocations of man-hours. Provided that it is possible to associate the progress of work with the deployment of resources, it can be said that the bulk of advance towards comple tion of the activities was made during a small proportion of their total duration.

A curve fitting exercise was conducted to produce a model for the relationship between cumulative resource usage and cumulative percent age duration. Various polynomial functions were succesfull in repre- sentig the shape of curve in figure 02; this sort of shape is also common to other phenomena in society or in nature, leading to what the industrial engineers call the ABC curve, or the economists call the Pareto's law. The following approximate equation was selected for its simplicity:

$$f(x) = 100^x \tag{1}$$

The cumulative percentage consumption of resources is represented by $f(x)$ and it varies obviously from 0 to 100%: x is the cumulative percentage duration divided by 100, thus assuming values in the interval 0 - 1.

If the weekly ocurrences of work were ordered according to de- creasing MISWARs, the following equation would be derived:

$$g(x) = 100 - 100^{1-x} \tag{2}$$

It is important to distinguish between the above relationships and the "S" progress curves usually employed in building programming and control. The latter considers the cumulative resource usage and the cumulative duration associated with the exact sequence of allocation of resources over time; the former first regroups the ocurrences of work according to the weekly allocation of resources and then reorders their sequence from the smaller allocations to the larger ones (or vice-versa).

Progress "S" curves and $f(x)$ type curves will probable never coin cide, since it is unlikely that the allocation of resources to an activity will increase ($f(x)$) or decrease ($g(x)$) continuously, time period after time period.

The "S" shaped curves of the literature suggest that small allo- cations are made at the start of the activity, they increase up to a peak towards the semi-duration of the activity, and then decrease towards its completion. As already mentioned earlier on, it was not possible to derive such sort of curves for the labour consumption of activities at the level of individual blocks, due to the random- ness and descontinuity of labour allocation at this level of aggregation. Summing up the total labour consumption per activity, week after week, irrespective of block being tackled,might produce more promising "S" curves; this is being tried at the moment and should be reported in a future paper.

For the moment, the $f(x)$ curve and its counterpart, the $g(x)$ curve, provide respectively a lower and upper bound for the "S" shaped resource allocation curve at the level of individual blocks; neither are the allocations during the first weeks likely to be smaller than the allocations predicted by $f(x)$, nor are they likely to be greater

213

than the allocations given by g(x).

While further developments in connection with real "S" shaped curves are not brought forward by research effort under way by the author, it will be interesting to discuss other implications of the f(x) and g(x) type of curves, as described below.

The Weekly Allocation of Resources vs. Cumulative Duration Relationship

The f(x) function represents a cumulative resource usage curve: its first derivative is thus related to the weekly allocation of resources. After the necessary mathematical transformations it comes that:

$$df/dx = (dR/dD * Dt * 100) / Rt \qquad (3)$$

$$df/dx = 4.605 * 100^x \qquad (4)$$

The first derivative of f(x) is equal to the weekly allocation of resources (dR/dD) multiplied by the total duration (Dt) * 100 and divided by the total amount of labour resources used by the activity (Rt).

The set of equations can be used to express the Minimum Significant Weekly Allocation of Resources (MISWAR = dR/dD) as a function of the cumulative duration, as in figure 03; in this particular case Dt = 22 weeks and Rt = 115 man-hours; the Ladygate Lane site has 10 blocks of houses, thus average duration per block was 2.2 weeks and average resource consumption per block was 11,5 man-hours for the Strip Top Soil operation. The area under the curve is obviously equal to the total amount of labour resources deployed to the activity.

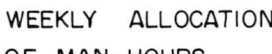

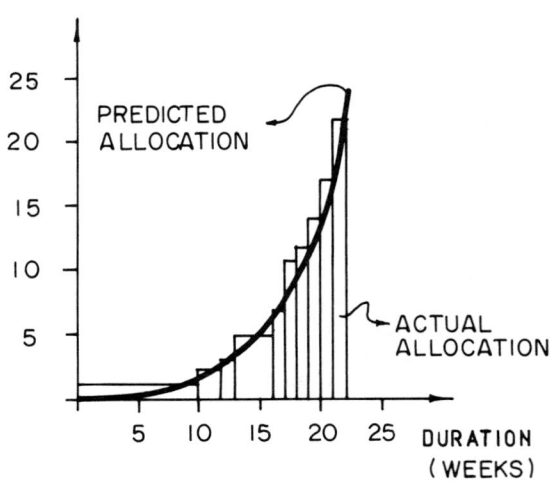

Figure 03. Predicted and Actual Weekly Allocation of Man-hours to the Strip Top Soil Operation, irrespective of Block, Ladygate Lane Site with a Total of 10 Blocks.

It has already been mentioned that the weekly allocation of resources varied wildly from week to week, with no apparent rule governing this variability. While it is still not possible to explain
and predict the allocation of resources week after week, the df/dx
equation is at least able to model the magnitude of the allocations
and their associate durations: the model is able to indicate the
various allocations that took place on site, but does not give any
information regarding the timing of these allocations. Further
studies are needed to determine the distribution of these allocations
over time.

The df/dx model behaved well for the majority of activities on the
3 sites. However, it should be noted that it is extremely sensitive
to the correct estimation of the total duration of the activity (Dt):
the string of allocations predicted by the model for an activity not
yet performed can be completely different from the actual string of
allocations, depending on the estimating accuracy for the total
duration.

The Percentage Resource Consumption (or Duration) vs. Weekly Allocation of Resources Relationship

A further straightforward development was the establishment of
models to predict the percentage of resources (or duration) associated with each MISWAR parameter. Given the f(x) and df/dx models described previously, the relationship between the cumulative percentage duration and the minimum significant weekly allocation of resources can be derived as it follows:

$$df/dx = 4.605 * 100^x;$$
$$\log(df/dx) = \log 4.605 + x * \log 100;$$
$$x = (\log(df/dx) - 0.663) / 2; \text{ from (3) it comes that:}$$
$$df/dx = 100 * dR/dD * Dt / Rt; \text{ assuming } dR/dD = MISWAR \text{ gives:}$$

$$x = (\log(100 * MISWAR * Dt / Rt) - 0.663) / 2 \qquad (5)$$

Equation 5 involves 3 independent variables, MISWAR, Dt and Rt;
the df/dx expression presented in equation 3 can be used to express
them into a single variate, as it can be seen in figure 04. This figure depicts the relationship between the cumulative percentage duration and df/dx for the Ground-floor Slab operation on the Pitcoudie
1 Site. For this site with 29 blocks, total duration for this activity
was 87 weeks and total resource consumption was 1627   hours, giving
and average of respectively 3 weeks and 56.10 hours per block.
Choosing MISWAR = dR/dD as 8 man-hours per week it comes that
df/dx = 29,01 and x = 0,40. Therefore it can be said that during 40%
of the total duration of this activity manpower allocations were
smaller or equal to 8 man-hours a week. Figure 04 would tell that
actually it was necessary to take into account weeks with allocations
somehow greater than 8 man-hours (a greater value of df/dx) to
explain 40% of the total duration; that is, actually this activity
did not have such a great number of insignificant allocations as
predicted by the model. Notwithstanding this, the correlation between
predicted and actual allocations seems to be good.

215

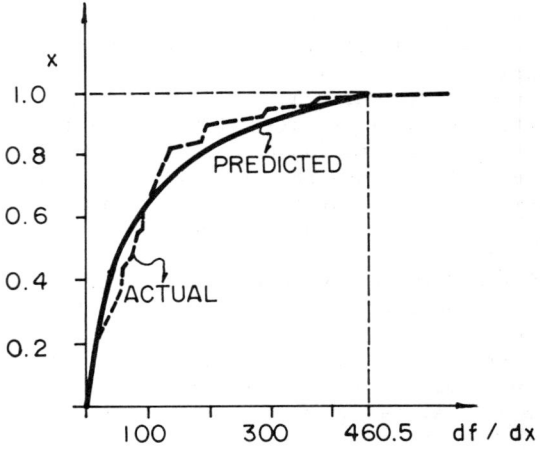

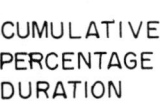

Figure 04. Cumulative Percentage Duration (x) vs. df/dx
Ground-floor Slab Operation, Pitcoudie 1 Site (df/dx is a
substitute for 3 independent variables, Dt, Rt and dR/dD =
MISWAR)

Given Rt and Dt it is possible to predict the cumulative percentage duration associated with any MISWAR. Furthermore, if the duration
of the activity is known for a particular MISWAR, it is possible to
derive the expected duration corresponding to any other minimum
significant allocation parameter. This capability of the model presented in equation 5 removes the need for defining objectively the
most suitable MISWAR for the calculation of durations; any parameter
can be used as the criterion: the resulting duration can then be
adjusted to the corresponding value associated with any other MISWAR.

DISCUSSION
     Suppose that the duration of an activity was only recorded on a
site for the weeks with an allocation greater or equal to 40 man-
hours. This could have been motivated by practical reasons; for example, if the production card method of recording information is being
used, it would only be practical to record the significant allocations of resources to the activities. Given the duration associated
with this MISWAR of 40 man-hours per week and the total amount of
resources deployed on a greater than 40 man-hours/week basis (that
is, the sort of information that the production card method could
have provided),it would be possible to predict, using the models pres
ented in this paper, not only the total duration Dl = Dt, but also
the total amount of resources used by the activity as if smaller
than 40 man-hours/week allocations were also recorded.
     Both the percentage resource usage and t   percentage duration
associated with each magnitude of weekly allocation of resources can
be predicted: however, the order in which these percentages (or the
actual allocations) will occur remain still unknown.

Due to the similar production characteristics of the 90 activities on the 3 sites it was possible to obtain good correlation coefficients for the various resource allocation models that were developed. It seems that despite the differences between the activities on the 3 sites, expressed by the physical and operational features they refer to, common rules governed the allocation of resources to them. One of the most important rules can be put as it follows: resources are not deployed to activities on a constant basis, as assumed by the majority of programming techniques, in particular by the Line of Balance method for repetitive construction; classical "S" shaped curves for the allocation of resources to individual units (houses or blocks) were not found particularly easy to identify on the sites under investigation.

Instead of the more useful "S" shaped curves, only upper and lower boundaries are proposed for the allocation of resources, time period after time period. Further studies are needed to evaluate possible "S" shaped curves for the activity as a whole on site, irrespective of houses or blocks being tackled. It is also necessary to investigate the influence of factors precluding the identification of "S" shaped curves at the level of activities being undertaken at each block or house; it might be worthwhile to sort again the activity sampling data bank in order to have the consumption of labour resources at the level of days rather than weeks, as it was the case for this research work.

ACNOWLEDGEMENTS

Thanks are due to the Conselho Nacional de Desenvolvimento Cientifico e Tecnoloógico, CNPq (Brasil) for the financial support and for the Building Research Establishment (UK) for making the activity sampling data bank available.

REFERENCES

1. Bishop, D. Productivity in the Building Industry, paper to the Royal Society Symposium, November 1971, Building Technology in the 80's, Philosophical Transactions nº 272, London, Royal Society, 1972

2. Forbes, W.S. Production Cost Information, chapter nº 7 in Aspects in Economics of Construction, edited by D.A. Turin, London, George Godwin, 1975, p. 186-201

3. Forbes, W.S. The Rationalisation of House Building, Building Research Establishment Current Paper nº 48/77, Garston, BRE, 1977

4. Heineck, L.F. On the Analyses of Activity Durations on Three House Building Sites, Ph.D. thesis, Department of Civil Engineering, University of Leeds, Leeds, UK, March 1983, 275 p.

BUILDING MARKET ORGANISATIONAL COMPATIBILITY TESTING

Augustin Marian Huska and Ladislav Palenik

The Institute of Economy and Organisation of Building, Bratislava, Czechoslovakia

Summary

Effectiveness of managerial reaction of building firms is, to a considerable extent, dependent on the causal context between the structure of building production, the structure of building technology and the building supplier organisational structure being taken into consideration. The paper demonstrates the method of testing this causal coherence by means of an expertise assessment of organisational compatibility. The testing method allows to take advantage of computer assistance in the mode CAA (Computer Aided Analysis) and CAE (Computer Aided Evaluation).

THE REASONS FOR ORGANISATIONAL COMPATIBILITY TESTING

Only the building firm which has the high adaptive capability of audit to building market flexibility is considered to be prosperous. The problem of organisational adaptation appears as the problem how to find the most appropriate compatability between the structure of building production, the structure of building technology and the building supplier organisational structure. The causal nexus of adaptation expects to find the answer to two kinds of questions :

a. If the building production structure is taken for a constant, what structure of building technology (processual organisation of the construction) is the most suitable and in what departmental structure of supplier it is more effective to realise it, or
b. If the supplier structure is taken for a constant, what structure of building technology it will cope with and what structure of building production it will realise in a most effective way.

To answer these two questions the present data base of building firms has only a few valid pieces of information. Moreover, in the above-mentioned questions there are more qualitative than quantitive aspects which are of importance in searching for organisational compatibility. The data base of a firm can answer the question "what" rather than "how". Therefore it seems necessary to find out and apply such a method of testing which in estimating the existing real and proposed target or model structure of adaptation could employ also statements which are difficult to be quantified and without laborious creation of a new, costly data base. Since these are complex and multi-branch phenomena, it is necessary to use the assessment of various experts. This expertise assessment is transferrable into a simplified fuzzy metrics and its causal-derivable character allows the use of computer assistance in the stage of an analysis (Computer Aided Analysis - CAA), in the stage of designing (Computer Aided Design - CAD) as well as in the stage of evaluation (Computer Aided Evaluation - CAE). The causal context is assessed in an expertise through the so-called organisational compatibility.

THE DYNAMIC MARKET AS SPACE OF CAUSALLY COMPATIBLE FORMATION

If we assume the building market is an area of choice, then we can distinguish at least 2 extensive sub-areas for choice :

a. the sub-area of a customer field (the field of demand for structures) and
b. the sub-area of a supplier field (the field of supply of structures).

Each field can be followed a a self-organising super-cycle consisting of 3 types of sub-fields :

a. the sub-field of demand for construction works defined with parameters of requested utility values,
b. the sub-field of processes of investment planning of demanded structures (investment, utility spatial and financial planning).
c. the sub-field of departments of investment planning (investment institutions).

The supplier field consists of 3 sub-fields :

a. the sub-field of competitive construction works (defined with parameters of constructional properties),
b. the sub-field of processual organisation of building (technology of construction),
c. the sub-field of departmental organisation of building suppliers (the institutional struccture of building suppliers).

In the conditions of co-evolutional self-organising each field as well as each sub-field is autonomous in the area of choice but in the causal nexus it can either accelerate or slow down the opppsite field, it can act either as an accelerator or catalyst on one hand or retarder and inhibitor on the other hand. Causality between the customer and supplier fields ensues from the fact that the sub-field of demand for structures is at the same time the cause - the sub-field of supply/demand of structures acts as a parametric requirement for utility properties of construction works and consequentially there reacts supply in parameters of construction properties project. It is evident that this sub-field forms interface between both fields. (See figure 1.)

Further in this paper we shall deal only with the supplier field of the building market.

Expertise Evaluation of Organistion of the Building Market Supplier Field by means of Fuzzy Metrics

In order to render complexity in organising the supplier field, it is necessary to choose such techniques which allow to get over ambiquity of organisation - forming factors and their low quantifiability by means of expertise evaluation. Through fuzzy metrics it is transferrable into common equivalent - the organisa-tional compatibility degree in a closed interval <0;1>, where 0 equals the full incompatibility and 1 equals the full compatibility of the property. In this interval assessments are transferred into the fuzzy metric scale as follows :

- high compatibility   1.0
- semi-high compatibility   0.7 - 0.9
- semi-low compatibility   0.4 - 0.6
- low compatibility   0.1 - 0.3
- indistinct/zero compatibility   0.0

The expertise assessment and the choice of the value from the scale are accomplished always by an instructed expert. It is an expert in constructional systems/designer for the evaluation of the building production structure, and expert in technology/ technologies for the evaluation of the building organisation structure and an expert for a supplier establishment/ organiser. In evaluation, the assessment values are then, by means of a selective reductional rule, limited only to the so-called significant assessments, ie, those whose organisational compatibility degree is higher than 0.6.

The supercycle of the co-ordination of the building market supplier field is causally derived from the interface state, ie, from the state of the demand sub-field and in a mirror-like way there is derived the choice of the supplier sub-field proper. Then according to the building production supplier sub-field there is derived the choice of the building technology sub-field/the processual organisation of construction. And from this there is derived the choice of the departmental/institutional construction organisation sub-field.

The Expertise Evaluation of the Construction Work Parametrics

The logics of the evaluation algorithm follows from the fact than an expert imagines himself in the postion of a supplier or an

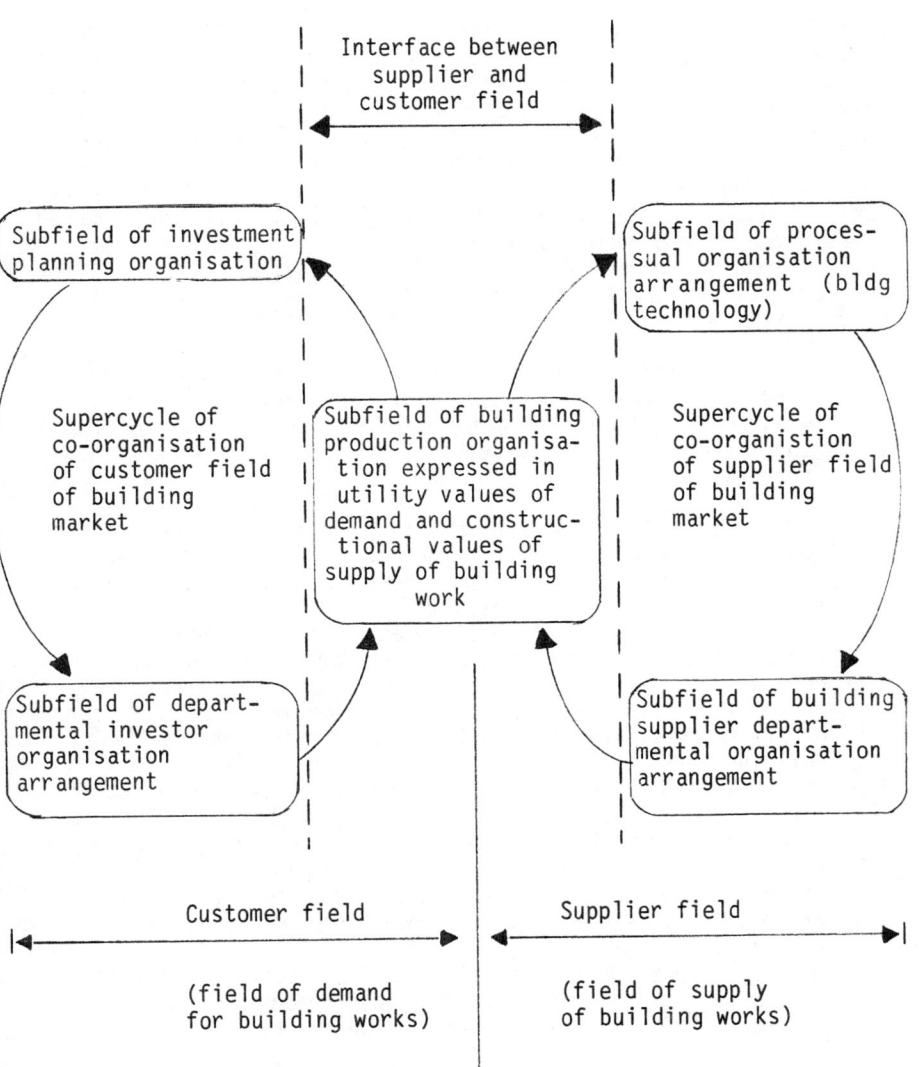

Figure 1. Space of building market

architect who reacts to utility requirements of demand in the algorithm of a construction project/supply of a building work. A building work in its constructional parametrics, whether it has been realised or only designed, can be immediately evaluated using the so-called expertise evaluation method with the application of the already-mentioned fuzzy metrics. it is the indistinct metrics which enables to follow and estimate properties which otherwise are difficult to be ascertained and especially difficult to be transferred to a common equivalent.

The expertise evaluation methodology with the indistinct metrics follows from the precondition that a constructional specialist/an expert - designer or designer engineer will evaluate the successive space/time properties of the building work constructional composition by means of the evaluation maquette/ scale and accordingly he will pronounce estimates on : 1. structural - allocation, 2. subject - specialised, 3. extent, and 4. temporal properties of the construction system of the evaluated building work.

1. In the structural - allocation dimension of the maquette observes flexibility or non-flexibility of the modular composition of a building work and rationality or irration- ality of the territorial layout.
2. In the subject - specialised dimension the maquette observes the share of building and technical work value in the worked comparison as well as the ecological and social burden extent caused by the realisation of a building work and the degree of application of progressive technologies in realising a building work
3. In the extent dimension the maquette observes the utility level of the operational performance (the ability of a quantitative meeting the utility demands compared with the world level), the price level in comparison with the world price as well as the level of the operational profitableness in comparison with the world profitableness of operation of similar buildings.
4. In the temporal dimension the maquette observes both the time limits of construction in the world comparison and the service life of a building work in the world comparison.

The total by expertise estimated values in numerator and the number of evaluating date in denominator forms and aggregative degree of the organisational arranagement of a building work

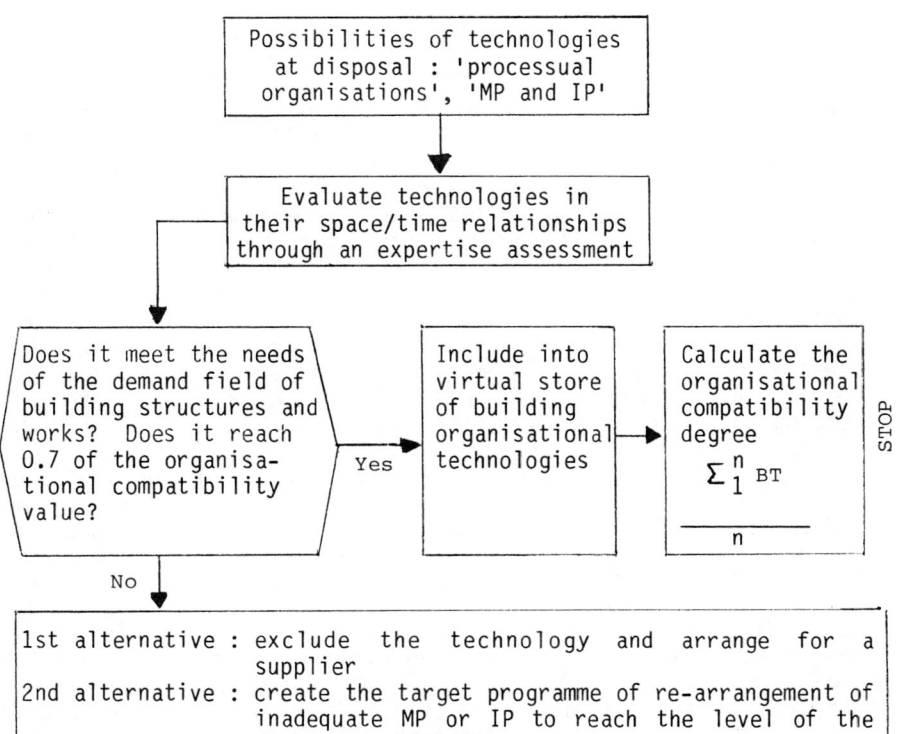

```
┌─────────────────────────────────────┐
│      Possibilities of technologies    │
│        at disposal : 'processual      │
│      organisations', 'MP and IP'      │
└─────────────────────────────────────┘
                    │
                    ▼
┌─────────────────────────────────────┐
│      Evaluate technologies in         │
│    their space/time relationships     │
│    through an expertise assessment    │
└─────────────────────────────────────┘
```

Does it meet the needs of the demand field of building structures and works? Does it reach 0.7 of the organisational compatibility value?

Yes → Include into virtual store of building organisational technologies → Calculate the organisational compatibility degree

$$\frac{\sum_1^n \text{BT}}{n}$$

STOP

No ↓

1st alternative : exclude the technology and arrange for a supplier
2nd alternative : create the target programme of re-arrangement of inadequate MP or IP to reach the level of the desired comptibility

The Expertise Evaluation of Parameters of Building Supplier Departmental Organisation

The evaluation maquette requires first of all the division of organisational institutions of construction into individual departments on the basis of the fact that the departmental arrangement is derived from the virtual store of the processual organisation, namely the so-called material departments (MD1 to MDn) and the so-called intelligence/superstructure departments (ID1 to IDn).

The maquette of evaluation of the level of the institutional organisation enables the organisational experts to deduce a mirror-like arrangement of the departmental organisation from the processual organisation. Also here the values are derived according to space/time properties of the building supplier departments and according to the fact whether they tend to the world level or they are deeply below it.

The selection of the depatmental organisation of the building supply is derived from the reqirements of the processual organisation/technology of construction and the choice of the most adequate microstructural organisational genotypes as well as the most adequate mezzostructural genotypes. The extent of the paper does not make a more detailed description possible, therefore we only mention that the organisational cybernetics derived the whole organisational genofund of the departmental forms both on the microstructural levels (from the basic working groups up to a size of profit centres) and on the mezzostructural level (from the small entrepreneurial firms up to inter-firm integration unions). In the genofund of the microstructural organisation there are 3 organisational genotypes :-

- MESOG1 - isolation-autarky unit
- MESOG2 - monocratic unit
- MESOG3 - functional unit
- MESOG4 - flexible unit

By means of a maquette an expert-organisor evaluates the selected possible departments - MD1 to MDn, or ID1 to IDn, from the aspect of compatibility with the virtual store of building organisational technologies and in the next step the departments which have a lower value of compatibility than 0.7 are excluded by means of a selective reduction rule. Then there is realised the expertise selection of the adequate organisational genotype to the selected set of departments and the total organisational ability degree is determined. See the scheme on page 9.

CONCLUSIONS

The submitted method of testing the organisational compati-bility results in an aggregate organisation arrangement degree

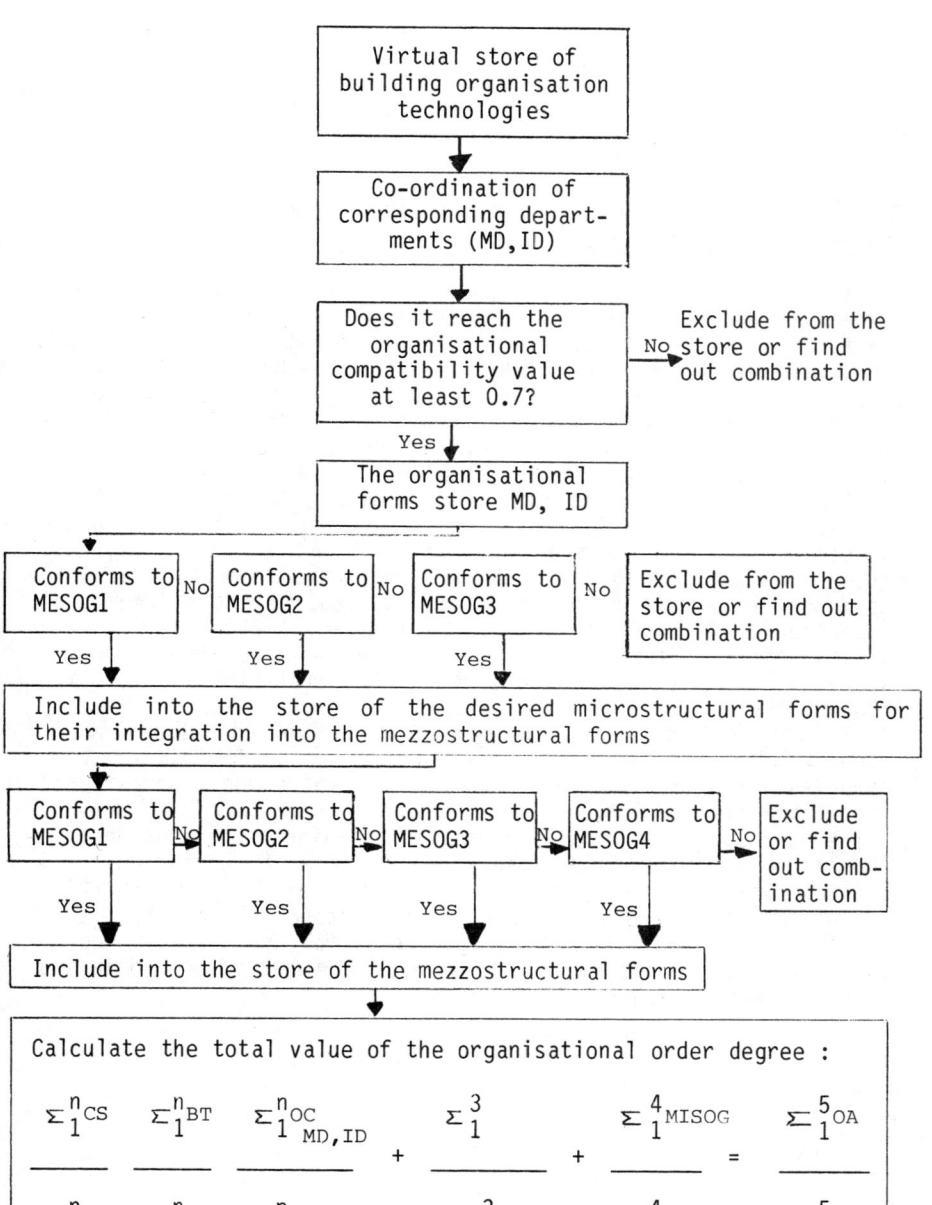

$$\frac{\sum\limits_{1}^{n} c_s}{n}$$

The Expertise Evaluation of the Processual Building Organisation Parametrics/Building Technology

The evaluation maquette requires first of all the division of organisation of a building process into individual flows on the basis of the fact that the flow in question includes such processes which are carried out in the same technology, same time, same space and with the same forces (the unity of time, space, technology, forces and means of production). Thus the individual types of material processes (MP1 to MPn) are separated from the intelligence processes (IP1 to IPn).

The evaluation maquette of the processual organisation level enables the technological experts to derive building technology space/time properties from the constructional characteristics, from the aspect of the structural - allocation dimension as well as from the aspect of subject - specialized, extent and temporal dimensions. The values acquire the similar stratificaton in the closed interval <0;1> according to the fact whether they tend to a world level or they are deeply below it, namely in all evaluated MPs and IPs.

In the next step the so- called selective-reduction rule is used which, from the furter evaluation, excludes those technologies whose properties reach the lower value and organistional compatibility then 0.7.

The selection of the processual building organisation-type (building technology) is closely derived from the constructional characteristics of a building work (mentioned in 'The Expertise Evaluation of the Constructional Work Parametrics' above) in such a way that the existing building technologies are co-ordinated to constructional characteristics of a building work in the following decision-making algorithm :

(OA). Owing to the fact that the method does not need to harness a cumbersome and costly information base but only dialogue algorithms CAA, CAE inserted in a computer and expertise assessments of specialists, it is very operative and flexible. Any building firm using this method can verify the compatibility degree between its real and presumptive structure of building production, th structure of building technologies and the strucure of supplier departments and thus to verify in a quick and more detailed way the causal context and adaptation requirements. In future we shall consider the similar procedure also in te more specifid designing of organisation in Computer Aided Design (CAD) mode.

PQA (PRICE, QUALITY ANALYSIS)

Armando C. Manso; Building Economy and Productivity Dpt;
Manuel S. Fonseca; Building Economy and Productivity Dpt;
Luis Arriaga da Cunha; Computer Dpt

Laboratório Nacional de Engenharia Civil
1799 Lisboa Codex, Portugal

Summary

This paper presents a proposal for an Expert System that prepares both technical reports and economic analyses on bulding and public works.

Reference parameters (quality, quantity, space and typology) are introduced in this model to enable the system to make simulations that will provide economic results and technical reports.

The data base relational model together with optimization algorithms are used as the basic implementation tools for the proposed model.

Sommaire

Cette communication présente une proposition pour un system expert qui prépare les rapports techniques et aussi les analyses économiques dans les édifices et dans les travaux publiques.

Paramètres de référence (qualité, quantité, espace et typologie) sont utilisés dans ce modèle pour possibiliter le système à faire des simulations qui présentent des resultats économiques et des rapports techniques.

Le modèle de registrés des données relationels conjointement avec les algorithmes d'optimisation sont utilisés comme implantation basique dans le modèle proposé.

Keywords

Expert System, Data Bases, Functional Requirements, Quality Levels, Costs.

INTRODUCTION

a) Present situation

Economic evaluation of buildings in their various design stages or during execution is carried out on the basis of automatic calculation programs and by consulting data bases of information on costs, normally constituted by building operations specified by sets of performances of resources involved in such operations.

These procedures lead to the evaluation of costs and quantification of quality parameters resulting univocally from the calculation methods applied and the specifications relating to the technical solutions adopted. The results are typical economic evaluation tables and technical reports, with different degrees of detail (e.g. building elements, technical characterization parameters or technical coefficients).

Applications of these programs in a cost/quality analysis involves a repetition of the calculation for the various solutions to be analysed, quality being evaluated by the comparative reading of the various technical reports prepared. It is an evaluation process by means of trials and successive approximations (Fig. 1) that involves various calculations in which closer and closer values of the desired quality parameter are obtained (final version) until the optimized solution in terms of cost is achieved.

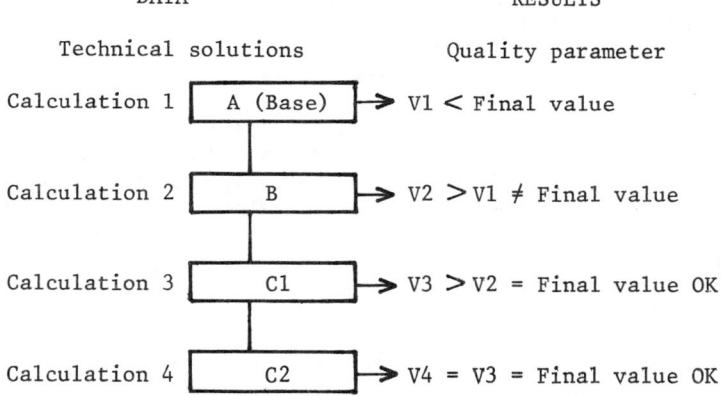

Fig. 1 - Results obtained after sucessive approximations

b) Development proposal
The "Expert System" proposed (Fig. 2) accepts as data the desired quality parameters, as well as the basic technical solutions adopted for the work, indicating as results the costs and respective technical reports of the various alternative solutions to those regarded as basis, and which comply with the quality parameters introduced as data, for each of the different levels required for the possible techological solutions.

Introduction of the data can be done by relational operators ($>$, $<$, $\neq$, $=$), to allow the results to correspond to different ranges of solutions and enable the analyses to be done selectively.

The set of results can be the object of statistical analysis and be presented in tables or schemes prepared by the user in the may best suited to the study to be carried out.

```
         DATA                        RESULTS

Quality parameter and        Alternative technical
basic technical solution          solutions

   Final
   value  ------------>  ┌─────────────────┐
                         │                 │
   ┌─ ─ ─ ─ ─ ─ ─┐       │           C1    │
   │ A (Base)    │----->  │              C2    │   OK!
   └─ ─ ─ ─ ─ ─ ─┘       └─────────────────┘
                                         Ci
```

Fig. 2 - Results obtained for the development proposal

BASIC CONCEPTS OF THE EXPERT SYSTEM
The basic concepts used in this system are as follows:
a) Data base of building operations (Base A)
This consists of a set of building operations defined in terms of performances of materials, equipment and labour and applicable in general
in Building.

   In the present study we refer to a data base that contains building
operations with validity in the construction of buildings, and in
which one can find information for about 90% of the works needed. This
data base is Known as Base A and is developed on the basis of the relational model of information processing.
b) Functional requirements
The functional requirements establish the general and particular conditions to the complied with by the constructional elements, the spaces
and building in general in order that each function is complied with,
and they also define the quality rules that are to be checked.

   Examples of lists of functional requirements to be checked for a
work are as follows:
b.1) Safety requirements
     - Structural safety in building, service and accident situations;
     - Safety against fire hazards and intrusion and use risks.
b.2) Habitability requirements
     - Proofness against solid materials, air, water and gases;
     - Thermal comfort, function of the location of the building and of
       the winter and summer climatic zones;
     - Acoustic comfort (levels of acoustic insulation against air-
       borne noise, percussion noise and noise of the functioning of
       installations);
     - Visual comfort (appearance of the wall facing, lighting level);
     - Adaption to use (resistance to scratching, chemical agents).
b.3) Durability requirements
     - Basic materials (natural durability, treatment or protection,
       mechanical strength);
     - Finishings (external, internal, floor, roof);
     - Window frames (materials, treatment and protection);
     - Installations and equipment (water, drainage, sanitary, electri-
       cal installations);

b.4) Space requirements
- Requirement as regards spaces and equipment (common spaces and dwelling units).

c) Technical characterization parameters

These are values that quantify or qualify the building operations.They are expressed in special units for each characteristic that together enable the various functional requirements to be evaluated.

Example:

Compliance with the functional requirement of thermal comfort can be evaluated through three characteristics that are quantified in each building operation associated with that requirement. Such characteristics are the thermal insulation expressed by the coefficient of thermal transmission in W/m2.K, solar protection, expressed by the solar factor in percentage and thermal inertia expressed by the mass of the element in Kg/m2 as shown in the table.

Thermal comfort requirements		
Thermal characterization of the building operation		
Thermal insulation	Solar protection	Thermal inertia
Coefficient of thermal transmission K (W/m2.K)	Solar factor Fs (%)	Mass of the element M (Kg/m2)

The technical characterization parameters are the values that define each characteristic of a functional requirement, and they are determined for all the building operations constituting Base A and are independent of the location or the type of work where the building operation is executed.

d) Quality levels

These are qualitative indicators that give the degree of compliance with each of the functional requirements by type of work or location, in a scale of VERY GOOD, GOOD, SUFFICIENT, TOLERABLE and BAD and with specific designation as regards the functional requirement concerned.

Classification by quality levels is based on the values of the technical parameters referred to in c) which, together or otherwise, characterize each functional requirement.

Example:

Attribution of the classification VERY GOOD to an internal facing, taking into account compliance with the functional requirement "Safety against fire hazards", in buildings constructed throughout the country, is done for all facings (Base A) that have as technical parameter of the facing materials the characteristic "reaction to fire" belonging to Classes M0 or M1.

The following table gives other quality levels for the other classes (M2 to M4).

231

Technical parameters	Specific designation of the quality level	Quality levels
MO, M1	Incombustible or non-inflammable internal facings	VERY GOOD
M2	Hardly inflammable internal facings	GOOD
M3	Moderately inflammable internal facings	SUFFICIENT
M4	Easily inflammable internal facings	BAD

In the same way, for the same functional requirement the building operations relating to structural or compartmentation elements (Base A) are characterized by the technical parameter for the characteristic "Resistance to fire", from which are defined the respective quality levels.

e) Data base for recording quality levels (Base B)

The quality levels are stored in a data base known as Base B with the following parameters:

1 - Operation code (Data base A)
2 - Type of work to which applied (List 1)
3 - Location (List 2)
4 - Functional requirement to be complied with (List 3)
5 - Specific designation of the quality level (text)
6 - Classification of the quality level of the building operation (List 4)

Parameter 1 gives the building operation code that constitutes Base A.

Example:

The building operation "External walls of perforated brick masonry 30*20*22 with thickness of 22 cm laid with 1:5 mortar" has the code 2037 in Base A.

Parameter 2 refers to the type of work and is organized in the form of a list that may be:

0 - All
1 - Housing buildings
2 - School buildings
3 - Industrial buildings

Parameter 3 refers to the site of the work and is organized in the form of a list that may be the designation of the administrative form of a list that may be the designation of the administrative District, for example:

0 - All
1 - Aveiro
2 - Beja
3 - Braga
4 - Bragança

Parameter 4 refers to the functional requirement to be complied with by the building operation, organized in the form of a list codified and

232

based on the elements mentioned in Paragraph (c) above, for example:
101 - (1= habitability, 01 = Winter comfort)
102 - (1= habitability, 02 = Summer comfort)
  Parameter 5 refers to the specific designation of the quality level
of the building operation, and may be a function of the type of work,
its location and the functional requirement analysed.
  For example, in the case of the functional requirement "Thermal
comfort", this is a function of the winter and summer climatic zones
of the place, and their field of variation in the country is shown in
the following table:

WINTER ZONES			SUMMER ZONES		
Altitude (m)			Altitude (m)		
<200	200-500	> 500	<200	200-500	>500
HIV and HV		HIII to HV	EII to EIV		

  Parameter 6 gives the list of quality levels to be attributed to the
functional requirements analysed, the classification used being as
follows:
  1 - Very good
  2 - Good
  3 - Sufficient
  4 - Tolerable
  5 - Bad
An example of constitution of Base B is as follows:

Oper. Code (1)	Type work (2)	Zone (3)	Functional requirement (4)	Designation qual. level (5)	Quality level (6)
2037	Hous	All	101	HIII	SUFFICIENT
2037	Hous	All	101	HIV	GOOD
2037	Hous	All	101	HV	VERY GOOD
2037	Hous	All	102	EII	GOOD
2037	Hous	All	102	EIII	GOOD
2037	Hous	All	102	EIV	GOOD

f) Reference parameters (Base C)
These are records of quality levels and dimension and space references
that are calculated on the basis of works considered to be reference
works or works with regulation specifications.
  The values determined on the reference works make it possible to

233

obtain reference parameters and the values determined from the regulation minimum quality rules enable minimum reference parameters to be obtained.

This information is stored by the Expert System in a data base called Base C.

Data Bases A, B and C are related to each other as shown in the figure below.

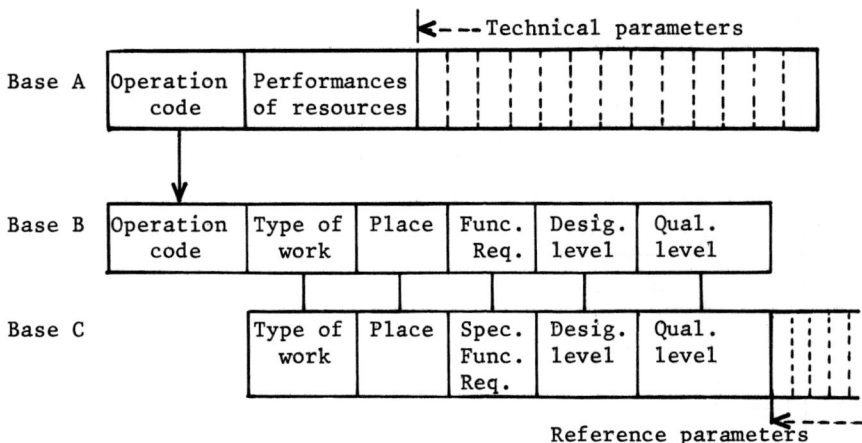

VALIDITY OF APPLICATION
The Expert System is applicable in the construction of buildings and public works whenever:
   1 – There is detailed information on performances for most of the tasks for the construction that are organized in the form of a data base (A) of building operations defined in terms of performance of materials, equipment and labour.
   2 – There are quality rules defined for complying with functional requirements that allow characterization of each building operation. Compliance with a given functional requirement corresponds to guaranteeing that all the operations used comply individually with the quality level required.
   3 – The technical characterization parameters are of a physical kind and are determined by building operation in specific units.

APPLICATIONS OF THE EXPERT SYSTEM
The Expert System is implemented on a set of technical information data bases containing building operations, functional requirements, technical characterization parameters and quality levels that can be accessible by direct consultation. Other information relating to lists of specifications, regulations and measurement rules can be introduced in order to wider the scope of consultation.

Direct applications of the Expert System in the various design stages have the following aims:
a) Evaluation of a project, given its dimension by quantities of building operations. In this case the results obtained will be:

- List of errors or anomalies in measurement, in relation to another project with reference values, e.g.
  . No earth shifting
  . Excessive amount of reinforcements in structural elements
  . No painting or facing in building elements
- Technical report on the solution planned, giving associated costs and quality parameters
- Report on alternative technical solutions owing to variations in the quality parameters introduced selectively by:
  . values
  . cancellation of values
  . above a value
  . below a value
  . between two values
  This report makes it possible to relate the values and quality parameters with the technological solutions and costs associated with them.
- Calculation of costs involved in alternative solutions (maximum, minimum, average and basic solution planned).
- Optimization of measurement of the work due to technological and dimensional alterations.
b) Evaluation of a set of projects, given their measurements by quantities of building operations (evaluation of projects in tenders). In this case the results obtained will be:
- List of errors or anomalies in measurement of each of the projects (see a) above).
- Technical report for each project, giving associated costs and quality parameters.
- Technical report on the set of projects, giving deviations of costs in relation to a reference project (typical reference projects to be analysed).
- Evaluation of overall quality indices of each project, given the weighting formula of each functional requirement.
c) Evaluation of projects in relation to a reference project. In this case the results will be:
- Calculation of the quality level of the project in relation to the reference project, with identification and justification of the deviations detected.
- Quantification of the deviations in costs in the ligh of the quality of the solution of the project analysed.
- evaluation of cost variations for the same quality levels.

SOFTWARE
The system is implemented based on a computer relational data base model.
The non computer specialist user can question the data bases formulating any logical condition on the data registered.
Technical reports, based on the information selected by the user, can be formated and prepared by that same user, already adapted to the design phase for which they are intended.
As an example technical reports can provide:

. Descriptive lists of adopted and/or alternative technological
  solutions
. Indicators of quality levels
. Exceptional analyses for detecting anomalies, on the basis of the
  values of the reference parameters chosen.
The calculation of real and alternative costs has a direct equiva-
lence with the various solutions that comply with the technical report.
The software enables the results to be presented with different levels
of detail, e.g., overall values, building elements, chapters, sub-
chapters, building operations grouped by type of resource, basic resources, costs and its incidence on the total costs.

Finally, statistical analysis of the results are available, as required by the user.

REFERENCES
1. D'HAVÉ, R. - Méthodes de comparaison et de classement des offres
   sur base des performances. Perform concept in building. Proceedings
   of the 3rd. ASTM/CIB/RILEM Symposium, Vol. 2, pg. 53-64. Lisboa,
   LNEC, 1982.

2. LABORATÓRIO NACIONAL DE ENGENHARIA CIVIL. Classification of tenders
   for design-construction contracts on basis of integrated criteria.
   An instance of application. Proc. 83/11/7330, Lisboa, LNEC, 1985.

3. ORSHAM, OSSY M.; SPACE - Quality-Cost in building. CIB W55 BUILDING
   ECONOMICS 13th. Meeting. Edimburgo, U.K., 1985.

THE MAINTENENACE OF INFRASTRUCTURAL SERVICES IN HOUSING
DEVELOPMENT FOR LOW INCOME GROUPS IN KENYA

Nicky M Nzioki, MSc

Department of Land Development, University of Nairobi, Kenya

Summary

This paper is divided into four sections. The first section
begins with an overview of what infrastructure maintenance is by
explaining some categories of infrastructure system. The second
part deals specifically with the current policies of the maintenance of infrastructure services in Kenya by discussing the
government capital investment in urban development and the
highlights of recent surveys on the provision and maintenance of
infrastructural services for low income housing development.
Several constraints related to infrastructure maintenance in the
country are described in the third section, while the final
section contains a series of recommendations for the local
authorities to institute if the current state of the level of
maintenance of infrastructural services is to improve appreciably.

Sommaire

Cet article est divise en quatre parties. La premiere commence
par un apercu general sur l'entretien de l'infrastructure.
L'auteur presente qualques examples de la deterioration de
l'infrastructure, et une analyse des parties constituantes d'un
systeme infrastructural.
La deuxieme partie traite specifiquement la politique actuelle
de l'entretien des services infrastructuraux au Kenya. Il y a une
discussion sur l'investissement par le gouvernement kenyen dans le
domaine de developpement urbain, et aussi sur la conclusion des
enquets recentes faites dans le domaine de la fourniture et
l'entretien des servies infrastructuraux etablis pour le
development d'hebergement a loyer modere.
La troisieme partie est consacree a une analyse des contraintes
relatives a l'entretien de l'infrastructure au Kenya.
La derniere partie de l'article comporte une serie de
d'ameliorer sensiblement le niveau actuel de l'entretien de
l'infrastructure.

Keywords

Infrastructure, maintenance policy, infrastructure deterioration, infrastructure system, urban development, public utilities,
standards, inventory, community participation.

INTRODUCTION

The theme of this paper is to show that capital investment in infrastructure is very expensive, particularly when considered as a proportion of total investment by a developing country. The investment, whether it is building municipal sewer mains or a road, will start to deteriorate the moment it is completed - for like all manufactured projects it has a life cycle. The life cycle of infrastructure will be influenced by wear and tear due to use and abuse, natural deterioration of the materials and the frequency of maintenance and care. When we consider which of these can we influence and which plays the biggest part - the likelihood is maintenance.

The purpose of this paper is therefore to outline the attempts made by the government in the provision and maintenance of infrastruture for housing development and the constraints encountered. The scope of the paper is limited to the maintenance aspects of urban infrastructure which are the responsibility of the local authorities in most urban centres.

BRIEF REVIEW OF INFRASTRUCTURE SYSTEM

Infrastructure is the collective term for the fixed installations and facilities to support a habitable environment for human settlement (1). Infrastructure services for housing development are considered to include the provision of community facilities and utilities, that is water supply, electricity (estate and street lighting), sewerage services, surface drainage, road and public transport, open spaces and refuse collection.

Infrastructure deterioration has several meanings. In its most publicised form, infrastructure deterioration refers to the gradual decaying of public service facilities. Some likely causes have been identified (2). First, although they may have been properly designed and well-built originally the infrastructural services/facilities become worn out from use. In some cases decay may have been hastened because of a lack of maintenance or neglect. A second aspect of the problem involves the capital facilities which, despite adequate maintenance, become obsolete as a result of changing needs, demands, standards or technology. These systems cannot meet today's standards nor handle the loads that population increases have placed on them. Overall the major component of our capital plant deterioration/decay appears to be that of decay from lack of maintenance. In most local authorities the problems stem more from overloading because of unexpected rapid growth and incremental unplanned extensions to systems that were never envisioned to be the backbone of major capital plants. The backlog in many local authorities is tremendous, and as quickly as the worst problems are resolved more problems surface. Therefore we can no longer build public facilities without planning for their maintenance.

Infrastructure systems contain three generic components : an origin, where some desired material or service is created or generated, a 'destination', where the material or service is transformed into useable products or converted into waste products for disposal, and a 'distribution network' from where they will be processed.   These three components are more clearly evident in some systems than others.   Wastes, for example, are generated in individual buildings, are transported by truck and sewer pipes to centralised processing facilities and there are either removed from the system for burial or dilution or chemically treated and converted into a useful item such as fuel or fertilizer (recycling).   Drinking water is generated in reservoir fed fil-tration plants, transported to individual buildings and there utilized for a wide variety of purposes - including drinking, washing and flushing wastes.   Electricity is created at central generating stations, transmitted through power lines to invididual buildings and it is then converted to some useful purpose such as activating light fixtures, running motors, and providing energy for electronic devices (2).
   Most of the recent concern about urban infrastructure decay has focused on the physical aspect. Yet the deteriorating performance may have its roots in the institutional and social aspects of infrastructure rather than in the physical systems themselves. Many of the improvements that modern technology can make possible will require a more comprehensive view of urban infrastructure than that of the past.   Most infrastructure experts agree that there is no national infrastructure crisis but rather a variety of infrastructure conditions varying in severity from local authority to local authority.   There is an urgent need not only for money for the repair and replacement of those portions of today's infra-structure that have deteriorated, but also for a more system-integrated approach to the technology of urban infrastrucure. There is a pressing need to redefine the requirements for urban infrastructure in a way that will encourage invention and innovation (3).

CURRENT POLICIES ON THE MAINTENANCE OF INFRASTRUCTURE SERVICES IN KENYA

   If the urban population continues to grow in Kenya at the same rate as during the decade between the censuses of 1969 and 1979, it will reach a total of 10 million by the year 2000 and account for over 25 per cent of the population, compared to 15 per cent in 1984.   This represents a massive shift from rural to urban areas and raises the question of where these new city-dwellers will work and where they will settle so as not to exceed the capacity of the towns to accommodate new residents.   Provision of transport net-works will be crucial to reinforce the marketing and other links between farms and market centres. Water supplies and electricity will be essential to permit such centres to run, as will housing

for the expanding urban population. In building such infrastructure, local materials, labour-intensive methods and
inexpensive designs must predominate especially in low cost
housing (4).

In recent years, Government capital investment of urban
development has not kept pace with the growth of urban population
- public investment in urban infrastructure - measured by gross
approved development estimates for water, urban land, energy,
roads and housing, together with gross fixed capital formation by
municipalities - declined as a share of gross fixed capital
formation from 14.3 per cent during the period 1971-77 to 12.1 per
cent for the period 1978-84 as given in Table 1. Per capita
spending fell from K£610 for each new urban resident during the
first period to K£507 per new resident during the second period,
measured in 1984 prices. Capital spending declined according to
both measures for five of the six sectors examined. The exception
is gross fixed capital formation by the city of Nairobi from 1981
onwards. As a result more and more urban families are lacking
basic urban infrastructure and the backlog in the provision of
such services has been steadily increasing. Data from the annual
rent survey, for example, show that the proportion of urban
dwellings serviced with water, sewage and electricity fell
dramatically between 1978 and 1982 (4).

Table 1. Public capital expenditure on urban infrastrcuture
          1971-84 (Constant 1984 Prices)

	1971-77			1979-84		
Sector	Capital Expend. (K£M)	Expend per capita (K£)	Share(%) total invest	Capital Expend (K£M)	Expend per capita (K£)	Share(%) total invest
Municipalities	90.6	221	2.0	184.4	261	2.7
Water	61.5	82	1.3	87.9	72	1.3
Urban land	14.1	19	.3	10.1	8	.1
Energy	34.2	45	.7	23.8	20	.3
Roads	357.2	115	7.8	451.1	80	6.5
Public housing	96.2	128	2.1	80.0	66	.2
Sub-total :	653.8	610	14.3	837.3	507	12.1
Total Investment	4585.6	-	100.0	6944.5	-	100.0

Source : Economic Management for renewed growth; Sessional Paper
         No 1 of 1986; Ministry of Economic Planning and Develop-
         ment, Nairobi, Kenya Government Printer, 1986, p.49

Most local authorities in Kenya do not appear to have a policy
on the maintenance of the bulk of their infrastructural services.

Recent surveys by the Housing Research and Development Unit of the University of Nairobi (5) and Sanitation Survey by the Ministry of Water Development (6) have found that most community facilities were not planned for in most of the low income housing programmes. Water supply in most of the estates was found insufficient. Present sewerage facilities are inefficient due to constant block-ages as a result of inadequate water in the sewer mains. Road and surface drainage in major public housing developments is hardly satisfactory. Recent floods as witnessed in April 1986 in Nairobi demonstrate the inadequacy of the present road and surface water drainage maintenance standards. Although the local authorities cite lack of funds as the root cause of the maintenance problems, it has been suggested there is complacency that has blinded the authorities against the roles they are meant to play in their towns and urban centres. The following editorial from one of the local dailys summarises the general public out cry about the poor maintenance of infrastructural services in Kenya.

"....Not one municipality, township or urban centre in the entire country can proudly proclaim that it is spotless. Street pavements, flower gardens, recreation areas, parks, name it, all are rubbish dumps. Cigarette butts, sweets and chocolate wrappings, maize cobs, newspaper cuttings, etc., are thrown carelessly everywhere. And the authorities look without any apparant concern. Probably the worse hit are public toilets. These are outright health hazards. Blocked sewers and flooded floors meet anyone entering them and the stench hits like a physical blow......" (7).

Refuse collection has been a major issue in all the local authorities. For Nairobi, the capital city, the situation grew so bad that late in 1986, His Excellency the President appointed a special cleanliness task force for Nairobi to save the city from becoming 'a huge dumping ground for all kinds of refuse'. While the situation in the capital has been arrested, the other munici-palities are yet to convince the public that something is actually being done.

Provision of infrastructure - mainly streets, water supply and sanitation - is a major component of housing development for low income groups in Kenya. About 75 per cent of the urban population has reasonable access to safe water supply from networks provided with individual connections, standpipes and kiosks, or from wells and pumps. Water-borne sewerage is available for some 25 to 30 per cent of the urban inhabitants. Some of the larger towns and urban centres own and operate their own water supply and sewerage works, but most networks are operated by the Ministry of Water Development (MOWD) in co-operation with the local authorities, who are in charge of billing and collection. Responsibility for urban roads belongs to the local authorities, but because of their precarious financial situation, road maintenance has become deficient (8).

Management, operation and maintenance of water and sewerage systems vary in quality from one local authority to another, from very good to inadequate. The Water and Sanitation Research Division of the Ministry of Water Development is now assisting local authorities with management training courses, regular supervision and technical training.

In 1983 the Ministry of Water Development (MOWD) carried out a sanitation survey of all gazetted towns in Kenya. With the exception of larger towns like Nairobi, Mombasa and Kisumu, the survey involved a house-to-house inspection of the sanitation facilities present as summaries in tables 2 and 3 (9)

Table 2 : Sanitation coverage in all Gazetted Towns in Kenya (1983)

Type of Sanitation	Number of people served	
	Incl. Nairobi	Excl. Nairobi
Waterborne Sanitation		
Sewerage	1,378,315	390,652
Septic Tanks	690,998	359,102
Aqua Privy	1,202	1,202
On-Site Sanitation		
Bucket Latrines	29,532	14,001
Pit Latrines	1,360,794	1,151,233
No. of Sanitation Units	31,311	31,311

Source : Water and Sanitation Research Division, MOWD

Table 3 : Number and Type of Sanitation Facilities in Gazetted Towns in Kenya (1983)

Type of Facility	Number of Sanitation Facilities	
	Incl. Nairobi	Excl. Nairobi
Waterborne Sanitation		
Sewerage Schemes	45	43
Septic Tanks	113,164	22,533
Aqua Tanks	82	82
On-Site Sanitation		
Bucket Latrines	5,769	702
Pit Latrines	149,900	93,429

Source : Water and Sanitation Division, MOWD

CONSTRAINTS ON INFRASTRUCTURAL MAINTENANCE IN KENYA

There are difficulties in an assessment of the size and scope of the nation's maintenance of infrastructure problem : the following four constraints appear to be the most crucial.

First, appropriate standards are a key issue. Standards capable of helping us measure the condition or adequacy of condition are not readily available in each key infrastructure area of concern. Where standards do exist, they often fail the test of relevancy, that is, generally time has passed them by. They reflect primary engineering criteria and/or criteria generated by producers of infrastructure. Rarely do they reflect the consumers' interests. Rarely do they concede the necessity to balance safety with costs and/or the need to respond to varied community needs in addition to the facility or system under consideration. In Kenya it appears difficult to enforce national standards because the local authorities enjoy a large degree of autonomy and are free to adopt or not standards proposed by the central authority. For example, the local authorities can prevent the low-cost housing provisions of the Building Code (Grade II by-laws) from becoming effective, simply by not defining zones where they apply. Another problem is that standards for sanitation come from different sources (mainly the Public Health Act, the Building Code and the various town planning laws and regulations) and are therefore ruled by several authorities. This makes their modification or relaxation a complex and lengthy process (8).

Secondly, projections of infrastructure need and condition are premised in part, on projections of use and related population and economic growth trends. Forecasting is not a precise science, the state of the art in demographic and economic projections, is at best marginal and at worst subject to 'mature intuition' than to predictable skills. Given this fact, it is almost impossible to secure 'hard' or reliable data concerning the number of future infrastructure users and/or the relevant characteristics associated with the intensity of their use pattern (9).

Thirdly, very few local authorities have a reasonably comprehensive inventory of infrastructure facilities - let alone a comprehensive analysis of the condition of these facilities. Several difficulties like absence of plans, drawings for certain infrastructure facilities and lack of a clear maintenance policy as to what are the maintenance needs or priorities (9).

The fourth constraint is a financial constraint in most local authorities with excessively high backlog on revenue collections especially for rates and water charges which includes sewer and refuse collection fees. This inefficient system of collection of these charges has contributed to the most rate of decay for of the services provided due to lack of funds for their maintenance (4). Another factor is the low pricing of the utilities and services provided by the local authorities. Failure to charge realistic prices which reflect the real costs of operation, maintenance and long-term capital stock replacement has contributed to the low funds available for maintenance of infrastructural services in most low-income housing estates (4).

RECOMMENDATIONS

Maintenance of infrastructural services in low-income housing development present a challenge and several policies have to be pursued. Local authorities should establish a maintenance policy for the maintenance and management of all their infrastructure. The objective of such a policy would be directed primarily at the improvement of shelter and the creation of complete human settlements and thereby ensuring a public health programme aimed at removing the various health hazards through the provision of clean drinking water, frequent refuse collection, and sewerage maintenance. The local authorities would be expected to adopt and follow more appropriate engineering standards for the construction of infrastructure such as roads, water supplies and sewage systems. The revised standards reflect the relative scarcity of capital and the trade-off between lower capital costs initially and higher maintenance costs later. Also, in order to stretch available funds to the maximum, resources would be concentrated on those projects which offer lower construction maintenance costs per beneficiary.

The Ministry of Local Government should issue instructions to local authorities to revise the pricing of utilities and services to ensure that they reflect the real costs of operation, maintenance and long-term capital stock replacement.

The private sector's contribution in the provision of facilities and services for low income groups should be recognised, encouraged and brought within legal bounds by the introduction of appropriate regulations and administrative procedures and better communication between public and private operators.

Local authorities should compile a comprehensive inventory of infrastructure facilities complete with details of the conditions of each facility.

For a successful maintenance programme of services in low-income housing development, community participation is crucial in the operation and maintenance of the facilities. In the case of communal systems, this involves regular operations, maintenance, occasional repairs, and the collection of funds to pay for recurrent expenses. The degree of community participation and willingness to pay for improved service levels by contributions of money, labour, or materials depends fundamentally upon the household income levels and perceived needs. Whether a feasibility study results in a project that properly meets the needs of the community depends on the accuracy, completeness, and timeliness of information exchanged between the residents and those who are conducting the feasibility study (10).

REFERENCES

1. Sykes, J.B., The Concise Oxford Dictionary, 7th Edition. Oxford, Oxford University Press. 1984.
2. Patton, C.V., Infrastructure decay in the United States, Built Environment, Vol. 10 No. 4, 1984, pp. 231-244.
3. Eberhard, J.P., et al; A conceptual framework for thinking about urban infrastructure; Built Environment, Vol. 10 No. 4, 1984, pp. 253-261
4. Republic of Kenya; Economic management for renewed growth; Sessional Paper No. 1, Nairobi, Kenya Government Printer, 1986.
5. Housing Research and Development Unit, Field survey evaluation report of sites and services schemes in Kenya. University of Nairobi, Nairobi, 1977.
6. Republic of Kenya; Report of the national sanitation survey by the Water and Sanitation Research Division, Nairobi, Ministry of Water Development, 1983.
7. The Sunday National, 25 January 1987 ; "Why are our Towns so Extremely Dirty". Editorial comment; Nairobi.
8. Nankman, Piet; 'National Housing Strategy for Kenya', Memorandum to the Sub Task Force on Planning, Infrastructure and Construction including Building Code, Washington DC, The Urban Institute, 1986.
9. Saad Yahya and Associates; 'National Housing Strategy for Kenya : Policy guidelines for planning infrastructure and construction', A report for the Ministry of Works, Housing

and Physical Planning, Nairobi, 1987.

10. Kalbermatten, J.M.; et al : Appropriate sanitation alter-
natives; A Planning and Design Manual; World Bank Studies in
Water Supply and Sanitation; No. 2. Baltimore, John Hopkins
University Press, 1982.

WORK AND TIME STUDIES IN PREFABRICATION OF CONCRETE PANELS

Svetlana Vuković, MTSc, Arch

University of Novi Sad, Faculty of Technical Sciences, Yugoslavia

Summary
This paper deals with the procedures of work and time studies in a real technological system for prefabrication of concrete panels - - walls and ceilings for housing construction.

The time measuring of work and time losses at the working place for concreting, for workers and machines, has been carried out according to the chosen time classification, corresponding to the nature of the process.

The measured data on effective working time and time losses have been processed using statistical methods as to establish the nature of the empirical distribution.

The carried out analyses show that the empirical distribution of measured data for the effective work and time losses can be, only in some cases, approximated by the normal distribution.

Sommaire
On discute en article les procedures de l'étude du travail dans un système technologique réel pour la prefabrication des panneaux en béton armé - murs et plafonds pour la construction des logements.

On a fait la mesure de temps du travail et de temps des pertes à la place d'ouvrage pour bétonné, pour les ouvriers et les machines, fondé à une classification choisi de temps, qui a correspondé le plus à la nature de processus.

Les données mesurées pour le temps du travail effective et pour le temps des pertes, avaient procedé avec des methodes statistiques pour établir la nature de la distribution empirique.

Les analyses faites montrent que la distribution empirique des données mesurées pour le travail effective et des pertes de temps peuvent, seulement en quelques cas, être approximées avec la distribution normal.

Keywords
Prefabrication, Concrete Panels, Distribution of Working Times.

INTRODUCTION
All research works presented in this paper are based on the results

of one real technological system. The investigated system MONTASTAN is today, in Yugoslavia, the only large panel reinforced concrete system which uses the charge of hollow ceramic blocks, whose production is carried out by industrial methods in a stationary factory. The system is designed for application in housing construction.

BRIEF REVIEW OF CARRIED OUT RESEARCH
Technological process in prefabrication of concrete panels
The reinforced concrete panels for walls and ceilings, intended for housing construction, are produced by industrial methods in a factory. This industrial production is characterized by an organized technological process, appropriate mechanization and equipment, good work organization, continual production and permanent quality control. The tested production of concrete panels develops along two tehnological lines. They are two aggregate flows where the elements and moulds are transported by bridge-cranes. The workers have their permanently determined working places. The working places on the technological lines (the ceiling elements are produced on one, and the wall panels on the other) are determined in advance for all working operations.

The production process of panels (walls and ceilings) starts with transportation and storing of basic and accessory material, preparation of moulds and placing steel reinforcement for concrete elements. The production technology and adopted prefabrication methods correspond to the type of elements - the wall panel (internal bearing wall or facade wall) and the floor ceiling. In this technology it is possible to define the following working operations:

- preparation of metal moulds;
- making mortar layer (on the internal side of the wall or for the surface treatment of the ceiling); for the facade panels a special tratment can be used;
- placing hollow ceramic blocks, depending on the type of panel (the blocks are different for the walls and ceilings);
- placing and binding of steel reinforcement bars;
- charging moulds with concrete; vibration of concrete;
- making mortar layer (at wall panels);
- resting before accelerated hardening;
- accelerated concrete hardening (by steam curing of concrete);
- resting of elements after accelerated hardening;
- extraction of elements from the moulds;
- correction of elements and finishing touches (building-in of carpentry and locksmith´s trade at the wall panels);
- storing of elements in the depot.

The said production of panels presents a cyclic process: the production is carried out by repeating working stages and working operations, stated above.

The process of concreting panels will be especially worked out in further analysis. The prepared mould charged with reinforcement steel bars and concrete blocks is transported to the vibro-table by bridge-crane, where the mould is filled with concrete and the fresh concrete mass is vibrated. The fresh concrete mass from the concrete factory, being outside the workshop, is transported to the workshop by a monorail basket. The finisher-distributor distributes the fresh concrete mass into the mould, placed on the vibro-table. In the workshop there are two vibro-tables, one on each production line. The fresh concrete mass is vibrated on the vibro-table. Filling and vibration are carried out using two stages. When the vibration of concrete is finished, the mould, with the fabricated element, is transported to mortaring (for the wall panels) or directly into chambers for steam curing (for the floor ceilings).

Applied research methods and measuring of work times
The designed scope of production on the lines for producing panels and the efficiency of these lines must be checked trough the fund of working time. Connected with this objective is the organized study and measuring of work - the time measuring of work and time losses on the technological lines.

Various methods can be used for studying the process of work in prefabrication. The application of different methods for studying the production process depends on the type of work, degree of the separation of production operations, as well as on the final objective for the purpose of which the study takes place.

As one of the research objectives was to establish time losses in the process of work in order to influence upon the process by certain measures, it was adopted to use the method of graphical photo-survey, i.e. the working day timing. By using this method it is possible to carry out the analysis of studied time (of work and losses), which can offer detailed data on the work on lines to the production organizers. On the basis of such analyses, it is possible to make technological and organizational improvements on the lines for prefabrication.

For the study (measuring) of work time, special forms are used, which are arranged in accordance with the method of studying the process of work. The forms must match the process which is studied, as well as the adopted time classification (of work time and losses). Usually the forms for the purpose of studying a choosen process are printed separately.

The studies were carried out on both production lines. It was foreseen to measure the whole day production continually. The working places shown in Table 1. were included in the study plan.

All working operations are precisely included in the graphical photo-survey: effective work, preparatory-final work, as well as time losses: waiting for machine, waiting for material (element), waiting and breaks during the work and other organizational problems. The graphical photo-survey enables a simultaneous observation of several workers. At the places for concreting the work of two workers was recorded. The duration of each working operation was recorded by the line graph. The accuracy of 1 minute for recording the time corresponds to the process in prefabrication. The obtained results were further processed by statistical methods.

Table 1.   Study plan of times on technological lines

Working places	Technological line	
	Wall panels	Ceiling panels
Preparation of panels	P_1	P_1
Preparation of panels	P_2	P_2
Concreting	C	C
Mortaring	M	-
Bridge-cranes	BC (C/125 and C/100)	

*In this analysis the working place for concreting is especially discussed, where concreting is carried out by the finisher-distributor and the vibration of elements also takes place.

Processing of the obtained data by statistical methods

The measured times of work and time losses, obtained by measuring on the real system, are given by numbers and represent variables.   These measured sizes form an empirical distribution of data can be grouped for analysis.

Measuring the times of work and losses was carried out under essentially the same working conditions of the technological system.   It can be said that the universe is homogeneous, i.e. an appropriate statistical analysis of the study results can be done.   The authentic (measured) data on times are given in minutes and are designated with x_i.   The data were grouped and absolute and relative frequencies (statistical probabilities) of the measured values were determined.

The frequency distribution can be graphically presented using the histogram of frequencies, as it is, for example, shown in Figures 1. and 2. for the effective work and the time losses at the working place for concreting wall panels.

A insight into the empirical distribution will be obtained by using statistical parameters calculated from ungrouped data.   They are: the arithmetic mean, the standard deviation, the coefficient of variation, the coefficient of asymmetry and the coefficient of excess.
The statistical parameters of the empirical sample class can be determined by means of the central moments as:

$$M_1 = \bar{x} = \frac{1}{n} \sum_1^n x_i \qquad \ldots \ldots (1)$$

$$M_2 = \sigma^2 = \frac{1}{n} \sum x_i^2 - \bar{x}^2 \qquad \ldots \ldots (2)$$

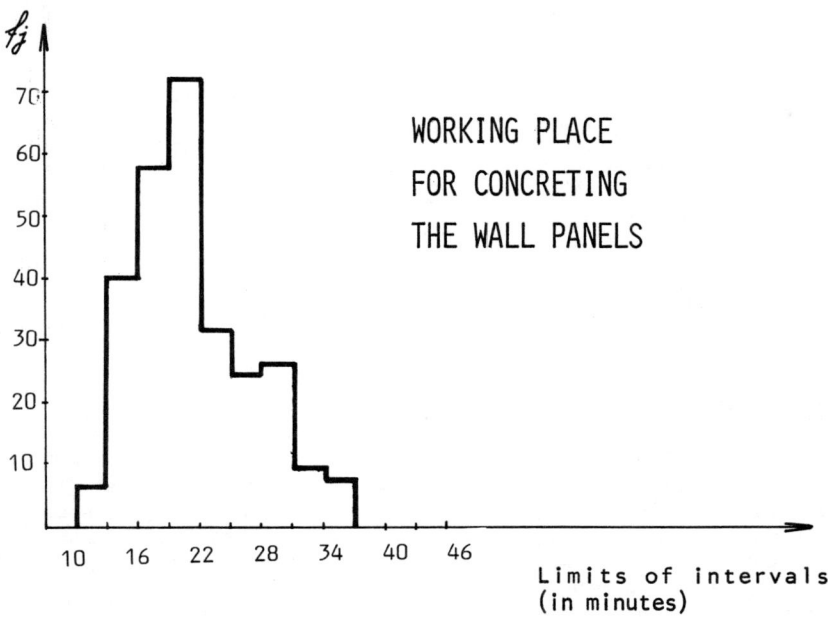

WORKING PLACE
FOR CONCRETING
THE WALL PANELS

Limits of intervals
(in minutes)

Figure 1. Histogram of frequencies for effective work

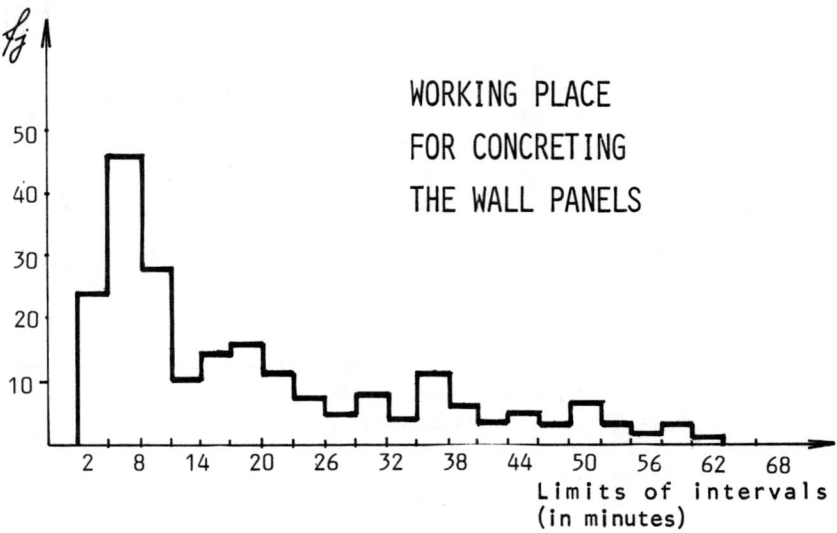

WORKING PLACE
FOR CONCRETING
THE WALL PANELS

Limits of intervals
(in minutes)

Figure 2. Histogram of frequencies for time losses

251

$$M_3 = \frac{1}{n} \Sigma x_i^3 - \frac{3}{n} \bar{x} \Sigma x_i^2 + 2 \bar{x}^3 \qquad \ldots \ldots (3)$$

$$M_4 = \frac{1}{n} \Sigma x_i^4 - \frac{4}{n} \bar{x} \Sigma x_i^3 + \frac{6}{n} \bar{x} \Sigma x_i^2 - 3 \bar{x}^4 \qquad \ldots \ldots (4)$$

$$a = \frac{M_3}{M_2\ 3/2} \qquad \ldots \ldots (5)$$

$$e = \frac{M_4}{M_2^2} - 3 \qquad \ldots \ldots (6)$$

Approximation of empirical data by normal distribution

The empirical distribution can be approximated by a chosen theoretical distribution. Testing of the approximation quality of one empirical distribution by the theoretical distribution is most effectively carried out using statistical tests. Pearson's χ^2 (Chi-squared) test was applied in this work. It is considered that the Chi-squared test is very strong when you should estimate the difference between the empirical curve and a theoretical curve by which the approximation is done. The obtained value χ^2 is compared to the critical values of χ_α for a chosen level of significance and the determined number of degrees of freedom.

In this experiment the measured times of work and work time losses were taken as variables. The observed values for all wall panels with and without openings for windows and doors, for wall panels with openings for windows and doors and for the ceiling panels on the working place for concreting were analysed and the approximation of the empirical distribution by normal distribution carried out. Theoretical frequencies were calculated for class intervals of 3 minutes. The χ^2 (Chi-square) values were compared with the critical values χ_α^2 for the level of significance $\alpha = 0,01$ and the estimate was done.

The results of the χ^2 (Chi-squared) test for the approximation by normal distribution are shown in Tables 2,3 and 4.

All dates were statisticaly processed by means of electronic computer and known formulas and standard computer programs were used.

DISCUSSION OF THE RESULTS

From the analysis of the obtained results it can be concluded that the empirical distribution of work times and work time losses in prefabrication only in some cases can be approximated by a normal distribution. For a greather number of the tested variables the approximation by normal distribution fails.

In our opinion in statistical test for this sort of operations the choosen level of significance $\alpha = 0,01$ is appropriate.

Further research works are required in order to find out which theoretical distributions might be used for the approximation of empirical distributions of work times and work time losses in prefabrication.

Table 2.   Results of the χ^2 (Chi-squared) test - approximation by normal distribution.
Working place for concreting all wall panels
with and without openings for windows and doors.

Name of variable	n	$\bar{x}$	s	Number of degrees of freedom	Calculated value χ^2	Criterion χ^2 $\alpha = 0,01$
Effective work	280	20,996	5,525	6	49,709	49,709 > 16,812 **
Preparatory-final work	50	22,879	9,367	3	8,574	8,574 < 11,345
Total work	280	24,764	10,999	9	216,850	216,850 > 21,666
Waiting due to machine	28	13,000	16,406	1	24,865	24,865 > 6,635
Break due to material	66	13,545	16,087	2	134,669	134,669 > 9,210
Waiting for object of work	135	20,637	18,661	10	91,802	91,802 > 23,209
Organizational problems	3	/	/	/	(*)	/
Lack of discipline	45	16,177	12,421	2	5,225	5,225 < 9,210 **
Vis maior	/	/	/	/	/	/
Total losses	218	21,651	20,880	12	212,627	212,627 > 26,217
Work - Losses	278	42,194	26,791	16	189,624	189,624 > 32,000

(*) χ^2 (Chi-square) impossible - number of intervals lower than 4.

** Approximation by normal distribution - g o o d.

Table 3.   Results of the χ^2 (Chi-squared) test - approximation by normal distribution.
Working place for concreting the wall panels
with openings for windows or doors.

Name of variable	n	$\bar{x}$	s	Number of degrees of freedom	Calculated value χ^2	Criterion $\chi^2_\alpha = 0,01$
Effective work	118	21,915	5,806	4	9,640	9,640 < 13,277 **
Preparatory-final work	23	25,000	9,224	/	(*)	/
Total work	117	26,119	11,137	6	72,802	72,802 > 16,812
Waiting due to machine	10	/	/	/	/	/
Break due to material	23	13,173	13,796	/	(*)	/
Waiting for object of work	55	21,490	20,025	3	10,790	10,790 < 11,345 **
Organizational problems	/	/	/	/	/	/
Lack of discipline	25	15,719	12,765	/	/	/
Vis major	/	/	/	/	/	/
Total losses	90	19,577	17,763	6	86,699	86,699 > 16,812
Work - Losses	115	40,356	21,906	8	43,506	43,506 > 20,090

(*) χ^2 (Chi-square) impossible - number of intervals lower than 4.

** Approximation by normal distribution - g o o d.

Table 4. Results of the χ^2 (Chi-squared) test - approximation by normal distribution. Working place for concreting the ceiling panels.

Name of variable	n	$\bar{x}$	S	Number of degrees of freedom	Calculated value χ^2	Criterion $\chi^2_\alpha = 0,01$
Effective work	153	19,686	4,381	3	9,052	9,052 < 11,345 **
Preparatory-final work	28	28,464	20,087	/	⊛	/
Total work	150	23,013	10,582	6	70,445	70,445 > 16,812
Waiting due to machine	18	20,388	27,964	/	/	/
Break due to material	57	9,280	6,421	/	/	/
Waiting for object of work	70	14,585	13,467	5	10,865	10,865 < 15,085 **
Organizational problems	3	/	/	/	/	/
Lack of discipline	19	13,526	8,624	/	/	/
Vis maior	2	/	/	/	/	/
Total losses	116	18,095	17,834	8	31,245	31,245 > 20,090
Work - Losses	152	39,243	23,626	12	88,041	88,041 > 26,217

⊛ χ^2 (Chi-square) impossible - number of intervals lower than 4.

** Approximation by normal distribution - g o o d.

REFERENCES

1. Fisz, M.S., Probability Theory and Mathematical Statistics, John Willy Inc, New York, 1963.

2. Flašar, A., Vuković, S., Brana, P., Study of technological processes in Building, Special Edition, No 8, Faculty of Technical Sciences, Institute for Industrialised Building, Novi Sad, 1985. (in serbocroat).

ORGANISATION OF CONSTRUCTION PROJECTS IN NIGERIA

Prof. Kunle Ade Wahab, Professor of Building

Obafemi Awolowo University, Ile - Ife, Nigeria

Summary
The paper discusses the evolution of project organisation in Nigeria
noting major lapses - absence of adequate planning, distorted pattern
of investment, unrealistic design standards, dominance of Foreign
designers and contractors, haphazard fund flow and general inefficiency.
These have prevented the construction industry from being responsive
to the needs of the clients in particular and the national economy in
general.
   In an attempt to find solutions to these lapses, the paper examined
contract procedures at Obafemi Awolowo University which emphasise the
use of committee system, for examples: users committee, projects
advisory and projects implementation committees for planning, controlling and monitoring of projects and reports for management.
   The adoption of such a procedure is recommended for the public and
private clients which are still at the development stage of procuring
construction projects. Such clients may include government departments
and their parastatals (ministries of construction, education, health,
defence and housing corporations) others are commercial banks, multi-
national industries and development companies.
   For small and medium size clients engaged in off-peg projects, the
use of project management consultancy as a direct service to clients is
advocated in place of the traditional separation of design consultants.
A guide to such a service to the client is provided to conclude the paper.

Sommaire
Cette etude discute l'evolution de l'organisation des projects au
Nigeria en notant des defauts ma jeurs - mangne de plan suffisant, plan
deforme d'investissement, niveaux irrealistes de projects, predominance
des entrepreneurs et des dessinateurs etrangers, circulation dangereuse
des fonds et l'inefficacity generale. Tous ces defauts out empeche la
construction d'etre sensible aux besoins des clients en particulier et
l'economie nationale en general.
   Afin de resoudre ces problemes, cette etude a examine les procedes
d'entreprise a l'Universite d'Obafemi Awolowo on l'on met l'accent sur
l'emploi du systeme de comite par exemple comite d'usagers, comite con-
sultatif et executif qui se charge de la planification et du controle
des projects et qui rapporte pour la direction.
   L'adoption de tel procede est a recommander aux clients publics
et reserves, qui sont encore en niveau du developpement d'obtenir des
projets de construction. Tels clients peuvent renfermer des

departements gouvernement aux et leurs annexes (ministeres de la
construction, del'education, de la sante des defenses et des
corporations de logement) les autres sont les banques commerciales,
les industries multinationales et les compagnies de developpement.
Pour les clients de dimention petite on moyenne et qui
s'engagent aux projets horschamp, l'emploi direct de consultation
de direction des projects aux clients est mieux que le systeme
traditionnel de separer les consultants dessinateurs.
Afin de conclure, on a mis le guide a tel service aux clients.

Keywords

Project Organisation, Adequate Planning, Design Standards,
Foreign Designers and Contractors, Fund Flow, Inefficiency, Construction Industry, Clients' Needs, National Economy, Contract
Procedures, Tenders' Manual, Committee System, Users, Projects
Advisory, Projects Implementation, Controlling, Monitoring, Reports
for Management, Development, Procuring Construction Projects,
Government Departments, Parastatals, Housing Corporations, Commercial Banks, Multi-national Industries, Development Companies, Small
and Medium Size Clients, Off-peg, Project Management Consultancy.

INTRODUCTION

The organisation of building projects have evolved throughout
the world. The primitive man of prehistory modeled his shelter along
the line of the cave; later each family unit used their own efforts
to build a family house while the construction of civic buildings was
the joint responsibility of all or selected members of a given
community(1). At the emergence of colonial intervention, public
projects were undertaken using direct labour approach through the
public works departments. Today, contract systems of varying options
have become the vogue. Each of the above mentioned evolutionary
stages had peculiar styles and varying degree of project organisation
and contract procedures.

The objective of this paper is to provide information on the
current procedures for the organisation of construction projects in
Nigeria, highlighting major bottlenecks and lapses which have made
the industry inefficient. In addition, the paper presents details
of contract procedures currently adopted by Obafemi Awolowo
University with a view to recommending its adoption by the large
clients since it has been shown to provide adequate responsiveness
to the needs of the University. Since such a procedure may be too
cumbersome and expensive for small and medium size clients, a project
management consultancy approach is thought to be feasible for these
groups. The implications of adopting the two procedures are explored.

THE NATURE OF THE CONSTRUCTION INDUSTRY

A brief discussion on the roles of the construction industry and
the manner in which its operations are carried out will facilitate an
understanding of its complex organisation and an appreciation of its
problems.

The importance of the construction industry

One of the greatest exponents of the interrelationships between
the building economy and the national economy has argued that the

importance of the construction industry can be appreciated from its size; that it provides predominantly investment goods and that government itself is the largest client(2). These three attributes when coupled with the in-built employment generation directly or indirectly and the fact of the multiplier effects of construction projects show convincingly the importance of this sector. In another analysis the issues were summarised as follows:

"The construction industry of any country straddles the public and private sectors of the economy. This is because most human activities involve a building or structure of one kind or the other: For examples - Housing, Education, Health, Religion, Entertainment, Sports, Agriculture, Industry, Transport, Commerce, Governance etc., in fact all amenities of civilization lay claim on the construction industry"(3).

For such a sector, it is not surprising that many developed countries have found it necessary to put their searchlights on it, in order to improve its operation, organisation and output. For the developing countries such efforts appeared to have been very limited and consequently the sector has become totally unproductive and infested with avoidable malpractices(4). Both in the developed and developing countries, the manner in which the industry operates its business has largely been responsible for major lapses and into this we now turn.

Procedures for organising construction projects

In its simplest form, project development and execution brings a contractual relationship between two "people" - the client (public or private) and the contractor. In this exercise, there are many available options. Traditionally, the Architect takes charge of the design and the contractor organises the site activities and production. Under this system, full drawings and specifications with a Bill of Quantities are prepared before tendering. The contractor then submits a tender taking into account all implications for construction. A construction contract is thereby created by an offer and acceptance as it is in any other contract.

The Package Deal, the Design and Build as well as Management contracting options are expected by their advocates to provide some improvements on the traditional approach. One advantage claimed by the proponents of the above options is that the contractors' knowledge of the building process is released to the design process. Other advantages include: buildability, savings in time, shorter lines of communication, informality in ironing out conflicts etc. Bad experiences have occured where the client was unable or unwilling to institute adequate checks and balances on cost escallation and exploitation(5).

Another option which has become attractive is the introduction of an independent person into the construction process to 'weld' both the Architects and the contractors together. In this system - Project Management Consultancy Service, the Project Manager is the team leader. He applies management skills and techniques to the organisation and control of all aspects of the project in order to optimise the use of resources to produce a well designed and generally well constructed facility which will meet the clients requirements of function, cost and time budget and future maintenance(6).

259

At this juncture, it needs to be pointed out that the modern building is a product of the efforts of many professionals, whose contributions have been aptly described elsewhere as follows(7).

"The Architects designs the proposed building on paper in terms of its spatial orientation, physical form and aesthetic appeal. The aesthetic considerations are sometimes overdone. When this happens, costs can be excessively high as the Sydney Opera House has shown. The Planner ensures that the building is well located in terms of essential facilities. The Land Surveyor identifies the relative topography of the site. It is on this topography that both the Architect and the Planner base their own work. For commercial projects involving reasonably high investment, the Estate Surveyor is expected to provide the initial feasibility studies before the commencement of the architectural design. He also comments on the viability of the location. The management of the project may also be entrusted to him. The Quantity Surveyor relates cost to design; advising on the specification of materials and components. The emphasis is to design to a cost and not costing a design. He is regarded as a kind of "accountant" in the building industry.

The structural engineer works closely with the Architect to ensure stability. He must address himself to the interplay between such requirements as aesthetic and structural form, division of space, optimum cost solutions and provision for services' runs. The Services' Engineer is concerned with the users comforts such as cooling, acoustics, as well as the lighting and plumbing of the building interior.

The Professional Builder is required in a variety of decisive roles within the building organisation. These are mainly in the area of middle and top management functions, estimating, buying, production planning, quality and costs control. Thus the dream of the client, conceptualised by the architect is realised through physical construction by the professional builder. It is after this, that critics and admirers can have a field day! Owing to the expertise which the professional builder possesses, the potential building owner may approach them for a speedy delivery of his building. Even when the formal procedure as described above is adopted the experienced professional builder may offer alternative construction solutions to those provided by the architect. The professional builder is enabled to achieve his goal by the comprehensive nature of subjects he must study in the University."

Project Execution in Nigeria

The procedure for projects development and execution in Nigeria, both in the public and private sectors is similar to that of the United Kingdom. A detailed analyses have been described elsewhere including short-comings and possible solutions(8). Only a brief review will be attempted here. The changes that have been made to the United Kingdom's practice are very often to assist in sharp practices resulting very often in corruption tendencies. Such practices occur in the selection of inappropriate tenderers; sale of contracts without the consent of the client/consultants, the granting of mobilization without adequate security, inflated tenders, and shoddy workmanship(9).

Except for the ministry of Defence almost all government projects are handled on behalf of the user ministry by the Federal Ministry of Works and Housing. On the other hand the organised private sector such as banks and business enterprises rely either on the private consultant or in-house arrangement. In the later such organisation have established premises/property department/unit to take charge of all their construction activities. Such departments are usually headed by Estate/Building Surveyors who perform other duties in addition to project management, for example repairs and maintenance of owned or rented premises.

The informal sector rely on varied systems of labour only contracting and or self supervision of building development.

There is little doubt that the bulk of all the construction activities can be traced to government projects. Until the oil boom, substantial proportion of design of government projects are carried out by technical officials of the Federal or State Ministry of Works and Housing. Similarly the construction of such projects were handled by the Public Works Department (PWD) of the same ministry by direct labour. Up to about 1970 each ministry of works particularly at the Federal level had a high concentration of highly trained and experienced Architects, Builders, Quantity Surveyors, Engineers, in direct employment. Nowadays only a few of these calibre of staff remain in government service and they very often firm out even works which can still be handled by them to outside consultants with whom they are in league. Besides the appointment of consultants and contractors has been politicised for selfish gains. Consequently the administration of government projects is loose and the control expected of professionals in the public sector projects has become grossly inadequate.

The problems which developing countries like Nigeria face in the management of construction projects may be traced to the blanket copying of the structure of organisation similar to that of their colonial masters. This was done with little or no change in the structure of component parts to reflect the special problems peculiar to their local situations. In many cases the adopted structure is inappropriate because of differing objectives and constraints(10). In addition, there is the problem of inadequate executive capacity which has been identified to have slowed down the pace of development(11). The shortage of manpower in the construction sector had led to two other major problems. First, the conditions for the registration of contractors for government projects have not been enforced leading to the use of untrained and emergency contractors with dissastreous consequencies; collapsed building, shoddy workmanship, abandoned contracts, corruption etc. In theory, contractors bidding for government projects are expected to possess technical knowledge, relevant experience from previous similar jobs successfully completed, organising ability, good reputation, access to adequate capital (funds, plant and machinery). The second problem relates to the domination of the industry by foreign expertise. The situation

was recently described elsewhere as follows:
> "Due to the slow and sometimes inaccessible technology
> transfer and the lack of effective indigenous competition,
> the construction activities in Nigeria has been dominated
> by the foreign expertise. The sky-line of Lagos and major
> state capitals as well as the new Nigeria Capital City at
> Abuja continued to display the presence of foreign partici-
> pation. In the case of Abuja, projects were conceptualised
> and designed for foreign participation except for the low
> rise residential buildings. In actual fact many of the
> consultants often recommend international contractors,
> sometimes justified by the speed with which the project
> had to be executed. In addition there were until recently
> turnkey projects for Hotels; Airports, Hospitals, etc.
> The Sharaton Hotels at Abuja and Lagos, the Concord Hotel
> at Owerri are few examples of turnkey projects."(12)

It is against the above background that the need arises to formulate new strategies and guidelines for the organisation of construction projects in Nigeria with a view to utilizing construction
resources in such a way as to achieve a systematic procedure in
project development, implementation and evaluation. As a first
step, the procedure adopted at the Obafemi Awolowo University will
now be examined.

TENDERS MANUAL OF OBAFEMI AWOLOWO UNIVERSITY, ILE-IFE
The tender's Manual(13) of Obafemi Awolowo University, Ile-Ife
is the first of its kind in Nigeria. This document was approved by
the University's Tenders Board in December 1977 and became effective
in February 1978. It has since become a major reference work since
then. The National Universities Commission in Nigeria adopted similar
document for controlling and monitoring capital projects development
among Federally funded Universities and other Institutions.
It is divided into seven chapters as follows:
Procedure for Registration of Consultants and Contractors
Chapter one deals with the following issues:
  (i)   the keeping of a register of consultants and contractors who
        are judged to have met the stipulations of the University;
  (ii) the award of contracts subject to registration;
  (iii) the removal of any consultant or contractors who break any
        laid down regulations;
  (iv) the eligibility of registration subject to previous
        registration with either the Federal or State Government;
  (v)   the classification of contractors into categories according
        to their capacities to finance projects;
  (vi) the advisory roles of Projects Advisory Sub-committee in
        recommending those to be so registered with the University.
Power to Award Contracts
Chapter two deals with the following:
  (i)   The body empowered by the University Governing Council to
        award building contract above ₦20,000 by the Tenders Board.
  (ii) Identification of Awarded Contracts by name and number as well
        as by type - new works, or minor capital projects.
  (iii) The power to award or reject any tender and in the case of

rejection of all tenders, the power to invite fresh tenders.
  (iv) The eligibility for award of contract subject to previous
       registration.

Procedure for Initiating Capital Project

Chapter three deals with the following issues.

  (i) The definition of capital projects which includes building and
      engineering projects as indicated in the approved Capital
      Budget.
 (ii) Those charged with the responsibility to initiate capital
      projects. These include, the Development Committee who shall
      consider recommendations from the Faculties/Departments/Units
      and decide on order of priority.
(iii) The roles of users committee to discuss and collate details
      of faculty/departmental needs.
 (iv) The responsibility for preparing project briefs which is
      vested in the Capital Projects Unit in the office of the
      Vice-Chancellor for the consideration and approval of the
      Building Works and Estate Committee.
  (v) The roles of Projects Sitting Sub-Committee in selecting
      appropriate sites for each project in line with the campus
      master plan.
 (vi) The roles of the Project Advisory Sub-committee with respect
      to recommendation of consultants for each project to the
      Building Works and Estate Committee.
(vii) The duties of Consultant Quantity Surveyors in the preparation
      of contract documents such as Articles of Agreement, Conditions
      of Contract, Bill of Quantities. He is also expected to submit
      to the Secretary of Tenders Board, pretender estimate. This
      will be opened at the same time as the invited tenders.
(viii) Criteria for selecting and appointing consultants based on
      previous experience, number of years of experience, existing
      commitments and revision after a previous complaint.
 (ix) Need for as-built drawings.
  (x) Condition for resident consultancy.

Procedure for Tendering and Award of Contract

Chapter four deals with the following issues:

  (i) Responsibility for inviting tenders and types of tender to
      be adopted such as open, selective or negotiated tendering.
 (ii) Guide for selecting contractors to include evidence of
      relevant skill, personnel, experience, equipment, adequate
      finance, current commitments, and capacity to undertake
      additional contracts.
(iii) The selection of contractors and their own confirmation of
      interest in the contract as a condition precedent to invita-
      tion to tender. Thereafter each contractor is sent tender
      documents – drawings, articles of agreement, bill of
      Quantities, trade preambles and general specifications and
      a tender form to be completed.
 (iv) The issuance of tender notice; the completion of tender form,
      the preparation of conditions of contract. At the close of
      tender, the tender's sub-committee opens the tenders received
      and have them stamped officially in the presence of the
      Quantity Surveyor and the Consultant Architect.

(v)   Report on opened tenders to be prepared normally by the Quantity Surveyor in strict confidence within a specified time limit. The report is expected to cover the following
- (a) Tender sum and its computation
- (b) Errors in the tender
- (c) Tenderer's experience of similar work
- (d) Experience of personnel of the tenderer in relation to the work
- (e) The equipment available to the tenderer for the work
- (f) Tenderer's reservations (if any)
- (g) Time required to take possession of the site
- (h) Completion period 'if noted'
- (i) Provisional and prime cost sums (if any)
- (j) Rating of tenderer in relation to other tenders with reasons.

(vi)   Attendance of Quantity Surveyors and Consultants at Tenders Board to explain and comment on Tenders Report respectively. These experts may be asked to withdraw from the meeting when decision on the award is being made. The Board to give reasons where contractor not recommended gets the award.

(vii)   Notification of successful tenderer as well as others as of necessity by the Secretary to tenders board who also should complete the contract documents which includes.
- (a) General University Condition for the award of contracts
- (b) Special condition relating to the contract
- (c) Working drawings – architectural, structural electrical etc.
- (d) Priced Bill of Quantities
- (e) Letter of award of the contracts
- (f) Articles of Agreement

Administration of Contract

Chapter five deals with the following issues.

(i)   Maintenance of contract register by the Directorate of Council Affairs.

(ii)   Director of Physical Planning to prepare progress reports based on records of site meeting and present same to Projects Implementation Sub-committee which may make recommendations on same to Building Works and Estate Committee.

(iii)   Frequency of site meetings pegged at monthly and report sent to University officers and Chairman Project Implementation Sub-committee.

(iv)   Certificate of completion issued by the Director of Physical Planning upon practical completion. Maintenance period specified as six months.

Financial Procedure Relating to Tenders

Chapter six deals with the following:

(i)   The University Bursar is expected to provide on request for funds for projects approved by the University Council.

(ii)   Fees for consultants are to be in accordance with Federal Government Scales of fees currently in force or otherwise negotiated initially or as a result of abandoned or modified projects.

(iii)   Condition for making mobilization or Advanced payments as

approved by the Tender's Board.
- (iv) Interim payments to reflect work done, refund of mobilization/Advanced payment and retention money as authenticated by the Director of Physical Planning.
- (v) Final payment will be paid after completion of contract on the recommendation of the Director of Physical Planning after all maintenance work has been satisfactorily completed.
- (vi) Insurance of Works and Materials by contractors as a condition for above payments by the Bursar.
- (vii) Conditions for payment of variation on contract to include previous approval by Tenders Board, if still within the contract sum or counsil, where cost limit is being exceeded.
- (viii) Audit Inspection of all certificates and payments is necessary before payment.
- (ix) Insurance of completed building by the Bursar.

Committees on Contract Awards

Chapter seven deals with the following committees.

- (i) Projects Users Committee
- (ii) Building Works and Estate Committee
- (iii) Projects Advisory Sub-Committee
- (iv) Projects Siting Sub-Committee
- (v) Tenders Board
- (vi) Tenders Sub-Committee
- (vii) Projects Implementation Sub-Committee

The terms of reference of four of the above committee and their membership – Building Works and Estate Committee, Projects Advisory Sub-Committee, Tenders Board and Projects Implementation Sub-Committee are indicated in Appendixes A – D.

ADOPTION OF OBAFEMI AWOLOWO UNIVERSITY'S TENDERS MANUAL

It would have been obvious by now that the exposition of the Tenders Manual procedure adopted at the Obafemi Awolowo University is a step in the right direction. It demonstrates that even the developing countries can correctly diagonise their problems and then adopt such solutions that is in their own interest. It needs to be pointed out that, like all committee systems of policy guidelines, enormous resources are called for. It is anticipated that the procedure is capable of being adopted by large organisations such as practically all Ministries of Works and Housing, Ministries of Defence, Health, Education etc., Government parastatals such as Universities, Corporations, Utility Companies, large private sector organisations such as commercial banks, multi-national companies, industries as well as property developing companies. These organisations/firms are expected to have one thing in common – that they need to be at a stage of rapid construction development.

It is not expected that small and medium size clients who are engaged in a rather few number of projects would be able to take advantage of the elaborate procedures described above. It will be too expensive and too complicated for them to adopt. It is for this reason that another attempt is made below to evolve a strategy that can take account of the needs of these categories of clients. In its place a project management consultancy is advocated instead. The where with all for this is briefly described below.

As mentioned above, project management consultancy is new and it has evolved as a private sector approach to management of construction projects as a total package instead of adopting the consultants versus contractors approach. A medium size client can engage the services of such a consultancy firm who will in turn manage the design, production and construction activities connected with the project including time scale and cost scale balancing at a negotiated fee.

Training requirements for project management

The existing degree programmes in Building, Quantity Surveying, and Estate Management come closest to the educational training required for a career in project management consultancy. Fortunately there exists many Universities in Nigeria and other developing countries offering courses in construction, the products of which can be encouraged to specialise in this area. Apendix E shows Nigerian Universities offering courses in Building and Construction related disciplines.

For adequate coverage of training in project management, the following major subjects must be included in the curriculum of studies: Land Law, Building Construction and Materials, Principles and practice of Quantity Surveying, Costing and Estimating, Principles and practice of Valuation, Principles and practice of Town and Country Planning, Construction Planning and Control, Management in Principle and Practice, Land Economics, Contract Administration; Structural Design, Budgeting and Financial Planning. In addition to the undergraduate courses mentioned above, Masters degree in Construction Management, Real Estate Appraisal and Construction Economics offer yet another opportunity for training those wishing to specialise in Project Management.

Organisation of Project Management

Project Management requires good organisation, leadership and co-ordinating ability on the part of the consultant.

To conclude this paper an attempt is made in table 1 below to provide a guide to Project Management Services.

Table 1: Guides to Project Management Services

1. Agree basis of appointment with client including terms of reference.
2. Determine the brief for the project with client.
3. Identify site, including its acquisition if necessary.
4. Arrange appointment of other professional team.
5. Arrange meeting of all the members of the project team with the client and her representatives.
6. Arrange site investigation.
7. Commission the Architectural/Engineering design with the recommended spatial relationships, floor area, specification and costs.
8. Carry out pre-investment studies.
9. Obtain preliminary cost estimate from the Quantity Surveyor.
10. Carry out market, economic and viability studies including financial requirements, income and expenditure pattern.

11. Update designs and establish the control budget.
12. Consider planning consent within the required statutory services requirement.
13. Conclude site investigation.
14. Consider type of tendering and type of contract.
15. Arrange Insurance for the project.
16. Prepare tender documents.
17. Finalise Budgetory control
18. Select contractor including Tender Report Analysis.
19. Conclude Viability analysis.
20. Arrange for performance bond.
21. Arrange for site possession.
22. Take inventory of existing building on site prior to demolition.
23. Conclude sub-contractor 'suppliers' contracts.
24. Apply for all temporary and final services required.
25. Carry out cash flows for stage payments.
26. Attend all site meetings and monitor resource positions - materials, labours, plant and management.
27. Analyse and approve all variations and report financial implications to client.
28. Arrange marketting strategies - lease, sales, and lettings.
29. Obtain certificate of practical completion.
30. Arrange occupation of premises.
31. Obtain as-built drawings and hand to client.
32. Analyse final cost.
33. Ensure necessary testing, inspections etc. during defects liability period.
34. Approve final account.
35. Analyse the project and supply feedback to the client.

CONCLUSION

The developing countries must now devote a good proportion of their resources to formulating indigenous strategies for efficient organisation of the construction industry so as to optimise the output of this important sector. This paper has suggested a number of ways to help in the achievement of such a goal. Hitch free, Project Execution requires adequate planning, working cooperation among relevant professionals in the industry. It is to be realised that Building process throughout the world has become so complex that it requires the corporate efforts of all the participants, Developing countries must not be left out.

ACKNOWLEDGEMENT

This paper has benefited from the ongoing research project on "Target Output Standards and Productivity of Nigerian Contractors" based in the Department of Building, Faculty of Environmental Design and Management, Obafemi Awolowo University, Ile-Ife Nigeria. The research is partly funded by the University Research Committee and partly by grant from the EEC-Ife-Trieste Universities Linkage Programme.

REFERENCES

1. Wahab, Kunle Ade (1983a) "More than Shelter" An Inaugural
    lecture delivered at the University of Ife, Ile-Ife Nigeria,
    In Press, University of Ife pp. 2.

2. Hillebrandt, Patricia M. (1974) "Economic Theory and the
    Construction Industry" London: McMillan, 1974.

3. Wahab, Kunle Ade (1983) "Specific Training Programmes for the
    provision of construction skills for African Region "Paper
    presented at United Nations Economic Commission for Africa
    Expert Group meeting on Regional Human Settlements Training
    Facilities and Mechanism. Addis Abbaba, November, 1983 p. 3.

4. The Nigerian Institute of Building (1987) "Finding Appropriate
    Remedies to the issue of Defaulting Contractors Handling Govern-
    ment Projects". A memorandum submitted to the Honourable
    Minister for Justice and Attorney General of the Federation of
    Nigeria. Unpublished, June, 1987 p. 4.

5. Titmus, P.D. (1982) "Design and Build in practice" Building
    Technology and Management, April, 1982 pp. 9.

6. The Chartered Institute of Building (1979) "Project Management
    in Building" Occasional Paper ISSN-0306-6878. CIOB 1979 pp. 10.

7. Wahab, Kunle Ade (1983a) Ibid p. 6 - 8.

8. Wahab, Kunle Ade (1987) "Alternative Strategies for Project
    Execution" In Press:Construction: The Journal of the Federation
    of Building and Civil Engineering Contractors in Nigeria.

9. The Nigerian Institute of Building (1987) Ibid p. 9 - 11.

10. Wahab, Kunle Ade (1977) "Construction Overseas, Hisorical cost
    information in Nigeria" Building and Quantity Surveying Quarterly
    1977 p. 61.

11. Wahab, Kunle Ade (1977) "Helping the indigenous building entre-
    preneurs" Quarterly Journal of Administration, Ife, 1977 p. 55.

12. Wahab, Kunle Ade (1987) "Urbanisation in developing countries
    carrying out Urbanisation Plans and Promoting Intervention in
    International Cooperation - The Case of Nigeria" Journal of
    Environmental Studies in West Africa. Vol. 6, 1987 p. 12.

13. University of Ife, Ile-Ife (1978) "Tenders Manual" University
    of Ife Press, 1978.

BUILDING, WORKS AND ESTATE COMMITTEE - OBAFEMI AWOLOWO UNIVERSITY

Terms of Reference:

1. To advise Council on the overall development of the University
   site and on the implementation of building, works and site programmes for which funds have been approved by Council;

2. To approve on behalf of Council plans and drawings for the
   construction or structural alteration of University buildings,
   works and site amenities, and the siting of buildings, roads,
   parks and other common amenities;

3. On behalf of Council to nominate for appointment, architects
   and other professional consultants as may be required for a
   project in accordance with the procedure laid down by the
   Tenders Board;

4. To supervise on behalf of Council all capital works after the
   contracts have been awarded;

5. To perform such other duties as may from time to time be
   required of it by the Council.

Membership

Vice-Chancellor   (Chairman)
Deputy Vice-Chancellor
Two Members of the Council (not being members of the Senate
   elected to the Council)
Two members of the Senate appointed by the Council on the
   recommendation of the Senate.
Chairman, Projects Advisory Sub-Committee
Chairman, Projects Implementation Sub-Committee
Chairman, Siting Sub-Committee
Two Students representatives appointed by the Students Union
Director of Medical and Health Services
Registrar
University Librarian
Bursar
Director of Physical Planning
Manager, Division of Maintenance Services

In Attendance

Director, Council Affairs
Principal Assistant Registrar (Tenders)
Architect
Planner
Quantity Surveyor
Civil/Structural Engineer

APPENDIX B

PROJECTS ADVISORY SUB-COMMITTEE — OBAFEMI AWOLOWO UNIVERSITY

Terms of Reference:

1. To advise the Building, Works and Estate Committee on all matters relating to Capital Projects as may be referred to it;

2. To discuss with the Deans and Heads of Departments principally concerned with a building project, the details of accommodation and other requirements of the project and to advise them on the possibility of their proposals within the limits of expenditure allowed;

3. To examine all architectural and engineering drawings prepared by Consultants and report to be Building, Works and Estate Committee on the acceptability of these drawings in relation to the briefs given to the consultants and bearing in mind the need for economy in the execution of capital projects;

4. To examine and report on estimates of cost of capital projects;

5. To advise and assist in the control, programming and execution of the University's capital works programme;

6. To perform such other duties as the Vice-Chancellor or the Committee may from time to time require;

7. The Dean and Heads of Departments principally concerned in a project to be co-opted when the project is under consideration

Membership
Chairman, nominated by the Vice-Chancellor
Chairman, Project Siting Sub-Committee
Chairman, Projects Implementation Sub-Committee
Director, Medical and Health Services
Director, Physical Planning
Manager, Division of Maintenance Services
Head, Department of Civil Engineering
Head, Department of Electronic/Electrical Engineering
Head, Department of Mechanical Engineering
Head, Department of Building
Head, Department of Estate Management
Head, Department of Quantity Surveying
Head, Department of Architecture
Civil/Structural Engineer
Two members to be nominated by Vice-Chancellor
Horticulturist
Principal Assistant Registrar (Tenders)
Architect, Capital Projects Unit
Planner, Capital Projects Unit
Quantity Surveyor, Capital Projects Unit

THE TENDERS BOARD - OBAFEMI AWOLOWO UNIVERSITY

Terms of Reference:

1. To invite and consider tenders and to award contracts for
    building projects and related works and services within the
    cost limit set by Council for the particular project;

2. To approve variation of tender on the recommendation of the
    Building, Works and Estate Committee and to approve fluctuation
    in contract price;

3. To award contracts on non-capital projects in excess of ₦20,000
    for any one contract to be charged to Recurrent Expenditure;

4. To determine the procedure for tendering and the award of
    contract;

5. To advise Council on any matter relating to tenders and the
    award of contracts either on its own initiative or on reference
    from Council.

Membership

Pro-Chancellor   (Chairman)
Vice-Chancellor
Deputy Vice-Chancellor
Four members of the University Council two of whom shall
 be members of the University Senate
Executive Secretary, National Universities Commission
Registrar - Secretary

In Attendance

Bursar
Director, Council Affairs
Director of Physical Planning
Manager, Division of Maintenance Services

PROJECTS IMPLEMENTATION SUB-COMMITTEE - OBAFEMI AWOLOWO UNIVERSITY

Terms of Reference:

1. To receive and consider regular reports on the due implementation of building contracts awarded by the University.

2. In respect of each contract, to co-ordinate the supervisory functions of the Director of Works, the Clerk of Works, the Architects and the Professional Consultants appointed for the project and facilitate the resolution of problems.

3. To advise the Building, Works and Estate Committee on all matters relating to the progress of any project awarded, having regard to obligations of the contractors/consultants appointed to work with the project.

4. To make such recommendations to the Building, Works and Estate Committee as may be necessary to ensure the due implementation of building programmes as approved.

5. To make periodic visits to project sites to acquaint itself with site conditions.

Membership
Chairman (nominated by the Vice-Chancellor)
Chairman, Projects Advisory Sub-Committee
Chairman, Projects Siting Sub-Committee
Two Representatives of Council
Dean, Faculty of Technology
Dean, Faculty of Environmental Design and Management
Dean, Faculty of Law
Bursar
Director of Council Affairs
Director of Physical Planning
Manager, Division of Maintenance Services
Head, Department of Building
Head, Department of Civil Engineering
Head, Department of Architecture
Architect, Capital Projects Unit
Planner, Capital Projects Unit
Quantity Surveyor, Capital Projects Unit
Civil/Structural Engineer
Horticulturist
Principal Assistant Registrar (Tenders)
One Students' representative appointed by the Students Union

NIGERIAN UNIVERSITIES OFFERING COURSES IN CONSTRUCTION DISCIPLINES

	ARC	BLD	CEG	EEG	ESM	LSR	MEG	QTS	URP
Obafemi Awolowo University	✓	✓	✓	✓	✓		✓	✓	✓
University of Lagos	✓	✓	✓	✓	✓	✓	✓		✓
Ahmadu Bello University	✓	✓	✓	✓		✓	✓	✓	✓
University of Jos	✓	✓							✓
Imo State University	✓	✓				✓			✓
University of Port-Harcourt			✓	✓			✓		
University of Benin		✓	✓	✓			✓		✓
Rivers State University	✓		✓	✓	✓	✓	✓	✓	✓
Bendel State University	✓		✓	✓			✓		
Ondo State University			✓	✓			✓		
Anambra State University	✓	✓	✓	✓	✓	✓	✓	✓	✓
FUT Owerri		✓	✓	✓			✓		
FUT Minna	✓	✓	✓	✓	✓	✓	✓	✓	

ARC = Architecture, BLD = Building, CEG = Civil Engineering,
EEG = Electrical Engineering,   ESM = Estate Management,
LSR = Surveying,   MEG = Mechanical Engineering,
QTS = Quantity Surveying,   URP = Urban and Regional Planning.

RESEARCH AND DEVELOPMENT IN BUILDING ROBOTICS AT THE
TECHNION ISRAEL INSTITUTE OF TECHNOLOGY

A. Warszawski*

Summary
Research and development program in building robotics at the
Building Research Station of the Technion I.I.T. is described. The
program includes a preliminary design of the robot, computer
simulation of the robot activity, analysis of its employment
problems on site, technological adaptation of selected activities,
and testing of their performance with a small scale robot.

Résumé
Le programme de recherche et de développement dans le domaine de la
robotisation dans le bâtiment à la Station de Recherche sur le Bâtiment du Technion (Institut Israélien de Technologie) est décrit. Ce
programme comprend un design préliminaire du robot, la simulation par
ordinateur de l'activité du robot, l'analyse de ses problèmes de
fonctionnement sur le site, l'adaptation technologique d'activités
choisies et l'essai de leur performance avec un robot de petite
échelle.

Keywords
Robots, Building Technology, Computer Simulation, Construction
Management.

1. INTRODUCTION
Possible employment of robots in building activities has been
receiving a considerable attention over the last few years as
evidenced by a large number of publications and four international
symposia devoted to this subject. The potential benefits from the
employment of robots are the productivity gains, improvement of
quality, and reduction or elimination of labor from hazardous
building tasks performed in risky, difficult or unhealthy
environments. Prototypes of construction robots have been already
developed and described in [5],[6] and a considerable effort in this
direction is expended also in U.S., France, Germany, Israel and
other countries.

* Head, Building Research Station, Technion I.I.T.

The building construction robots have been divided in [9] into 4 generic types: (1) robots for assembling of large components - beams, columns etc, (2) robots for finishing of building facades, (3) robots for finishing of large horizontal floors and (4) robots for execution of various interior finishing tasks. The last type was selected as the main subject of research at the Building Research Station of the Technion, because it complements the largely industrialized erection process of a prefabricated "shell" of floor slabs, vertical supports and facade components which can be produced off site.

The particular problems involved with the employment of an interior finishing robot have to do with its configuration, mode of operation, and adaptation of the construction technology to its constraints. Consequently, the development program consisted of the following projects, as shown on fig. 1:

a. Performance specifications of robot performance.
b. Preliminary design of robot features.
c. Computer simulation of the robot operation.
d. Physical testing of selected applications.
e. Analysis of methods for robot employment on site.
f. Adaptation of building technology to the robot constraints.
g. Detailed design.
h. Prototype construction and testing.

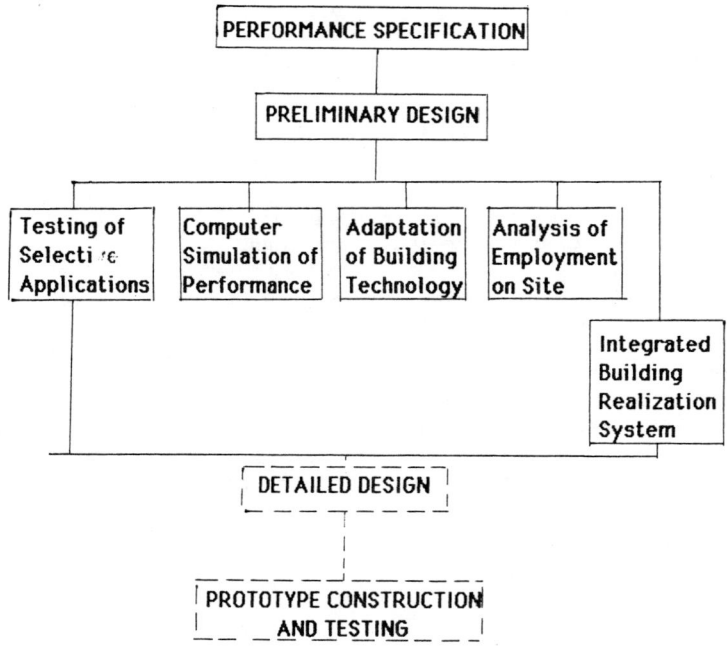

Fig. 1 - The construction robotics program

An additional related project examines an automation of integrated design build process which involves robotization at its final stage. The subjects a, b have been completed; subjects c,d,e,f are in progress. All of them will be now reviewed briefly.

2. THE PERFORMANCE SPECIFICATIONS AND PRELIMINARY DESIGN

The purpose of the specifications was to define the robot's performance in the execution of tasks assigned to it as a guide for its subsequent preliminary design. The robot was intended to perform the following group of activities on the erected prefabricated shell of slabs, vertical supports, and envelope:

a. Building of partitions - i.e. interior non-bearing space dividers. The same activity could be used for building of exterior walls.

b. Painting of interior surfaces - walls and ceilings.

c. Finishing of the structural floor slab surface.

d. Connecting between erected structural components.

e. Jointing between space dividing elements - walls, partitions and horizontal slabs.

The robot was intended to perform these activities in residential and similar buildings which are characterized by enclosed spaces not exceeding $15-20m^2$, and an interior height of 2.50-3.00m. The manner of performance, desired productivity and tolerances were defined in the specifications.

The robot which was eventually designed on the basis of these specifications is depicted in fig. 2. The design involved the arm structure, carriage, control unit and sensors. Two alternatives were offered - both employing an arm with a reach of about 3.00m, 7 degrees of freedom (later reduced to 6), and a payload of 20 kgf. It employed a variety of sensors for identifications of work locations, and prevention of collisions. The performance specifications and preliminary design of the robot are described in [7],[10].

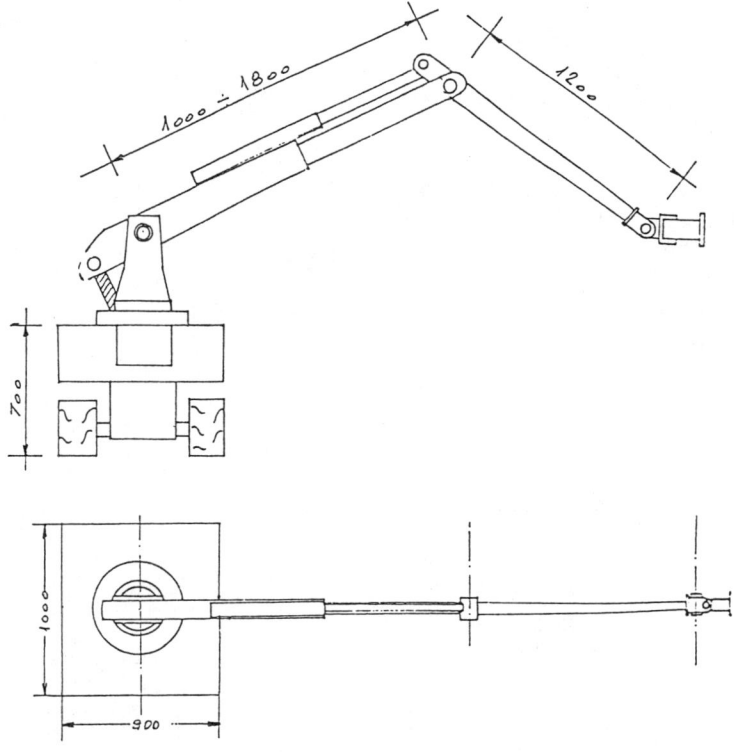

Fig. 2 - Schematic representation of interior finishing robot

3. THE SIMULATION OF ROBOT PERFORMANCE

The purpose of this stage of the development process which is
described in [4] was to test the various assumptions made in the
preliminary design. Its main objectives were as follows:

-   To test the functional feasibility of selected configurations,
    i.e. their capacity to physically perform the required tasks.
-   To determine the optimal value of several parameters which could
    not be determined in the preliminary design.
-   To compare the performance of the robot with the performance of a
    manual worker in the conventional construction process.

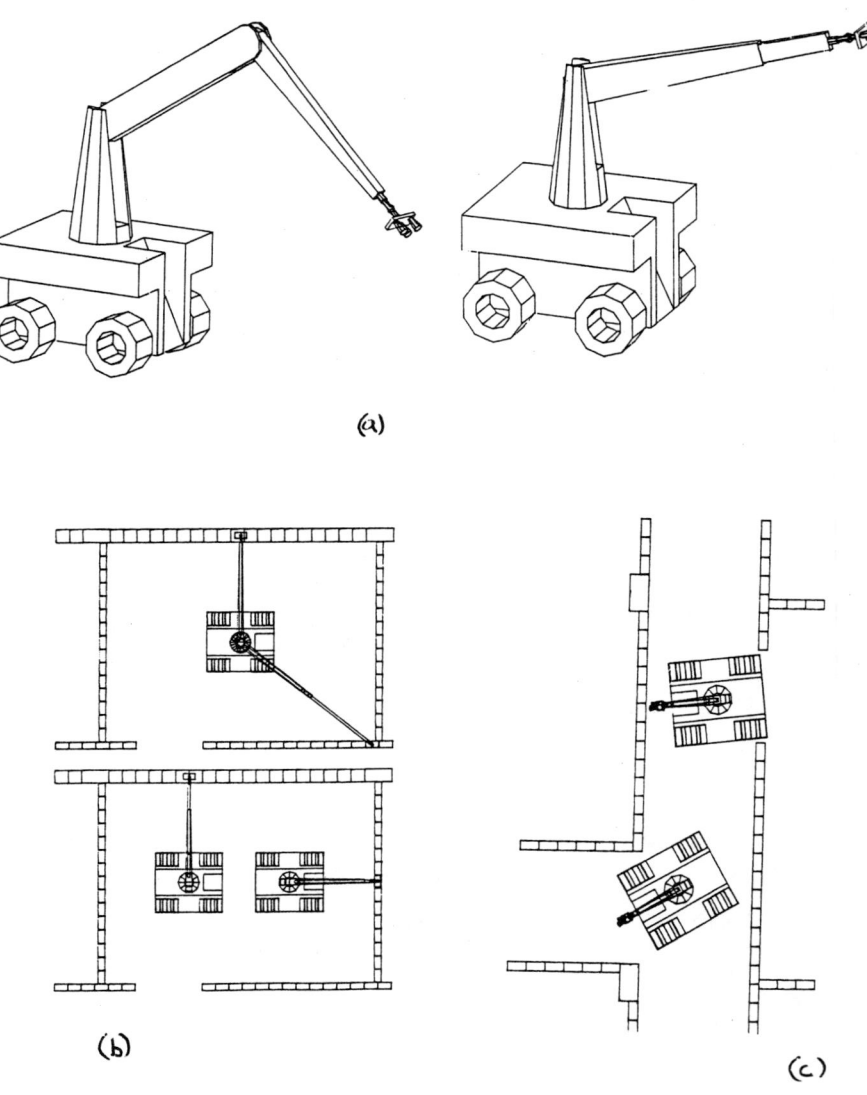

Fig. 3 - Views of simulation process
a. Robot configurations, b. arm reach alternatives.
c. Maneuverability test.

The parameters specifically addressed in the process were the robot arm configuration, the length of its links, the tradeoff between the cost of longer arm and the utility of larger work envelope, the maneuverability of the robot in the building interior, the velocity of movement of joints, the building technology employed, and the tolerances of the existing infra structure of building. The different solutions alternatives were simulated with an aid of a three dimensional animation system ROBCAD and evaluated in terms of impact on the productivity, cost and convenience of operation of the system. Some views of the simulation process are shown in figure 3.

Some of the immediate benefits of the simulation process were the reduction of the degrees of freedom of the robot from 7 to 6, and the reduction of the arm length from 3.00 to 2.80.

4. THE SCALED TESTING

This project should be viewed as additional facet of the robot performance testing which complements the simulation process described above.

The employment of robots for the execution of various specific construction task may create problems which could be identified and evaluated only within physical application experiments. The ideal experimentation would be performed with full scale prototypes, which is however a very costly method and should be undertaken rather at a final stage of development. Another preferred alternative is to perform the experimentation with a reduced physical model which presents both the robotic system and the built environment in a 1:2 - 1:4 scale.

As an intermediate stage to the creation of a complete modelled enviornment it was decided to test several selected activities with an available hardware adopted to the specified building tasks.

The tasks which were selected for this purpose included wall building - with a "dry" method explained in the next section, covering of walls with paint or plaster, and sealing of joints between prefabricated or built on site horizontal and vertical components. The performance of the robotic system included automatic (preprogrammed) execution of the designated tasks, and at a later stage - movement between work stations and interaction with environment through built in sensors.

The hardware which was selected for this purpose included a small SCORBOT robot with 600mm arm and 5 degrees of freedom and a set of work tools - grippers, sprayers, sensing guns especially constructed for this purpose. The movement and sensing capacity were built into the system at a later stage.

The exprimentation is described in (2).

279

5. TECHNOLOGY ADAPTATION

Most building activities as they are performed today are well suited to human capacity but ill structured for robotic performance. In order to make them more robot "friendly" it is necessary to restructure them in such manner that they could be performed with a single tool, at a single pass, and with a simple work pattern. This problem is extensively discussed in [9].

The tasks which were selected in the project to make them technologically suitable for the robotic use were partitions building, interior walls covering, sealing of joints between components , floor finishing, and connection between structural elements.

Fig. 4 - "Dry" wall building

A suggested "dry" alternative for conventional partitions building used lightweight interlocking blocks which after their placement <u>without mortar</u> are binded together either by a fiber reinforced plaster or by filling the joint in a completed wall by a binding substance as shown in fig.

An alternative for conventional jointing between elements involved filling nonstructural joints 20-50 mm wide between the elements with strong elastomeric fillers. For structural connections the solution involved application of adhesives with hight tensile strength to steel plates fixed in elements during their fabrication off site.

The covering of walls was to be done by spraying of a single layer of cover with desired appearance, and for walls - spreading of self levelling screed with specified characteristics.

The development of the conceptual solutions based on plastic and cementitious compounds for the above mentioned finishing methods is described in [3]. Their testing is now under progress.

6. THE ORGANIZATION OF ROBOTIC WORK

The robot employment on the construction site poses many organizational and logistic problems which must be addressed within the course of construction planning. These problems include among others:

a. The determination of the activities to be performed by the robot.
b. The pattern of the robot employment - autonomous or in conjunction with single operator, or with a gang of workers. Those distinctions are explored in [9].
c. The materials supply - blocks, plaster etc. to robot work stations.
d. The transfer of a robot between various levels and sections of the project.

The solutions to all those problems obviously depend on the type of project to be built - its size, geometry, composition etc. The method of analysis of these dependencies is described in [1] and is presently under development as a formalized procedure.

7. THE INTEGRATED DESIGN - BUILD SYSTEM

The purpose of the automated integrated design - build system is to automate the realization process of a building project. It is assumed that a building is erected from prefabricated elements of a specific system according to a preliminary design prepared by an architect. The complete process is shown on fig.5., and described in [8].

281

The robotization related stages involve the automated production of elements in an offsite plant and their robotized jointing and finishing on site with the methods described in the former sections.

AN INTEGRATED BUILDING REALIZATION
PROCESS

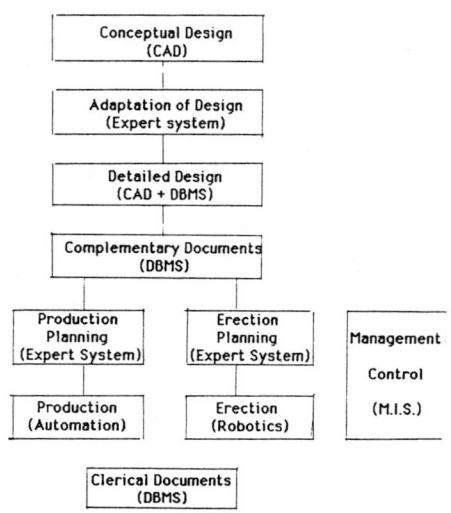

Fig. 5 - Automated design - build process

8.   CONCLUSIONS

The employment of an interior finishing robot can complement an industrialized building process which uses prefabricated concrete components for structural and exterior envelope components. It is very useful to commence the development process with a precise formmulation of the robot performance specifications, which enumerate the tasks for the robot to perform define its work environment, and the existing operational constraints. The performance requirements form the basis for a preliminary design, which results in the description of the robot configuration and its main features. The preliminary configuration can be then analyzed with an aid of a computer simulation which allows to evaluate possible alternative solutions. The conventional finishing activities should be restructured to make them adaptible to the robot operational constraints. Most efficient use of robots on a given construction site should be sought by an analysis of its employment pattern, and of the supply of its work materials.

9. REFERENCES
1. C. Argaman, "Employment of Robots on Construction Site", Interim Report, Building Research Station, Technion, I.I.T., Haifa, 1986.

2. C. Argaman and A. Warszawski, "Teaching Robotics in Building", Proceedings of the Fourth International Symposium on Robotics and Artificial Intelligence in Building, Haifa, 1987.

3. A. Benture and M. Puterman, "Adaptation of Special Materials for Construction Automation", Proceedings of the Fourth International Symposium on Robotics and Artificial Intelligence in Building, Haifa, 1987.

4. R. Navon and A. Warszawski, "Development of a Robot for Interior Finishing Work", Proceedings of the Fourth International Symposium on Robotics and Artificial Intelligence in Building, Haifa, 1987.

5. S. Suzuki, et al., "Construction Robotics in Japan", Workshop Proceedings of the Third International Conference on Tall Buildings, Chicago, 1986.

6. T. Ueno, et al., "Construction Robots for Site Automation", Proceedings of the International Joint Conference on CAD and Robotics in Architecture and Construction, Marseille, 1986.

7. A. Warszawski, A. Yavnai and R. Navon, "Performance Specifications and Preliminary Design of an Interior Finishing Robot", Building Research Station, Technion, I.I.T., 1987.

8. A.Warszawski, "A Comprehensive Design Build System, Proceedings of the 5th CIB Symposium, Washington DC, 1986.

9. A. Warszawski, "Application of Robotics to Building Construction", CIB Report No. 90, International Council for Building Research Studies and Documentation, Rotterdam, 1986.

10. A. Yavnai, "Sensor Architecture for Mobile Construction Robot", Proceedings of the Fourth International Symposium on Robotics and Artificial Intelligence in Building, Haifa, 1987.

TURNKEY CONSTRUCTION FOR BUILDINGS IN MALAYSIA

Paul M H Yong, Prof, Dip Bldg, PhD, AFAS, SISV, AFS, AEE, ACI, IMCM,
MCIOB (London)
Promet Consultancy Sendirian Berhad, MD, Malaysia

Summary
The turnkey system of contract for buildings is presented.
Development of this innovative system in Malaysia is discussed.
As a case study, the experience of a Malaysian Company - in this
area is emphasised. The application of this system relating to
management, design and construction techniques is examined in
detail in the building of the Shell Headquarters in Kuala Lumpur

Sommaire
Le contrat sous forme de Clef en main pour les batiments a ete
presente. Developpement de ce systeme innove en malaisie en
etait discute. Comme une etude de cas, l'experience d'une
societe malaisienne dans ce domaine a ete soulignee. La mise
en application de ce systeme a propos de la gestion de la
conception et les technologies de la construction ont ete
examine en details sur la construction du siege social de
SHELL a Kuala Lumpur.

Keywords
Turnkey Construction, Expertise, Speed, Reliability, Trust,
Management Competency.

INTRODUCTION
As distinguished fellow participants are aware, speed and
efficiency are the particular contributions of a turnkey builder.
Turnkey construction is fairly new to many developing countries
especially in the Commonwealth, but already it has shown its
value as a positive innovation. The turnkey builder's
responsibility to the Government and the client is immense
compared with that of the traditional builder. The expectations
and trust placed in him are high. Therefore he must provide
quality management in building construction, ensuring good
design and build as well as early completion of a project, in
accordance with the highest of standards.

THE MALAYSIAN EXPERIENCE
The object of this paper is to share with fellow participants
the Malaysian experience in the turnkey system of building. Malaysia

was once under British rule and influence. Therefore various regulations, by-laws and contract documents for the building industry were modelled on those of Great Britain. In fact, most of the qualified professional personnel related to the building industry, in one way or another, have been trained in the British system. As a result, standard agreements for a building contract and the building by-laws adopted by the Government, architects and engineers in Malaysia are strictly in the British tradition. Any attempt to change this by some progressive professional persons within the building industry will always meet with a lot of resistance.

The construction industry in Malaysia is among the most active and fast growing industries. It currently accounts for 4.7 per cent of the GNP. There are indications of the contribution growing to 5.2 per cent in 1990 with the 337,000 job opportunities created at present rising to 413,000 by that year.

Given the reluctant attitude of the Malaysian majority, particularly the bureaucracy, towards the revolutionary turnkey system of building, it is no exaggeration to say that this innovation would not have made much headway or impact if not for Malaysian Prime Minister Datuk Seri Dr Mahathir Mohamad.

He gave the necessary push to the implementation of the system. In a speech prepared for the opening of the 35-storey Promet H.Q. building on October 15, 1983, he explained the rationale behind the Government's decision to introduce the turnkey system of construction. The points mentioned by the Malaysian Premier on that occasion best summarise the Malaysian situation. Therefore, I have taken the liberty to quote extensively from that speech.

The Prime Minister says a fast but efficient and orderly construction system is a crucial qualification in situations where inflation has become a common factor. Malaysia is not spared this.

He regrets the fact that too many construction projects are taking longer than scheduled to be completed, resulting in not only high cost overrun but also loss of anticipated revenue. "Many Government projects are experiencing this problem with the consequences that the expenditure sometimes doubled or escalated even higher. We can no longer accept projects being abandoned like in the case of several school projects in some States (Malaysia is a federation of 13 states)," he said.

In view of the situation, the Government decided to introduce the turnkey concept with its principle of fixed costs to ensure cost overrun would not occur and construction kept to schedule. "The era of the individual or family business in the construction industry has ended," he declared.

He says the Malaysian government will consider local construction companies for multi-million ringgit turnkey projects if they have the expertise for fast and efficient construction of buildings. This means only contractors with a high level of financial, engineering, technological, designing and management competency will qualify.

285

Because of the high level of expertise required for such projects, the smaller construction firms in the country are not given the opportunity to participate in them except as sub-contractors or on a partnership basis according to the conditions of the contract awarded by the Government.

He hopes that Malaysian companies would restructure themselves to achieve the capability for undertaking turnkey projects successfully.   He urged local contractors to change their conservative attitude and adopt new technology aimed at improving the process of construction.

CONTRACTS IN MALAYSIA'S BUILDING INDUSTRY
There are two types of contracts commonly adopted by the Government of Malaysia and the private sector in this industry : The traditional system of contract and the turnkey system of contract.
The Traditional System of Contract (See Figure 1)

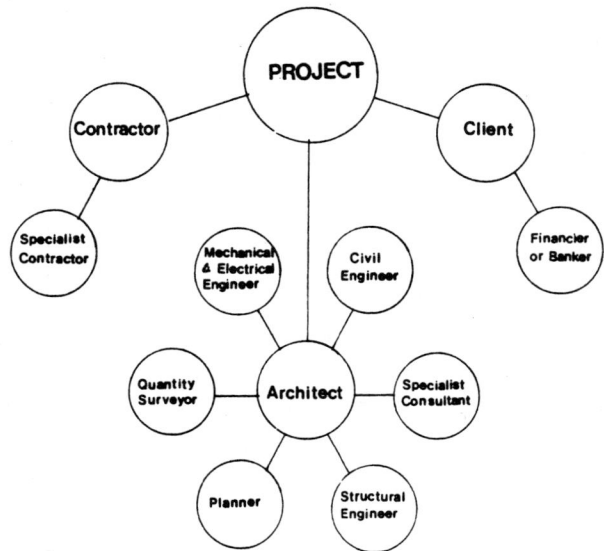

Perhaps here I should summarise the disadvantages from the builder's viewpoint.
1.   The contractor or builder is usually in a position opposed to the designers and owners.
2.   The contractor or builder's experience and expertise are not made use of, owing to the 'superiority complex' of the design team i.e. architects, engineers and quantity surveyors.
3.   The contractor or builder often meets with delays of decisions or insufficiency of details and clarification or discrepancies in certification of payment owing to poor coordination among the professional persons in the design team.

4. There are too many general contractors or builders who can execute a contract in this system, resulting in too competitive sums being tendered.
5. The contractor or builder has no authority to change to materials of lower cost even with similar standard and performance without prior approval from the architect.
6. The contractor or builder may suffer abuse from the owner and design team members, being made to use the services or materials related to these people at a higher cost.
7. When site staff are employed by the owner or designers to supervise the work to discharge his duty theoretically, the contractor or builder will suffer extra cost and time delay.
8. The contractor or builder has to approach the owner or designers and surveyors or site staff very tactfully all the time in order not to hinder the progress of his work or to spend extra money to comply 100% with unnecessary specifications.

TURNKEY SYSTEM OF CONTRACT FOR BUILDING CONSTRUCTION INDUSTRY

It is a design-and-build contract and is known to the Government as Accelerated Implementation Scheme (AIS). In this system, all phases of a project from pre-contract through post-contract is carried out by the same organisation. This form of contract can be used for lump sum or cost plus a fixed fee of contract. In this system there are only the owner and the design-and-build contractor or builder. The chance of an adversary relationship between two parties is surely less than in the three-party system, where there are the owner, the contractor or builder plus the team of professionals like architects, engineers and quantity surveyors, paid by the contractor or builder.

As the traditional form of contract has been practised in Malaysia for years, the turnkey system of contract only becomes possible with the consent of the clients. This can be achieved when the client has sufficient trust in the design-and-build contractor or builder.

The turnkey system of construction is to integrate the various aspects of the building industry into a unified discipline of project management.

The projects in building industry get larger and more complex each day. Problems accompanying these projects include the need for improved management, technology and research. The need to meet social, economic and environmental requirements has increased. One of the most basic obstacles is that the fragmentation and divisiveness among its participants inhibit the type of programmatic efforts that can help to improve the building industry's long-term prospects.

To implement the turnkey system of construction, the contractor or builder must have the personnel, qualifications and applicable construction experience to develop and implement a well thought out programme for successful accomplishment of the project.

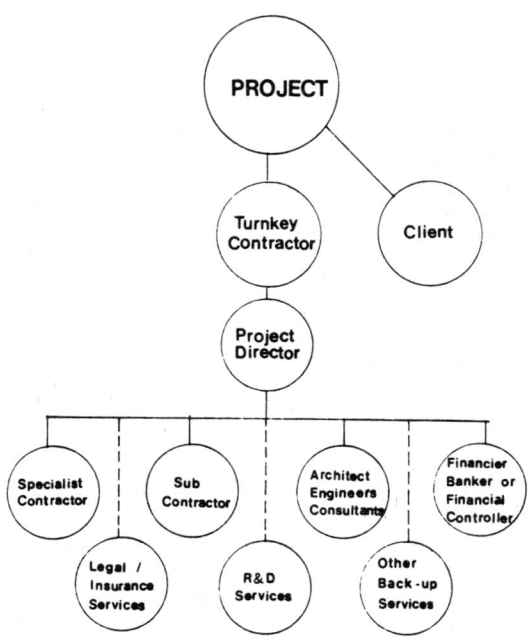

Figure 2.   Turnkey System of Contract for Building Construction

In this system, the Project Director is the supreme commander of the project; he sees that all parties are achieving the goal with authority and responsibility.

The Advantages From the Builder's Point of View

1.   The builder has the opportunity to direct his design team to design economically and in such a way as to make the building work easier.
2.   The chance of an adversary relationship with the design team is omitted.
3.   The builder can share his experience constantly with his designers to achieve better output.
4.   Any research and development towards new materials, criteria of design and construction can be shared by both contractor and designer.
5.   The builder can implement a project within a much shorter time than the traditional contractor.

Examples of Projects Using Turnkey System of Contract

The company has completed many turnkey contracts for buildings in Malaysia, Asean Countries and the Middle East. There are two types of turnkey contracts undertaken by the company:

1.   Turnkey contract on agreed percentage of fees based on the total construction cost.
2.   Turnkey contract based on a Lump Sum Price.

288

A. Under turnkey contracts on agreed percentage of fees based on
    the total construction cost, the company has completed three
    significant projects. These are:
(a) M$80 Million Saberkas Building in Kuching, Sarawak, Malaysia
    (See Figure 4)
(b) M$110 Million Karamunsing Complex in Kota Kinabalu, Sabah,
    Malaysia (See Figure 5)
(c) M$68 Million Promet Tower in Kuala Lumpur, Malaysia
B. Under turnkey contracts based on Lump Sum Price, the company
    has completed four significant projects. These are:
(a) M$16 Million Extension of Kuala Lumpur International Airport
    Terminal Two, Malaysia
(b) M$18 Million The Island Defence Project in South China Sea,
    Off Sabah, Malaysia
(c) M$8 Million Wholesale Market in Kuala Lumpur, Malaysia
(d) M$130 Million The Bukit Naga Complex - i.e. Shell Headquarters
    of Malaysia (See Figure 3)

Introduction To An Example Project - Bukit Naga Complex

This project is a joint-venture between the Shell Pension Fund and
the company. The complex has two blocks of 12-storey buildings
including basement floors. One tower block has 367,146 sq.ft to
be used by Shell as their headquarters in Malaysia and the other
tower has 493,139 sq.ft. to be developed for sale or lease. The
two buildings sit on 139,664 sq. ft. land on top of a hill. They
have a total built-in area of 885,335 sq. ft.

Each tower block is made of prefabricated steel structures with
metal deck for slab, slip form construction for the lift-core, the
precast reinforced concrete fins for the exterior with glazing
window. Each floor of the building is served by air-cool air-
conditioner in segmental system to cut down capital cost and easy
maintenance without affecting performance. The high speed computer-
controlled passenger lifts are installed to minimise waiting time.

Figure 3

Figure 4

Figure 5

This project will be discussed under the following stages of the contract:
1. Marketing of a Project
2. Pre-construction Period
3. Construction Period
4. Post-construction Period

MARKETING OF A PROJECT
In order to be successful in marketing the turnkey system of contract, one has to convince the client that this system of contract has all the advantages in comparison to the traditional system eg. Shell Headquarters history.

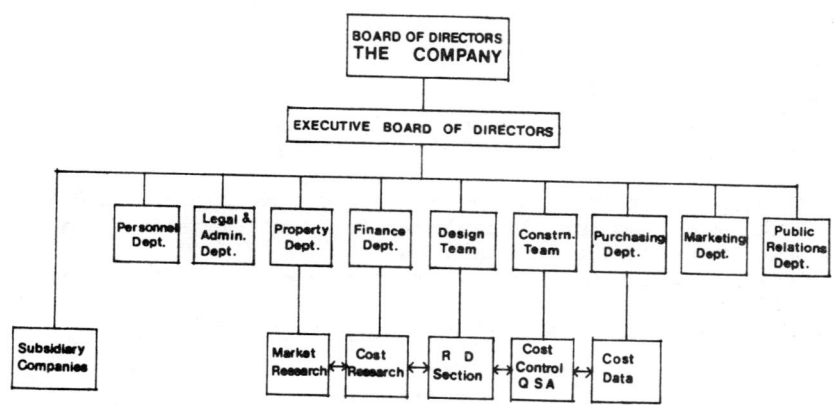

Figure 6. Marketing of A Project

THE COMPANY ORGANIZATION CHART
FOR TURNKEY SYSTEM OF CONTRACT

PRE-CONSTRUCTION PERIOD
A project team to handle this turnkey system of contract was formed.

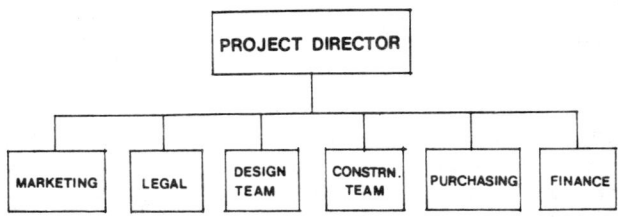

Figure 7.   Pre-Construction Period
Organisation Chart

PROJECT DIRECTOR
During this period, the following items must be agreed:
1.   An Agreed turnkey system of contract based on established
     conditions.
2.   An agreed procedures to approved sub-contractors and specialists
     work, and in addition, the design team and contracting team
     must have constant dialogues for:
(a) Design to cater for speed of construction e.g. 3 floors-one-lift
     concept of steel columns
(b) Identify critical material and equipment to order early

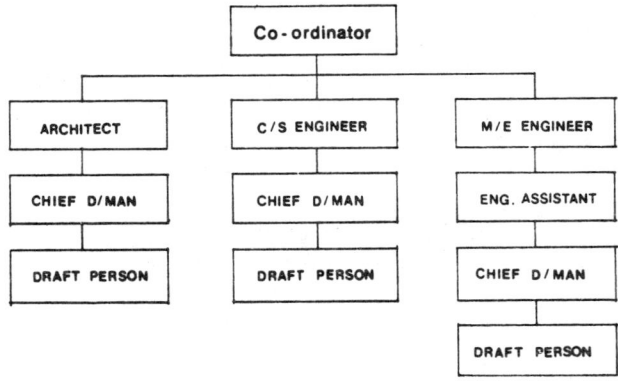

Figure 8.   Design Team Organisation Chart

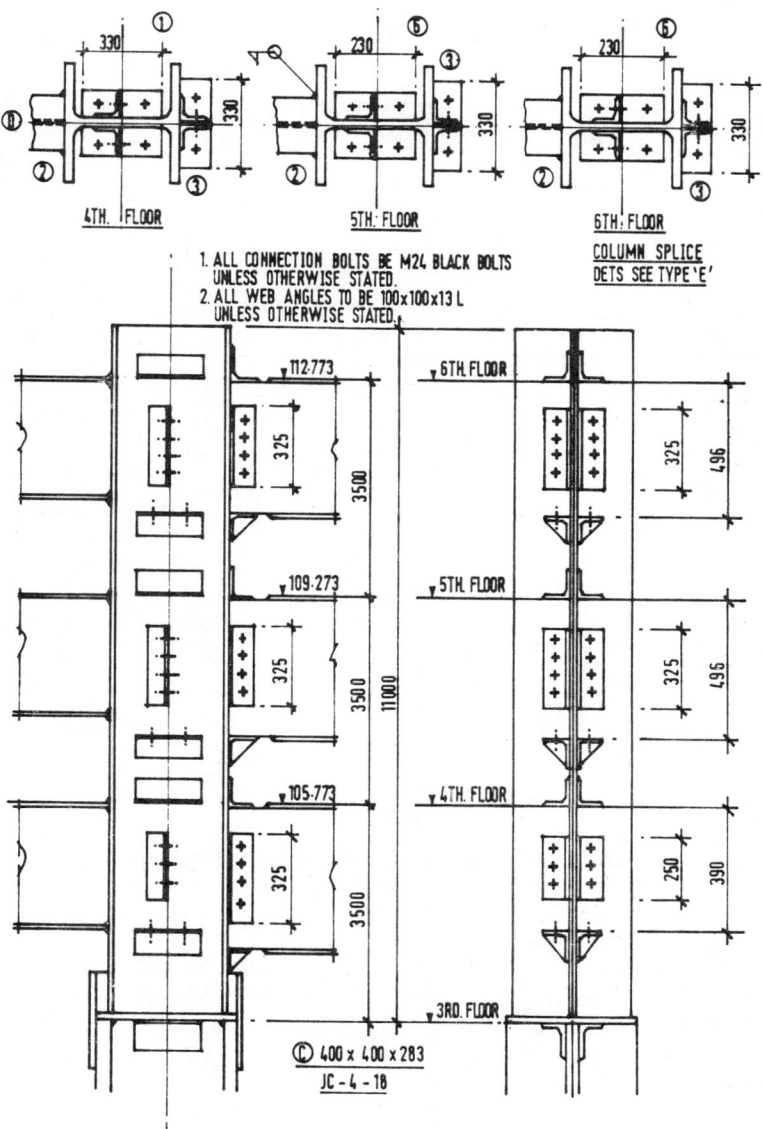

1. ALL CONNECTION BOLTS BE M24 BLACK BOLTS
   UNLESS OTHERWISE STATED.
2. ALL WEB ANGLES TO BE 100x100x13 L
   UNLESS OTHERWISE STATED.

4TH. FLOOR

5TH. FLOOR

6TH. FLOOR
COLUMN SPLICE
DETS SEE TYPE 'E'

Figure 9.   Example of 3 Floors-One-Lift

CONSTRUCTION PERIOD

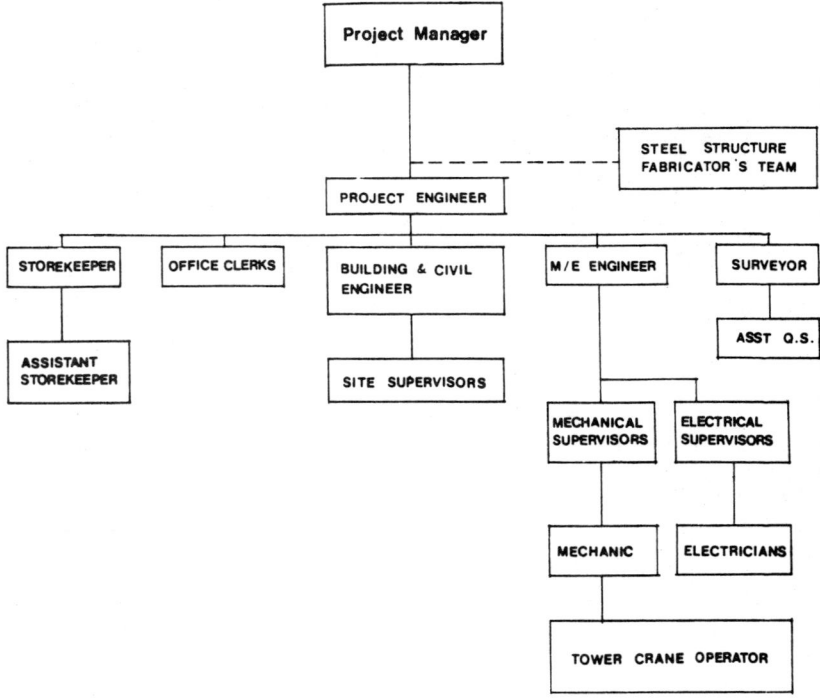

Figure 10. Project Site Organisational Chart
For Bukit Naga Complex

POST-CONSTRUCTION PERIOD
Upon completion of the project, the Project Director's function
does not end. He must form another maintenance team to carry out
the post-contract function.

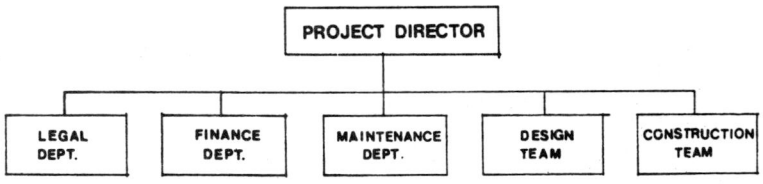

Figure 11. Post-Construction Management Chart

CONCLUSION

After going through the various stages of the contract, in my opinion, the following steps must be taken by the builder so that the turnkey system of contract can be commonly accepted and implemented in the developing countries:

1. To have standard contract for the turnkey system of construction
2. To review the various Professional Acts within the building industry to facilitate turnkey construction;
3. To provide training facilities or short courses in institutions for practising professionals within the building industry to fit into the turnkey system of contract;
4. To establish an accepted body similar to Lloyd to classify the contract undertaken so that insurers or bankers will support this system of contract;
5. To produce a building management team for an owner to audit his contract;
6. To have a single insurance cover for the turnkey system of contract;
7. To form a professional body for turnkey builders.

The success and survival of a professional builder promoting the turnkey system of contract are dependent on his ability to offer quality, speed, a very competitive price and trustworthiness.

ACKNOWLEDGEMENTS

The work described in this paper has the support of Prof. V.B. Torrance, Dr. Bernard T.H. Wang and the professional staff of the Promet Group of companies.

REFERENCES

1. General Conditions of Contract - the existing building contract used by the Public Works Department Malaysia.

2. Berger, Horst, Dr., "Design-Build" Takaneka's Approach.

3. Muramatsu, Teijiro, Professor at Tokyo University - A Pioneering Contractor With A Tradition.

4. Takahashi, Teiichi - Principal of Architects Co-Partnership Daiichi Kobo and Professor at Osaka University of Arts - A Step Towards Post Industrial Society.

5. Takaneka, Renichi - The Japanese Approach to Quality Control - Total Quality Control in Our Company.

6. Tatsumi, Kazuo, Professor at Khoto University - The Importance of Architectural Planning.

7. Wakita, Mamoru, writer on Business Affairs in Japan - "A Building is not a Product but a Work of Art". The Company Doctrine of Takaneka Komuten.